Out of America

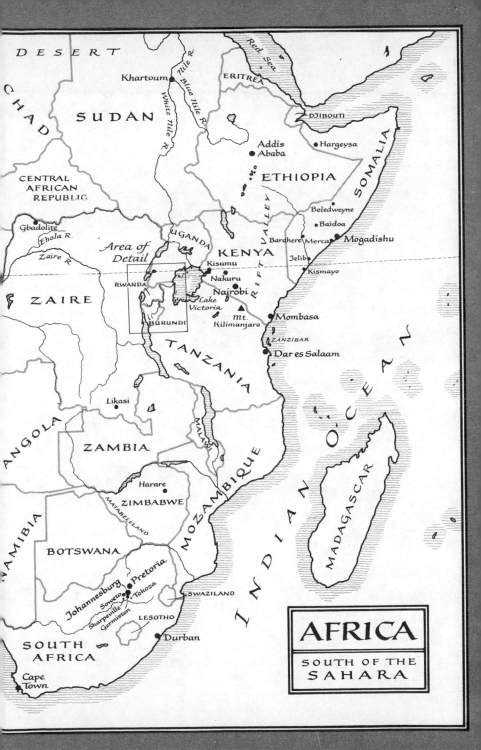

KEITH B. RICHBURG

Out of America

A Black Man Confronts Africa

A HARVEST BOOK
HARCOURT BRACE & COMPANY
San Diego   New York   London

Requests for permission to make copies
of any part of the work should be mailed to:
Permissions Department, Harcourt Brace & Company,
6277 Sea Harbor Drive, Orlando, Florida 32887-6777.

Lyrics from Peter Tosh's "African" are reprinted with permission
from the Estate of Winston McIntosh p/k/a/ Peter Tosh.

Portions of this work have appeared previously
in the *Washington Post Magazine*.

Reprinted by arrangement with BasicBooks.

Library of Congress Cataloging-in-Publication Data
Richburg, Keith B.
Out of America: a black man confronts Africa/Keith B. Richburg.
—1st Harvest ed.
p.   cm.—(A Harvest book)
Originally published: New York: BasicBooks, 1997.
Includes index.
ISBN 0-15-600583-2
1. Africa, Sub-Saharan—Social conditions—1960–
2. Richburg, Keith B.—Journeys—Africa, Sub-Saharan.
3. Africa, Sub-Saharan—Description and travel.
4. Human rights—Africa, Sub-Saharan.   I. Title.
HN773.5.R53   1998
306'.0967—dc21   97-47710

Printed in the United States of America

First Harvest edition 1998

F E D C B A

To my mother, Katie Richburg, in loving memory

Contents

Prelude

I WATCHED THE DEAD float down a river in Tanzania.

It's one of those apocryphal stories you always hear coming out of Africa, meant to demonstrate the savagery of "the natives." Babies being pulled off their mothers' backs and tossed onto spears. Pregnant women being disemboweled. Bodies being tossed into the river and floating downstream. You heard them all, but never really believed.

And yet there I was, drenched with sweat under the blistering sun, standing at the Rusumo Falls bridge, watching the bodies float past me. Sometimes they came one by one. Sometimes two or three together. They were bloated now, horribly discolored. Most were naked, or stripped down to their underpants. Sometimes the hands and feet were bound together. Some were clearly missing some limbs. And as they went over the falls, a few got stuck together on a little crag, and stayed there flapping against the current, as though they were trying to break free. I couldn't take my eyes off one of them, the body of a little baby.

We timed them: a body or two every minute. And the Tanzanian border guards told us it had been like that for a couple of days now. These were the victims of the ethnic genocide going on across the border in Rwanda. The killers were working too fast to allow for proper burials. It was easier to dump the corpses into the Kagera River, to let them float downstream into Tanzania, eventually into Lake Victoria, out of sight, and I suppose out of mind. Or maybe there was some mythic proportion to it as well. These victims were from the Tutsi tribe, descendants, they say, of the Nile, and more resembling the Nilotic peoples of North Africa with their narrower noses, more angular features. The Hutu, the ones conducting this final solution, were Bantu people, shorter, darker, and tired of being lorded over by the Tutsi. Maybe tossing the bodies into the river was the Hutus' way of sending them back to the Nile.

Sounds crazy, I guess. And I suppose you, the reader, find this image disgusting—the bloated, discolored bodies floating down a river and over a waterfall. If I'm disgusting you, good, because that's my point. Because it was that image, and countless more like it, that I had to live with, and go to sleep with, for three years—three long years—that I spent covering Africa as a reporter for the *Washington Post*. Three years of watching pretty much the worst that human beings can do to one another. And three years of watching bodies, if not floating down the river in Tanzania, then stacked up like firewood in the refugee camps of Zaire, waiting to be dumped into a mass pit. But sometimes the ground would be too hard and there wouldn't be any construction equipment around to dig a hole, so the bodies instead would just pile up higher and higher, rotting and stinking in the scorching African sun until I'd have to walk around wearing a surgical mask over my face. Or the bodies lying unburied along the roadsides in Somalia, people dropping dead of starvation as they tried to make it just a few more miles into town where the foreign-aid agencies were handing out free food.

Is this depressing you, all this talk of death and dead bodies? Do you want to put the book down now? No, please, press on. I have more to say, and I want to put it all right out here, right in your face.

I want you to walk with me, hold my hand as we step over the rotting corpses together, stand beside me as we gaze into the eyes of a starving child. Then maybe you'll understand a little better what it is I am trying to say.

Maybe now you're asking yourself: How does he deal with it? How does he cope with seeing those horrific images every day? Does he think about it? Does he have nightmares? What on earth must go through his mind?

I'll tell you, if you'll let me describe it. Revulsion. Sorrow. Pity at the monumental waste of human life. They all come close, but don't quite capture what I really feel. It's a sentiment that began nagging me soon after I first set foot in Africa in late 1991. And it's a gnawing feeling that kept coming back to me as the bodies kept piling up, as the insanity of Africa deepened. It's a feeling that I was really unable to express out loud until the end, as I was packing my bags to leave. It was a feeling that pained me to admit, a sentiment that, when uttered aloud, might come across as callous, self-obsessed, even racist.

And yet I know exactly this feeling that haunts me; I've just been too embarrassed to say it. So let me drop the charade and put it as simply as I know how: *There but for the grace of God go I.*

You see, I was seeing all of this horror a bit differently because of the color of my skin. I am an American, but a black man, a descendant of slaves brought from Africa. When I see these nameless, faceless, anonymous bodies washing over a waterfall or piled up on the back of trucks, what I see most is that they look like me.

Sometime, maybe four hundred or so years ago, one of my ancestors was taken from his village, probably by a local chieftain. He was shackled in leg irons, kept in a holding pen or a dark pit, possibly at Goree Island off the coast of Senegal. And then he was put in the crowded, filthy cargo hold of a ship for the long and treacherous voyage across the Atlantic to the New World.

Many of the slaves died on that voyage. But not my ancestor. Maybe it was because he was strong, maybe just stubborn, or maybe he had an irrepressible will to live. But he survived, and ended up in forced slavery working on plantations in the Caribbean. Generations on down the line, one of his descendants was taken to South Carolina. Finally, a more recent descendant, my father, moved to Detroit to find a job in an auto plant during the Second World War.

And so it was that I came to be born in Detroit and that thirty-five years later, a black man born in white America, I was in Africa, birthplace of my ancestors, standing at the edge of a river not as an African but as an American journalist—a mere spectator—watching the bloated bodies of black Africans cascading over a waterfall. And that's when I thought about how, if things had been different, I might have been one of them—or might have met some similarly anonymous fate in one of the countless ongoing civil wars or tribal clashes on this brutal continent. And so I thank God my ancestor survived that voyage.

Does that sound shocking? Does it sound almost like a justification for the terrible crime of slavery? Does it sound like this black man has forgotten his African roots? Of course it does, all that and more. And that is precisely why I have tried to keep this emotion buried so deep for so long, and why it pains me so now to put these words in print, for all the world to see. But I'm writing this so you will understand better what I'm trying to say.

It might have been easier for me to just keep all of these emotions bottled up inside. Maybe I should have just written a standard book on Africa that would have talked broadly about the politics, the possibilities, the prospects for change.

But I'm tired of lying. And I'm tired of all the ignorance and hypocrisy and the double standards I hear and read about Africa, much of it from people who've never been there, let alone spent three years walking around amid the corpses. Talk to me about Africa and my black roots and my kinship with my African brothers and I'll throw it back in your face, and then I'll rub your nose in the images of the rotting flesh.

Come with me, if you're willing, and I'll take you on a journey—it's my own personal journey, much of it taking place inside my head. It won't be pretty, but that's my point. I want you to feel it like I did.

Touch it, smell it. Let me be your guide, and try to follow along as I lay out for you here why I feel the way I do—about Africa, about America, and mainly about myself and where it is I now know I belong.

But first, let me put one thing plainly so that I'm not misunderstood: I am not making a defense of slavery. It was an evil institution that heaped the greatest indignity on my race, and it was a crime that must never be repeated. But condemning slavery should not inhibit us from recognizing mankind's ability to make something good arise often in the aftermath of the most horrible evil. It does not offer any apologies or excuses for the Holocaust to say that in the aftermath of Hitler's evil, the state of Israel was created. One can deplore the loss of life of the Second World War, and the death and destruction of the atomic bombs on Japan, and still say that from the debris of conflict emerged a more stable world order, a process of decolonization, and a Japan and Germany firmly anchored in the democratic camp.

Maybe it is because of the current condition of blacks in America that you instinctively recoil at what I'm trying to say. Blacks now form the core of America's urban underclass. One-third of all young black men in their twenties are in prison, on probation, or on parole. Drugs are ravaging the black community. We are told by some of our supposedly enlightened, so-called black leaders that white America owes us something because they brought our ancestors over as slaves. And Africa—Mother Africa—is often held up as some kind of black Valhalla, where the descendants of slaves would be welcomed back and where black men and women can walk in true dignity.

Sorry, but I've been there. I've had an AK-47 rammed up my nose, I've talked to machete-wielding Hutu militiamen with the blood of their latest victims splattered across their T-shirts. I've seen a cholera epidemic in Zaire, a famine in Somalia, a civil war in Liberia. I've seen cities bombed to near rubble, and other cities reduced to rubble, because their leaders let them rot and decay while they spirited away billions of dollars—yes, billions—into overseas bank accounts.

I've also seen heroism, honor, and dignity in Africa, particularly in the stories of ordinary, anonymous people—brave Africans battling insurmountable odds to publish an independent newspaper, to organize a political party, to teach kids in some rural bush school, and usually just to survive. But even with all the good I've found here, my perceptions have been hopelessly skewed by the bad. My tour in Africa coincided with two of the world's worst tragedies—Somalia and Rwanda. I've had friends and colleagues shot, stabbed, beaten to death by mobs, left to bleed to death on a Mogadishu street—one of them beaten so badly in the face that his friends could recognize him only by his hair and his clothes.

So excuse me if I sound cynical, jaded. I'm beaten down, and I'll admit it. And it's Africa that has made me this way. I feel for her suffering, I empathize with her pain, and now, from afar, I still recoil in horror whenever I see yet another television picture of another tribal slaughter, another refugee crisis. But most of all I think: Thank God my ancestor got out, because, now, I am not one of them.

In short, thank God that I am an American.

Out of America

I

On Native Ground

"When I was at home, I was in a better place, but
travelers must be content."
—WILLIAM SHAKESPEARE,
As You Like It, Act II, Scene iv

"WHAT'S THAT SMELL?" I asked.

My colleague, Neil Henry, and I were in Neil's battered brown
Range Rover, driving toward downtown Nairobi, the capital of
Kenya. I was a newcomer to Africa, and Neil was the guy I had been
sent out to replace as the *Washington Post*'s bureau chief. He had just
picked me up at the airport, tossed my bags onto the backseat, and
was giving me a quick tour of the city that would be my home for the
next three years.

We were somewhere on the edge of downtown—I wasn't sure
quite where—and it looked, and smelled, as if we were driving
through some vast garbage dump. On closer inspection, I could see

the corrugated tin roofs atop tiny shacks, and I knew we were actually in the middle of a sprawling squatter community. It had been raining in Nairobi, and the dirt road had turned to a brown muddy slime. A rotten, fetid stench hung in the air.

"The smell?" said Neil, and I could see he was enjoying himself, breaking in the novice. "Hell, that's Africa!"

Neil had had enough. He was quitting—not just the Africa job, but daily journalism. A gifted young black writer from the *Post*'s national staff, he had come to Nairobi to try his hand at foreign reporting. Now he was leaving, exhausted, beaten down by Africa. That should have been a warning to me.

It was Liberia that had worn out Neil Henry. He had been there in 1990 during the savagery that followed the fall from power of the U.S.-backed dictator Samuel Doe. He had seen too many massacres, too many bodies—black bodies—stacked up like firewood. And he told the editors he was quitting, getting the hell out of there, going home.

By contrast, I guess I seemed eager and a bit naive. After all, I was a veteran of the Third World, or so I thought. I knew I would encounter poverty, despair, and, yes, violence in Africa. But I had not spent my career at the *Post* cocooned in easy places. I had covered the fall of "Baby Doc" Duvalier in Haiti. And after that, I had been assigned to the *Post*'s Southeast Asia bureau, based in the Philippines. I had witnessed the suffering at the sprawling Cambodian refugee camps on the Thai-Cambodian border, and I had seen enough poverty in the rural Philippines and in the slums of Manila to convince myself that I was as emotionally battle-tested as the most hardened foreign correspondents.

But I got my first lesson in Africa as soon as my British Airways flight touched down at Nairobi's Jomo Kenyatta International Airport. That is to say, I learned how to lie.

Africa is a continent of endless, mind-boggling rules and regulations—sometimes contradictory, often based on no reasonable, modern-day foundation, or at least none that I could ever discern. Take, for example, the huge painted sign over the customs area at the

Nairobi airport, informing arriving passengers of all the items that are prohibited inside the country. Among them are fax machines, recording devices, cordless telephones—pretty much everything I was carrying for what would be a three-year assignment. And not to mention my Toshiba laptop computer—surely if they spotted that, the "duty" charged would be more than the machine itself was worth.

I was also carrying a rather large sum of cash and several thousand dollars in traveler's checks. Neil had warned me of what would become one of my favorite Kenyan government "catch-22" situations. When you go to Kenya to work, you need a work permit. But the approval of the work permit for a journalist can take about six months if they like you, and usually much longer. While you're waiting, you of course still need to do your job, run the office, pay the bills, and hire the local staff. But—and here's the catch—major banks refuse to allow foreigners to open an account without a valid work permit. So for six months or more, you run around town like a drug dealer or an international money launderer, paying all of your bills in cash and keeping hundred-dollar bills deposited around your body in different pockets, in your shoes, and in a secret pouch on the flip side of your leather belt. Of course, if you declared at airport customs that you were bringing in thousands of dollars in cash, the custom officers on duty would no doubt find some dubiously legal excuse for you to part with a major portion of it. And, of course, there would never be any receipt.

So you learn to lie. And over the years of traveling in and out of African airports—often without the correct visas, usually without whatever the latest inoculation that some health ministry had decided to require—I got quite accomplished at the art of the African lie.

"Do you have anything to declare?"

"No, nothing."

"What is your purpose here in Kenya?"

"Tourism."

"Is that a computer?"

"No, it's a typewriter."

"I think it is a computer."

"Oh, come on now," I said, trying my best to sound exasperated. "Have you ever seen a computer that small?"

A pause, and he finally heaved, "You are right," and waved me through.

He probably knew it was a computer. And he knew that I knew he knew. And that little vignette formed the basis for what longtime Africa hands confirmed to me was a key rule of thumb for traveling around the continent: It doesn't matter how big the lie as long as you stick to it. Over the months, I would end up traveling into Kenya with a fax machine, answering machines, pretty much everything you can think of tucked away in my shoulder bag. The fax machine I told them was a child's toy. The answering machines were too small to be detected.

There's a corollary to the Big Lie rule: It doesn't matter how fake your documentation looks as long as you present it with authority. This rule would come in particularly handy when traveling to cover the latest coup or refugee crisis in a country for which I had no valid, updated visa. Or to a country—Uganda comes to mind—that often checked the yellow health vaccination cards of incoming passengers. One colleague of mine started a bit of an industry with a fake hospital stamp she had made in Nairobi; when you were set to travel in a hurry and heard that country X was suddenly spot-checking for yellow fever shots, she would stamp your yellow card with the name of some totally fictitious but official-sounding hospital, then scribble a name above it.

I guess the larger point here is that I learned something about why a lot of the countries in Africa don't work. We, the foreign journalists, were not the only ones involved in this web of deception; in many places, it's a national pastime, forced upon people by layers and layers of bureaucracy and archaic, oppressive rules. Even generally honest people learn that you have to find ways to beat the system, or the system grinds you down. Consider: A Kenyan businessman of Indian descent explained to me that he needed a fax machine for his office. But because the Kenyan government imposes such ridiculously high duties on fax machines, he smuggled one in from London after a business trip. Soon he had enough friends demanding fax machines that he had set up a small side business selling imported models at about half the local price. So the government—by not charging a reasonable levy—was losing money, and this businessman essentially became a smuggler.

There's something else I learned, too, through my experience of African airports. It was a truth that was to haunt me for much of the three years I traveled the continent. Simply put, my colleagues in the foreign press corps—my white colleagues—rarely complained of the same hassles as I routinely faced. A few boasted to me how they typically would just barge right through, maybe with a few gruff words. White people traveling in East Africa are rarely stopped, rarely questioned, rarely instructed to open their bags. They jump to the front of lines, they scream and shout for seats on overbooked flights, they walk around with a kind of built-in immunity, the immunity of their skin color. If you're black or Indian, you get stopped. You get the once-over. Your bags get searched. And if you're black, trying to barge your way past an airport customs officer might very well get you a truncheon to the back of your head.

But I would find out about that much later. First I had to get settled into the place that would be my home for the next three years.

Nairobi is at once the center of everything and the center of nothing. Perhaps that's owing to the capital's strange founding, as a midway point on the railroad line between Kampala, now the capital of Uganda, and the Kenyan port town of Mombasa on the Indian Ocean coast. There is, in fact, no particular reason for a city to be here at all. It wasn't really planned, it just grew, from a dusty colonial outpost and transit point at the turn of the century to now the major capital and listening post for East Africa and headquarters for regional offices of the United Nations, the International Red Cross, most international news agencies covering Africa, and major foreign companies with branch offices spread out around the continent.

Despite the knot of downtown high-rise office buildings, though, Nairobi retains the flavor and feel of a large village, not a cosmopolitan capital city. It's a slow-paced city where everything shuts down on Sundays and where it's hard to find a restaurant serving a meal after ten at night. New Mercedes and BMWs, the symbol of Kenya's corrupt class, share the narrow streets with black London taxis, dilapidated pickup trucks, and minivans painted in zebra stripes shuttling khaki-clad tourists from their air-conditioned hotels to the game parks of the Masai Mara. And at the far edge of the city, giraffe and wildebeest roam freely against the silhouette of the capital's skyline, punctuated by the spiraling Kenyatta International Conference Center.

Along Kenyatta Avenue, Moi Avenue, Koinange Street, and the other main drags, European backpackers with tie-dyed baggy pants and colorful sandals over dirty feet fend off filthy beggar children of indeterminate sex who cling to their shirtsleeves crying for a single shilling. Shady-looking Indian shopkeepers suspiciously beckon passersby to step inside to browse at tourist curios or exchange money illegally at the best rates in town. Inside the dark and cavernous central marketplace, hawkers implore visitors to check out their latest collection of Kenya T-shirts, while Dave, the vegetable vendor, offers his own particular tourist favorite, powerful "bang"— marijuana—ready-rolled into joints and shoved into an old Marlboro pack. There are sidewalk vendors, newspaper hawkers, hustlers and swindlers, shoe-shine boys who'd just as soon pick your pocket as polish your loafers, grimy street kids sniffing glue out of large plastic containers, Somali exiles arguing politics over pasta at the corner table of an Italian restaurant, leggy prostitutes with fake weaves and perms winking at tourists from their street-corner perches, and occasionally the odd Masai *morani,* a lanky warrior wrapped in red cloth and looking seriously out of place on the streets of Nairobi.

Some of the old British travel writers and explorers used to extol the great beauty of the African plain. I found a more apt and up-to-date description in the book *Going Down River Road* by a Kenyan novelist named Meja Mwangi, who depicted a new, more urbanized—and to me, more realistic—Africa, one of tin-roofed squatter slums and sleazy bars where day laborers waste away their cash on cheap beer and cheaper whores. It was seedy, funky, dangerous, sometimes depressingly dreary.

But more than anything else, Nairobi was East Africa's premier listening post and staging area, the armchair of stability from which one could keep a watchful, if somewhat distant, eye on the surrounding turmoil. From Nairobi a journalist can take a taxi out to Wilson airport, hop on a twin-engine prop plane, and whip off in a couple of hours to the famine in Somalia or the war in southern Sudan. I could leave home before dawn, be at the airport by six, on the ground covering the latest disaster by nine, back on the plane by four in the afternoon, and in the safety of my own office filing my story well before dinner. And still have time for a shower and shave and the soul-music party at the Carnivore disco that night. Or the Florida 2000 disco. Or Buffalo Bill's. Or any of the handful of sleazy bars where reporters rubbed elbows with aid workers and UN bureaucrats and crazy white expat pilots and assorted adventurers out here for the cold Tusker beers and the easy African women.

For reporters, Nairobi was the perfect ringside seat to Africa's chaos, a place just at the edge of the various catastrophes without ever really being swept up in them. Rarely had Kenya itself been the story, and that's exactly the way President Daniel arap Moi liked it. But that was about to change.

Before my arrival in Nairobi, my exposure to Africa had been limited, to put it generously. I had taken courses in African politics in graduate school, at the London School of Economics, and I had taken some African studies courses as an undergraduate at the University of Michigan in the late 1970s, just after "Afrocentrism" and "Afro-American studies" curricula had been introduced at American universities. Beyond that, I knew very little—and if truth be told, cared very little. I was always more fascinated by European history and Asian politics than that vast, unknown continent south of the

Sahara. I knew that Zimbabwe was once the white-ruled colony of Rhodesia, that South Africa was still ruled by its white minority, and that Nelson Mandela was the world's number one political prisoner. In all, I was pretty ignorant about the land of my roots. Most of what I knew came from watching reruns of the old *Tarzan* series on television and *Daktari*—all of which were essentially about white people in Africa, with the blacks, the natives, reduced to the role of background cutouts.

I was born a black kid in white America. I grew up in the 1960s, in Detroit, when the United States was convulsed by the great movements of the time—antiwar, feminism, civil rights, and black pride. I was too young to remember anything about Malcolm X, and I was only ten when Martin Luther King was assassinated. I remember watching the news bulletin flash across the television screen and asking my mother who Martin Luther King was. And I remember asking if it was a white man or a colored man who shot him.

My family would probably be in that vague category they call "working class"—not really poor, but not particularly well off either. Like a lot of other blacks, my father came up from the South in the 1940s, selling off his dry-cleaning business and a small restaurant to come north and work in an automobile factory, the Ford Motor Company's Dearborn Engine Plant. The war was on, and the plants needed all the help they could get in meeting the demands of the World War II military machine. My father worked just briefly putting tags on engines, then realized, as he later told me, "I knew I was smarter than that." He joined the United Auto Workers, got elected as a committeeman, and stayed involved in union politics as an elected official for the next forty years.

Mine was not what you might call a particularly "black" childhood—just a childhood, an average American childhood. My neighborhood as I remember it growing up was racially mixed, if anything mostly white, Irish and Polish. Mr. O'Neil lived across the street and always sat out on his porch and waved when I came walking home from school. A white guy named Fred ran the corner store—there really was a corner store—and he recognized all the kids from the neighborhood when we came in to buy candy and potato chips.

My parents became Catholic after they moved to Detroit, and I attended a nearby Catholic school called Saint Leo's from first through seventh grades. Saint Leo's was one of those huge and ornate old urban churches, with the high school, grade school, convent, and rectory attached. And the church was packed for all three masses every Sunday. Most of the parishioners, and all the priests and nuns, were white.

Detroit got oppressively hot in the summers, and our small house on the west side had no air conditioning. So sometimes my brother Mel, who was four years older than I, would take me with him up Grand River Avenue to the Globe theater, where for a single admission price we could sit all day in cool, air-conditioned splendor, watching the same films over and over again until it was time to walk home for dinner. I especially remember the time the film *Zulu* was playing, and Michael Caine was leading a group of British soldiers in red tunics against hordes of attacking Zulu tribesmen who were sweeping down on their little fort. Mel and I took turns rooting for opposite sides, the British and the Zulus. And since we of course knew the ending of the movie, neither of us really wanted to root for the losing side. So when it was my turn to cheer on the Zulus—and that meant letting out a loud hoot every time a Zulu killed a British soldier—I would usually just sit there sullenly, knowing what fate was in store for the unfortunate Africans. Then came the credit roll and the heady knowledge that, after the cartoon break, the movie would come on again and I would be able to cheer the British side once more.

That was it, mostly a typical American boyhood.

Then the riot happened.

I didn't really know what a riot was—I was only nine years old in 1967. I remember my father taking me up the road to West Grand Boulevard and Grand River Avenue, a main commercial center a few blocks from my house where we used to go to buy comic books at Cunningham's drug store on weekends, or ornaments and wrapping paper at Kresge's before Christmas. Now the whole block was on fire.

"I want you to see this," my father said. "I want you to see what black people are doing to their own neighborhood."

The white guy who ran the corner store was sitting outside on his stoop holding a shotgun. The few black businesses around, like the barber shop, put hastily drawn cardboard signs in their windows reading, "Soul Brother." At night we turned out the lights and stayed away from the windows because my father was worried about "snipers." We had heard that some people had been shot standing too close to their windows.

The National Guard came in and put down the riot. They took up positions on street corners and rode around in their Jeeps. They imposed a curfew, which, I was told, meant we couldn't go outside or else we might be shot by a soldier. It was the worst urban riot in American history, with more than forty people killed and much of the inner city, the shops and stores I knew, burned to the ground.

Something else changed after the riot. The city, the neighborhood, turned blacker. The white people I knew started moving out to suburbs that sounded really far away. The church, where you sometimes couldn't find a seat on Sunday if you went late for mass, got emptier and emptier. They cut back from three masses to two, and soon most of the faces were black. The school became blacker, too. And, ironically, less Catholic. To keep the doors open despite the massive population loss, the school started admitting more kids from the neighborhood regardless of religion. But it wasn't enough. Eventually, before I ever made it there, the high school was forced to close down.

Our family went through a tragic change, too, just a few months after the riots. Mel, who was a safety patrol boy at Saint Leo's school, was hit by a car that ran through a red light across a broad intersection. Mel would always walk out first with his bright orange belt and beckon the other kids when it was safe to cross. He raced out too quickly this time and never saw the car coming; it hit him once and knocked him in the air, and hit him again as he fell down.

Mel died on November 22, 1967, after three days in the hospital. I was only nine years old at the time, and kids my age weren't allowed into the intensive care ward of the hospital. My last sight of Mel was him lying on his side on the street, kind of in a fetal position, with a big scar on his head above his eye. When I next saw him, he was lying in a casket, and they buried him in the black cassock and white surplice he used to wear so proudly as a Saint Leo's altar boy. It was the first time I had ever seen a dead person, and it was my best friend and brother. Suddenly, I was an only child. I felt all alone.

There was still another change going on at the time, although it would be some time before I could grasp the significance of it.

Before the riots—in fact, all through my childhood—black people were "colored." Or Negroes. Never "black." When I was a kid, the word "black" had kind of a negative connotation to it. Someone who was considered handsome would be invariably described as "brown skinned." To call someone "black" or "black skinned" was the lowest form of derision. It meant field hand. Ugly. Country. And when it was tossed around in the rhyming, singsong cadence of my southern relatives during those fun family gatherings, "black" would often come out in description as "that ugly black nigger," or "sit your black ass down."

I remember growing up thinking that we black people, colored people, whatever, often seem obsessed by our own color. We refer to each other by color. It was in our jargon, the southern idioms, as when mothers warned their children, "I'll beat the black off you." Or the tired statement of resignation, "I ain't got to do nothing but stay black and die."

But sometime, maybe it was after the riot of 1967, the term "black" took on an entirely different meaning.

Colored people, Negroes, began referring to themselves as black, not as a term of derision but with pride. James Brown had told us, "Say It Loud, I'm Black and I'm Proud," and then we got songs like "Young, Gifted and Black . . . that's where it's at!" There were the Black Panthers, black men in black leather jackets and berets looking menacing and scaring the hell out of white people. There was the Black Power clenched-fist salute.

There was also a new consciousness about Africa and things African. The dashiki, a colorful, loose-fitting robe, became popular. Young men—my father used to call them "jitterbugs," using a term from another era—stopped going to the barber shop to have their hair put into a slick "process," which was a painful straightening operation involving, from what I could tell, a lot of heat and a lot of grease. The new hair trend was called the "Natural," or the "Afro." Afro combs—"picks"—often came in red, black, and green, the colors of liberation, of Africa, and sometimes the handles curved up into an angry clenched fist.

The movies in Detroit changed, too, after the riots. Going to the movies was a regular family weekend outing, but after 1967, the theater audiences became blacker, and the movies took on decidedly black themes. There was *Mandingo*. There was *Shaft*, "the black private dick that's a sex machine to all the chicks." There was *Cotton Comes to Harlem*. There were a lot of hard-talking, mean black dudes on screen, giving it to whitey and "The Man."

All of this was part of Detroit changing rapidly from a white city to a black one. A black mayor would not be elected until 1973. But that, too, became inevitable with the massive shifts under way after the riots of 1967.

Now fast-forward to my high school. It looks more like a small college campus, actually, with its manicured lawns, spacious parking lot, tennis courts. Even the name implies something a bit loftier than your typical high school: "University-Liggett" it was called, and it's nestled away in a well-heeled, pristine suburb called Grosse Pointe Woods. I wasn't excited, at first, at the thought of leaving the city to go to a school so far from home, from neighborhood friends. But my parents saw the declining state of the city schools, and they said they knew what was best.

I was not the first black kid in the school, not by a long shot. Nor was I the only one at the time. In fact, there were quite a few of us—

a doctor's daughter, the son of a Detroit school principal, the son of a Michigan state senator. A minority, surely, but never made to feel unwelcome, never subject to any hostility. We were all just kids. We complained about the school dress code—neckties for the boys, skirts for the girls. We used fake IDs to buy beer on weekends, went to house parties, drove too fast on the freeways. Not exactly Boyz 'N The Hood.

Only occasionally in my high school years was I made conscious of my place in America's other world. In the eleventh or twelfth grade, a group of us organized a class trip to see a roller derby competition. The arena, Olympia Stadium, was smack in the heart of the city—the "inner city," as it was now called—in a rundown neighborhood that by the mid-1970s had become almost exclusively black. It was my neighborhood; I lived about a block and a half from the stadium.

Most of my white suburban friends from high school had never been to my house in Detroit. Not that I was particularly ashamed of the house, or the neighborhood. But it was pretty far from most everything; I had to take a bus for a half hour to school until I was old enough to drive myself. But most of the social life, the after-school activity, was centered around the school. I'm sure few of my friends even knew where I lived, except in the vaguest sense that I was from the city, the other side of the invisible line.

Bringing a bunch of sheltered, suburban white kids to the heart of the inner city for a school outing was probably a dumb idea in the first place. And it was probably inevitable that something would go wrong.

After the game, I decided to walk the short distance home. But as my classmates were coming out of the arena to board the bus back to Grosse Pointe, they crossed the path of a group of black kids. Kids from my neighborhood. One of the white girls saw one of the black girls with an Afro comb, a pick, stuck in the back of her hair, and made some ill-advised comment like, "Why do you have that comb in your hair?" Probably not hostile—I didn't hear it. Maybe she was really just curious. But of course, all hell broke loose.

So now you've got a bunch of white kids, clambering onto their bus back to the suburbs, and a bunch of angry black kids hitting at the windows with chains and bottles and anything else they can get their hands on. There were shouts and slurs flying in both directions. And there I was, on both sides, on neither side—not wanting to have to take sides. I got the hell out of there as fast as I could.

When I think back to that incident, I think about how I've often felt trapped between two worlds. I suppose I could say that it was always easier to walk away—to run, really—than to have to choose sides. But that would be only partially true. I'll tell you what I was really thinking then: I was embarrassed. Humiliated. These were my friends and schoolmates—my white friends—who had come into my neighborhood, less than two blocks from the house where I had grown up, where I still lived. And here's a bunch of black kids smashing the windows of their school bus. This is how black folks in the ghetto behaved. This is how they would see me. I was so ashamed that I wanted to cry. Instead, I just ran away.

Okay, now fast-forward one more time, to the University of Michigan in Ann Arbor. I picked U of M because it's big. Huge. Forty thousand total, if you count all the grad students. And after four years in a high school with just over three hundred kids (seventy-six in my graduating class, the class of '76), I wanted to feel like I could get lost in a crowd.

By the time I got there, "Afrocentrism" was already well entrenched in the university curriculum. There was a fairly large department devoted specifically to African and Afro-American studies, and several prominent black professors, including Dr. Ali Mazrui, perhaps the best-known African scholar in the West. Michigan also had a fairly large black student population, which succeeded in pressing onto the university's agenda questions like divestiture of school stocks and holdings from companies that continued to do business with the racist regime in South Africa. Much of the political consciousness-raising on campus was the result of an earlier struggle, when an earlier group of black students formed the BAM, the Black Action Movement, to demand more specific minority recruitment and staffing goals. I arrived in the "post-BAM" era, and the signs of the new black student awareness were pretty evident. It seemed to me almost like a kind of voluntary resegregation—we want to be equal, but separate. There were black fraternities and sororities that on weekends held black parties with black music. Most of the black students lived together, clustered in certain dormitories or sharing apartments. And when I walked into the dorm dining room, I had to decide whether to sit at the black table with my black friends or to integrate the white table so I could sit with my white friends. This for the kid coming out of a predominantly white high school, the one who hates having to take sides.

I became active on the staff of the campus newspaper, the *Michigan Daily*, which was published every day except Monday and was staffed and run almost entirely by students. I was following a high school interest in writing and journalism, and at college I found it enormously rewarding, if time-consuming; the newspaper became the center of much of my college life. The *Daily* offices on Maynard Street became something like a home, and all of us who worked there became something like a family.

One semester, I signed up for one of the African studies classes. Africa was hot on the student-activist political agenda at the time, and at the *Daily* we student editors were wrestling with what we considered some pretty weighty matters of state. The divestment issue was coming to a head, with students planning a disruption of the meeting of the board of regents. South Africa's black townships were exploding, and the John Vorster regime was responding with even harsher repression. The civil war in Rhodesia had forced the breakaway white regime to agree to negotiate a transition to majority rule in historic talks at Lancaster House in London. And Tanzanian troops had invaded Uganda to topple the brutal buffoon Idi Amin Dada—a clear violation of the cherished African precept of sovereignty, but an action just as clearly justified given Amin's butchery inside his country and his frequent military forays into Tanzania.

Given all that, it seemed like a pretty good idea to take a course or two in African politics.

One of the classes was held in a tiny classroom so crammed with desks that if you got there late, you'd have to weave through an obstacle course to get to an open seat. And of course I usually arrived late. I'd walk over there from the *Daily* office with a friend and colleague, Judy Rakowsky. Judy was from Polish Jewish stock, from Lima, Ohio, where her father, Rudy, ran a plant called Buckeye Rubber. And she looked about as much like the middle-American ideal—huge blue eyes, straight blond hair that hung to her waist, and a gymnast's perfect figure.

So here's the picture: Me, then a skinny black kid with big glasses, and Judy Rakowsky, this lanky blond gymnast, walking together, late, into an African politics class and having to jostle for a couple of open seats. I don't think she was the only white person in the class—but pretty darned close. And certainly the only white person, white woman, who was friends with a black guy. No, who came in every day with a black guy, who sat next to a black guy, who whispered to me during class and laughed at my jokes. Maybe it was my imagination, but you could cut through the thick layers of hostility with a butter knife. Hostility toward her just for being there, a white woman in a black studies class. And hostility toward me, it seemed, for breaking rank, for preferring the company of the enemy, the oppressor. It was the dining hall test, and I had failed. I had chosen the wrong side.

During my college years, I did come to be introduced to one African friend, and it happened in a rather strange way. His name was Conrad Bruno Njamfa, from Cameroon, and he had been my pen pal.

Remember pen pals? They were big in the 1960s, supposedly a way of fostering international cooperation and understanding. You sent in your name, enclosed a few bucks, and they matched you up with some kid about the same age from another country. And you exchanged letters and photos and had the excitement of getting those red-white-and-blue, thin-paper air-mail envelopes delivered to your house with your name on them. And you usually kept up the correspondence until you got to be a teenager and discovered girls and beer and forgot all about your faraway friend.

That's pretty much what happened to me until my pen pal from a decade earlier moved to the United States.

Bruno had been accepted to Eastern Michigan University in Ypsilanti, which was just a few minutes drive from Ann Arbor. He was from the Anglophone minority of Cameroon, a divided country where the dominant language and culture is still French. He could speak passable French, but an English-speaking Cameroonian was always made to feel a bit of an outsider in his own country, even though Cameroon was officially bilingual. For higher education, it was easier to go abroad, and Bruno ended up in Michigan.

I was a little wary when I drove down to meet him face-to-face. I'm not sure why, really. Maybe it was the idea of having to meet someone who was essentially a total stranger, whose only link to me was a series of letters written more than a decade earlier. Or maybe there was a twinge of guilt that I hadn't kept up the correspondence, and now my past was here to revisit me. Maybe he would hit me up for cash, or expect some other form of generosity from his long-lost correspondent. Maybe I wouldn't like him. Or maybe I was afraid that he wouldn't like me.

But what worried me most was that he was African, and I a black American. I was worried about how I would relate to him, but uppermost in my mind was how he would relate to me. I was worried that this African might not consider me black enough.

Sounds crazy, I suppose, which is why I hesitate even to put it into print. But to understand these feelings, I have to take myself back to the times, back to the hostility I described in the eyes of black students in the African studies class. Perhaps my African friend had come to America—to Michigan—purposely to find in his former long-distance friend a black soul mate. And perhaps he would see in me someone too assimilated for his liking, a black man with white roommates and white friends, who spurned the black dining table in the dorm cafeteria. Maybe he would look down on me as a black man who had lost his roots, his African-ness. Or maybe worse, he would shun me as a traitor.

As it turned out, Bruno did not shun me as a traitor or anything else. We did reestablish the acquaintanceship, but never became anything like close friends. Later on, when I went to work in Washington for a summer, Bruno ended up spending a few months in Detroit, living in my old room in my parents' house. He disappeared sometime after that, and we never heard from him again.

I am reminded now of a train trip I took across Europe several years later when I was already a reporter on the staff of the *Washington Post*. I was on vacation, taking advantage of a monthlong rail pass, and somewhere between France and Spain I ended up in a compartment with a smartly dressed West African. I wanted to practice my French, and we struck up a conversation.

The West African asked me if I had ever visited Africa. Yes, I told him—Morocco, Algeria, Tunisia, and Egypt. "No," he said. "I mean black Africa."

I made up a few lame excuses. Not yet. I was waiting until I had more time. The continent was so vast I didn't know where to begin. But he kept repeating to me: "A black man, speaking English, a little bit of French. You must visit Africa. You could travel everywhere. Yes, English and a little French. You should go."

He was right. I knew I must one day go. But I also knew—and I'm not sure he could tell—that the thought of Africa filled me with dread. No, something approaching terror. Partially it was a fear that I would not like it, that I would find the poverty there too depressing. But the other part of it was the same fear I had that night driving along the freeway in Michigan to meet my Cameroonian pen pal. Perhaps Africa would reject me and my lifestyle. Perhaps Africa would force me to choose which side of the dining hall I would sit on, and it was a choice I didn't want to make. It was easier to turn and run.

There was, of course, another reason for my reluctance to visit Africa. There's no nice way to put it, so I'll just state it plainly: I was uncertain what it would be like, how I would feel, for once not standing out in a crowd.

Being black in white America, you walk around constantly aware of your difference, defined by the color of your skin. By the time I went to Africa for the *Post,* I had lived in Asia, too, where, for better or worse, whites and blacks alike are outsiders, foreigners, strangers. In some places, like the Philippines, being a foreigner accords you special treatment, and it hardly matters if you're black or white. You can walk to the front of a line at an airline counter. Doors are held open for you. You can't convince a cop to give you a ticket, even if he catches you speeding through a red light without your license. It's because you're a foreigner, and you are accorded special treatment.

But to be black in Africa?

Would they be able to tell that I was not from the place? Would I still be accorded that preferential treatment that foreigners abroad enjoy? A friend of mine named Debbie Ichimura, a fourth-generation Japanese American, once confided to me her own private fears of going to Japan, her ancestral homeland. "I don't know what it would be like to be just another face in the crowd," she said.

Yes, that's it. Without intending to, Debbie captured the essence of my anxiety: the fear of being one in the crowd. Losing my identity. My individuality.

I had finished my assignment in Southeast Asia and was taking a year off living in Hawaii when the editors at the *Post* asked me in early 1991 to consider going to Africa. I asked for a few weeks to mull it over, took a trip back to familiar stomping grounds in Asia, and ended up in Thailand, where I sought out my friend Kevin Cooney, a big, hard-drinking Irish American reporter for the Reuter news agency who had spent several months working in the Reuter office in Nairobi. He was in Bangkok now, and we met in one or another of the sleazy go-go bars on Patpong Road.

We talked first about women—natural enough, I suppose, when you're slamming down Kloster beers in a Patpong bar. But then the talk turned to Africa. What was the scene like in Kenya? Was there any scene at all?

A few more beers. Then the question that was really on my mind. What would it be like—really like—to be a black man in Africa? How would the Africans relate to me, a long-lost cousin?

And Cooney was ready with a response. "In Africa," he said, "you'll be just another nigger!"

If it was crude, well, that was typical Cooney—I took no offense, and none, I'm sure, was intended. His warning was well intentioned, and even prophetic. I'd often find myself recalling it as I traveled around the continent.

And it was against that background that I stepped off the plane at Jomo Kenyatta Airport, and into Africa.

2

Welcome to Tara

"No matter where you come from, as long as you're a
black man, you're an African.
Don't mind your nationality, you have got the identity
of an African."
—From the Peter Tosh reggae song, "African"

As I STARTED my new assignment, I knew that the next few years
promised to be the most exciting in Africa since independence. The
fall of the Soviet Union and the effective end of the divide between
East and West meant that Africa was going to have a chance for a
second awakening, freed from the grip of Cold War superpower
rivalries. Socialism was in retreat not just in Eastern Europe but in
places like Angola and Mozambique, where longtime Marxists were
announcing their new embrace of free-market capitalism and democratic elections.

Africa's old dictators were also on the ropes. In the months before

I got to the continent, Mohamed Siad Barre had fled Somalia, and Haile Mengistu Mariam had fled Ethiopia. Kenneth Kaunda of Zambia—one of the continent's independence-era heroes—was forced to hold that country's first truly democratic election in three decades, and he was trounced by a diminutive trade union leader largely unknown to the outside world. And the premier strongman, Mobutu Sese Seko of Zaire, looked likely to fall next after a bloody riot by unpaid soldiers who rampaged through Kinshasa, the capital, forcing the French and Belgians to intervene.

Why all the upheaval? Simple. The continent was changing because the foreign donors, Western countries mostly as well as international lending institutions like the International Monetary Fund and the World Bank, were finally getting tough.

In the Cold War days, the excesses of Mobutu and the incompetent economic management of Kaunda went largely overlooked. African countries were little more than pawns on the chessboard in the global competition between Washington and Moscow. We had our dictators and they had theirs. Mobutu may have been a corrupt son of a bitch, but he did let the CIA use an airstrip in southern Zaire to funnel supplies to the anticommunist UNITA rebels in Angola. Siad Barre may have been brutal—his son-in-law, Mohamed Said Hersi Morgan, carried out a particularly ruthless aerial bombardment against the breakaway northern town of Hargeysa—but Somalia was strategically located on Africa's north-northeastern tip, facing a potential arc of instability across the Indian Ocean and the entire Persian Gulf region. We needed Siad on our side.

But by late 1991, things were different. Donors were starting to demand accountability for how their funds were spent. African strongmen were finding that with their strategic utility spent, the Americans, the European Community, the World Bank, and the IMF were no longer so willing to turn a blind eye to rampant state-level corruption. New terms like "conditionality" and "governance" entered the lenders' lexicons, terms that effectively translated into greater concern with how donated money was spent They also meant that the donors, led by the United States, were no longer willing to keep political matters like free elections and human rights separate from strictly economic criteria for the granting of aid. To the African autocrats, who had become accustomed to a blank check over three decades, this new attention to accounting smacked of renewed Western imperialism and interference in their internal affairs.

And if Africa was caught up in the global sweep toward democratization and reform, then Kenya had become a frontline state in the struggle. Since 1978 Kenya had been ruled by Daniel T. arap Moi, a former schoolteacher who took over after the death of the country's independence leader and first president, Jomo Kenyatta. Moi came to the presidency by accident—Kenyatta had selected him as vice president mainly as a compromise choice between various political factions lining up to succeed the old man. Moi is a member of the Kalenjin tribe, one of the country's smallest, and at best he was seen as an interim ruler, a seat-warmer.

But Moi proved more tenacious than anyone at the time gave him credit for. He was also more ruthless. As he consolidated his power, he slowly set about purging political rivals and critics. That paved the way for a constitutional amendment enshrining his ruling Kenya African National Union (KANU) as the sole legal political party. After an aborted coup by air force officers, mostly from Kenyatta's dominant Kikuyu tribe, Moi disbanded the entire air force and set up a new one. He also became more thorough in his consolidation of power, placing loyal tribesmen in key government posts and cracking down hard on his perceived enemies within.

As a leader, Moi has never been considered particularly smart or worldly. He's never been described as personally charming, like Mobutu. And he has no real governing philosophy, except an oddball vision he calls "Nyayoism," which literally means "footsteps" and is supposed to inspire the *wananchi*, the masses, to follow along. The large government office building downtown is called "Nyayo House." In its basement, human-rights advocates and dissidents say, are the police torture rooms.

What Moi lacks in charm and intellect, however, he more than makes up in guile. He has clung to power by cleverly manipulating three key and interrelated levers. The first is tribalism. Even in a relatively modern state like Kenya, tribal animosities bubble just an inch beneath the surface. The Kikuyu are the largest tribe and until Moi took over, had been at the forefront of the country's independence struggles and its early postcolonial politics. Jomo Kenyatta was a Kikuyu, and he was by all accounts a particularly harsh autocrat, a tribal chieftain of the first order who believed it was the Kikuyus' natural right to rule. Many Kenyans, non-Kikuyu, are deathly fearful of another Kikuyu presidency, and Moi has managed to tap into that fear and present himself as the only alternative. Moi has likewise been willing to allow more than a few tribal eruptions to make his point to Kenya and the world—that he alone represents stability for Kenya, that without him the country becomes just another African tribal killing zone.

The second lever relates closely to the first: Moi has been able to play the international community and the country's foreign donors like a virtuoso plays the violin. Somewhere, he figured out exactly how to allow just enough superficial reform to keep Western embassies happy while at the same time reminding them that Kenya, for all its faults, was still an anchor of stability in a pretty turbulent neighborhood.

It was a fair point, and one not lost on the foreign community. Look northeast from Kenya and you have Somalia, and northwest is Sudan, both racked by civil wars. To the west across Lake Victoria is Uganda, which suffered under the brutality of two successive dictators, Idi Amin and Milton Obote, both of whom seemed intent on grinding "the pearl of Africa" into the ground. And to the south is Tanzania, a favorite of Scandinavian do-gooders and armchair socialists, but whose economy essentially collapsed after decades of Marxist mismanagement. With neighbors like that, Kenya and Moi actually start to look pretty damn good. And that's precisely why Nairobi became the regional headquarters for a host of international aid agencies, such as the International Red Cross, Save the Children, and UNICEF. The UN Environment Program is headquartered in Nairobi, along with the Habitat group. And foreign media organizations—including the *Washington Post*—have made Nairobi their main base for covering the rest of the continent.

Moi had one final lever he could pull: money. Many politicians who opposed him were bought off and co-opted. Throughout Africa, I would soon discover, loyalties and principles often last only as long as it takes the ink to dry on a bank check. Some of those who oppose Moi today made their fortunes when they were on the opposite side of the fence, which makes me wonder if the reason for their current shift in allegiance is simply that they've lost their turn at the trough. And many who might have considered opposing the regime would think twice before seeing their livelihoods cut off.

By the time I arrived in Kenya, Moi was losing his privileged position. The foreign-aid donors were scheduled to hold their regular meeting in Paris in a few weeks' time, and all indications were that they were tired of Moi's stalling, his repression, his empty promises. This time, it appeared that they were finally going to shut off the aid pipeline until he made good on genuine reforms.

Moi's political opponents had also become more brazen, in part emboldened by the fall of Kenneth Kaunda in Zambia. The Kenyan opposition formed a broad alliance called the Forum for the Restoration of Democracy, or FORD, which was defying the government by holding unlicensed political rallies and attracting thousands of supporters. FORD members were demanding that Moi lift a ban on opposition political parties and hold a snap election that they were convinced they could win.

Much of the impetus for the change in Kenya, and the pressure on the government, was coming from the United States embassy in Nairobi, headed by the scrappy ambassador, Smith Hempstone. Hempstone was a former journalist, a die-hard conservative who had been editor of the defunct *Washington Star* and later the *Washington Times*. He had also had long experience with Africa, having served as a foreign correspondent in Kenya a few decades earlier.

Now back in Nairobi as ambassador, Hempstone, with his ruddy complexion, craggy features, and white beard, even looked the part of a modern-day Ernest Hemingway. He became an articulate pro-democracy advocate, often undiplomatically criticizing the excesses of the regime.

Moi was also feeling the heat on another front. A few years earlier, Robert Ouko, the popular foreign minister, had been killed under mysterious circumstances. His burned and mutilated body had been found in February 1990 in a bush near his hometown of Kisumu. Suspicion immediately had fallen on Moi's henchmen, who, according to the most popular theory at the time, may have been trying to silence Ouko because he was beginning to speak out about the mounting corruption of the ruling clique. Under pressure, the government agreed to an outside inquiry by a retired Scotland Yard investigator named John Troon. And Troon's conclusion turned out to be a bombshell, pointing the finger of blame at some of the politicians closest to Moi.

How odd, I thought as I scanned the papers my first day in Kenya. The two men splashed across the front pages, the two individuals who have more than anyone shaken the foundations of this regime, are Hempstone and Troon—two white guys.

The irony wasn't lost on the Kenyan government either. I was to learn on my first day on the job that race was never far from the surface of any discussion in Kenya. And Moi and his cronies were not above playing their own race card.

The foreign minister, Wilson Ndolo Ayah, responded by calling a press conference for the foreign reporters in town. That, in itself, I was told by my colleagues, was an unusual occurrence, since this government rarely saw any particular need to talk to the foreign press. I followed along with a group of reporters, but we momentarily got lost along the way. "Sorry," someone in the group apologized, "but we so rarely get the chance to go to the foreign ministry that we've forgotten where it is."

We soon learned the reason for the unusual summons. Ayah was angry, and his ire was directed at the U.S. embassy. Hempstone was acting like "a racist," the foreign minister thundered. "He's one of those white men who likes to come to Kenya to look at the animals, but not the people." Hempstone, Ayah said, "has the mentality of a slave owner."

For his part, Hempstone was able to laugh off the criticism, as he did most of the rants from the Kenyan government. The next day, Neil Henry and I went to the U.S. embassy—ironically situated on Moi Avenue—so I could introduce myself to the ambassador and Neil could say one last farewell. The ambassador greeted us at the door to his spacious office with a warm, wide grin and said, "Welcome to Tara," a reference to Scarlett O'Hara's antebellum plantation.

Maybe, I thought, this is going to be a fun assignment after all.

The *Post*'s bureau in Nairobi was a small and rather cramped one-room office on the second floor of a rundown building called Chester House, where many of the foreign news organizations kept offices lining a long and somewhat dingy corridor. At the end of the hallway was a little canteen and coffee bar, where seemingly any Kenyan political dissident, Sudanese guerrilla, Somali faction leader, or Rwandan rebel could come to hold an impromptu press conference for the assembled foreign correspondents. Two burly and badly dressed Kenyans usually sat at the end of one of the wooden tables sipping coffee, and Neil told me these were the Kenyan government security guys whose job it was to keep an eye on the foreign reporters and the various goings-on at Chester House.

One of my neighbors across the hall was Gary Strieker, who was kind of a one-man operation for CNN. He was cameraman, correspondent, producer, and even tape editor, assisted only by a friendly Kenyan named David, who was the sound man and helped lug the heavy TV gear, and sometimes by Gary's Kenyan wife, Christine. Gary had been an American banker in Beirut, had taught himself how to use a TV camera, and for the last several years had covered wars and famines around Africa. When I met him, he was already talking like a guy who had seen too much and was ready to go home;

he would speak longingly of moving to his ranch in the American West where he could cover environmental stories and features instead of tribal massacres and starving kids.

Also across the hall was Julian Ozanne, the correspondent for London's *Financial Times* newspaper who, though only in his mid-twenties, was already something of a legend among the Africa-based press hacks. His adventures had already included getting tossed into a Sudanese jail, surviving a plane crash, getting shot at, being wounded. When Julian wasn't out chasing guerrillas in the bush, he could usually be found at the Carnivore disco, dancing until dawn with the latest love of his life—and then he'd still somehow manage to make it to Wilson airport a few hours later to hop an early-morning aid-agency flight to southern Sudan or to Somalia so he could start tromping through refugee camps before noon.

Like so many others I met in Kenya, Julian was a white African; the accent was vaguely British, or from something out of the Queen's once far-flung colonies, but, as he liked to tell me, he was born in Africa and felt more at home on the African continent than moving among the pubs of London's West End or the denizens of Fleet Street. Julian and his best friend and roommate, Aidan Hartley, a white Kenyan working for the Reuter news agency, were buying a house in the Karen-Langata section of Nairobi. To me, that showed some kind of commitment. They could be cynical about the continent, and often downright cruel in their pointed barbs about the foibles of the black Africans, but it was clear that this was, after all, their home.

Another twenty-something white reporter who always felt more at home in Africa than London was Sam Kiley, the flamboyant East Africa correspondent for the *Times* of London. Sam was distinguishable by his completely shaved scalp, which he usually kept covered from the scorching African sun by some colorful bandanna. Sam rode a motorcycle around Nairobi's treacherously potholed streets, he boasted of having once worked as a male model in Japan for extra cash, and, like his rival Julian, he was another great lover of women. And since the number of available young white women in Nairobi was limited—Kenyan locals were considered risky because of the high rate of HIV infection—Julian and Sam often seemed in quiet competition on the female front, always scouting for fresh opportunities or sometimes resorting to short-term imports from the U.K. Nairobi seemed to me a bit incestuous at the time, like a scene out of that old movie appropriately titled *White Mischief.*

Like so many of the others in the press corps, Sam, too, could be brutally sharp in his commentaries on Africa and the Africans. Once, he came up to me in the hallway at Chester House wildly excited about his latest idea. He was going to write a book about his experiences in Africa, he told me. He would tell the real story of the guerrilla movements and rebel armies. "I've got the perfect title," he said. "I'm going to call it *Baboons with Rifles.*"

I hope I don't stay so long that I become so cynical, I thought.

The *Washington Post*'s stringer in Nairobi, whose job was to back me up when I was away from the story, was a former longtime wire service reporter named Todd Shields. A lanky American with a booming radio-voice baritone, he was the resident wit of the press corps. He and his wife, Didi, a reporter for the Associated Press, had been in Africa among the longest, and they too were tired and ready to leave. On more than one occasion Todd told me that he no longer found journalistic exhilaration in narrowly avoiding having his head shot off watching two African factions battling each other on some dusty street corner.

The news agency bureaus—AP, Reuter, Agence France Presse—all employed a number of black Africans on their staffs as reporters and photographers. One of the first photographers I met, just days after arriving in Nairobi, was Hos Maina of Reuter. I had written a quick-hit little feature story about the Miss Kenya beauty pageant and the debate the contest had ignited over African versus Western standards of beauty. But I didn't have a photograph of the winner, and I was desperate. I called the Reuter bureau late on a Saturday and found Hos there at work. I explained my dilemma, and he told me not to worry—he had taken a picture himself of Miss Kenya, and he was willing to come in the next day, Sunday, his day off, just to dig the photo out for me and transmit it to Washington. And Hos had never even met me before.

I always remembered that favor Hos did for me as one of those endless little acts of kindness I would later discover all over the continent. After that, I always considered Hos a friend and a good colleague.

But everyone's favorite in the Nairobi press corps was a young photographer named Dan Eldon. His father was British, his mother American, but Dan was in his heart an African, a white kid raised in Kenya who spoke Swahili and was the only one I met who seemed to move easily across the divide that separated black Africans from the white expatriate world. He was just twenty-one and could have passed for a teenager, but he had already established himself as a talented, up-and-coming young photojournalist, willing to go anywhere for the picture. He was a prankster with a wicked sense of humor and a trunkful of disguises. Once, at a party, I didn't recognize him when he came up to me wearing a fake mustache and glasses and spoke in a thick, indistinguishable accent. He introduced himself with a throaty "hello," then whipped off the glasses totally pleased with himself. "Had you going, didn't I?" he said, obviously delighted with himself. It was vintage Dan.

The stories of Dan's masquerades became legend. When his father, Mike Eldon, was briefly hospitalized, Dan managed to bully his way past the Kenyan hospital staff well after visiting hours, first by dressing up in a white coat and pretending to be a doctor, and then the next time by wearing American military "chocolate chip" desert fatigues and announcing brusquely, "Colonel Fred Peck, United States Marines!"

My own "bureau" in Africa consisted of myself and a Kenyan office assistant named George. Neil Henry had found George by accident one day while doing a story in one of the sprawling Nairobi squatter slums. He thought George bright, if not formally educated, and decided to try an experiment by giving him a job well beyond his capabilities to see if George would rise to the occasion. For the most part, he did, since his job was largely confined to reading and clipping important articles out of the local Kenyan newspaper and once a month carrying piles of money around town to pay the electricity bill, the water bill, and the bills for the house and office telephones, which seemed in perpetual danger of being disconnected for late payment.

There was another part to George that I started to figure out only much later. Within my first few weeks on the job, he told me that Neil had promised him a raise. Sounded reasonable to me, since his salary was only about eighty U.S. dollars each month. Then Christmas rolled around, and he asked me for an advance on his next month's salary, which sounded reasonable, too. As the months went by, George's requests for loans, for salary advances, for pay raises, continued to escalate. I mentioned it to Todd and Julian, who were astonished at how much I was paying George. A hundred and fifty bucks a month sounded like a pittance to me, but George was making twice what all the other Kenyan office assistants were earning, and for far less work, since I was constantly traveling. After checking my own books, I also discovered that I had "loaned" and "advanced" George so much money that he would have to work for me for free for about a year to pay me back.

I started thinking I now had a good idea about how Western governments must have felt after pumping money into Africa for years only to discover that it had been siphoned off and the hand was still extended. But it would get worse. Soon some of my colleagues in the press corps began complaining to me that George had been borrowing money from them, too! Sometimes, when I would leave town for a reporting trip, George would tell my friends that I had not left enough money to pay a phone bill or an electric bill, and he would ask them to advance some cash to the office until I returned. It was a lie—I always left enough cash on hand—but a convenient way for George to use my name to get personal loans from my friends. Now they were coming to me demanding repayment.

I uncovered other scams as well. Sometimes, when I gave George cash to pay the bills, he would pay only half the bill and put the remainder on credit, pocketing the other half. I discovered this once when I strolled by the shop of the Indian merchant who supplied my daily newspapers. He asked me when I was planning to catch up on my back bills. I was flabbergasted, knowing I had always paid my bills on time.

I had given George the benefit of the doubt. Part of my motivation, I admit, was guilt. I felt bad that Kenyans earned so little that they had to resort to shaving the edges of propriety for a little extra cash here and there. Then I felt that as a black boss to my African assistant, I should show a little more understanding, a little more generosity. A white guy probably would have fired George long ago. But for some reason I felt I had to care a little more. And he played on that, constantly leaving me notes telling me how kind I was after the latest raise, wishing me all God's blessing for being so understanding, pouring it on thick. Using me. Just like an African potentate plays the guilt strings of white aid donor countries. Now, after I found out about the newspaper scam, I was boiling mad. Like the World Bank and the IMF, I was about to start my own campaign for financial accountability.

When I confronted George about his pattern of lies and deceit, I was ready to fire him on the spot. But I didn't. My guilt came back. He told me that he was very poor and that his many children—I forget how many exactly, but a lot—needed books for school, medicine when they were sick. Part of the problem was that George, like many other Kenyan men, had more than one wife. Taking new wives and siring children accorded respect, even in a squatter slum. Whether one could afford the additional burdens of a new family was never part of the equation.

I realized that George and I were talking across a great cultural divide. I could never understand his world. I was thirty-four years old, never married, and had no children. George, a couple years younger than I, had three wives and at least eight kids. He probably felt that my life was incomplete.

He also felt that since I was the boss, I had an obligation to help him, to be his patron. It was a common sentiment around a country, and a continent, with little in the way of a social safety net like we know in the West. When a family member got sick, the patron, the boss, was expected to pay the medical bill. At school time, the boss helped out for the school fees, the books, the new clothes for the kids. When a parent died, the boss pitched in to help pay for the funeral. That's just the way it was in Africa. It was what George, through the prism of his culture, expected of me, the new *bwana*, or sir. I was angry at being put into a role that I never expected or asked for. My Western way of thinking said that I just wanted to pay him a fair wage for a fair day's work and that his family problems were not my responsibility. I resented being made to feel guilty when what I really wanted to do was fire him. But the cultural gap was too wide; I simply wasn't thinking about it in the African way.

I learned much the same lesson from my other household employees, who, while far more honest than George, seemed to have a seemingly endless series of personal and family crises all of which required large amounts of financial outpouring on my part. My house in Nairobi was kept clean and comfortable by a kindly and elderly live-in housekeeper and sometimes cook named Hezekiah. While I lived alone in the spacious three-bedroom house, Hezekiah lived in a little one-room shack behind the kitchen, his wife and children far away on his *shamba*, or farm, in the countryside. I never set foot inside Hezekiah's little cabin. I told myself that this was to allow the older man some modicum of privacy. In truth, I knew I would have felt guilty seeing his humble surroundings—probably just a thin cot and a tiny radio, in a room the size of one of my closets—compared to my own rather ostentatious lodgings.

The gardener, who walked to work each morning from a nearby slum, was a soft-spoken younger man named Reuben. He also substituted as my messenger and all-around helper. If I needed a taxi, Reuben would run—literally—for a mile or more to a main street to flag one down and bring it back to my house. He would walk uncomplaining through the rain to buy extra milk if I ran out.

Reuben walked and ran endlessly, while I drove or took taxis even the shortest distances.

Considering how George, Hezekiah, and Reuben lived, seeing just a glimpse of their hardship, I knew I could never truly understand what it was like to be an African.

Another fact of life in Nairobi that separated me from my African help was crime, or rather, the perception of crime. Foreigners in Nairobi—as well as white Kenyans—live in constant fear of it, of "the natives" coming over the walls with panga knives to slash you into a dozen little pieces and steal whatever money you may have in your nightstand. Everywhere you went—to dinner parties, to press conferences, just bumping into expatriates on the streets—you were constantly hearing new and horrific stories of families, white people, sleeping in their homes when "they" came in. If you were lucky, "they" simply tied you up and stuck you into a closet while they ransacked your house. A few brave souls apparently kept firearms at hand to resist the intruders, but invariably—or at least that's how the stories went—"they" would get the weapon first and the homeowner would end up dead for his efforts.

The other most talked-about problem was car theft. Everyone, it seemed, had a car theft story, involving themselves or someone they knew. "They" jumped into your car at shopping centers while you were loading your bags. "They" often forced you to drive with them to the outskirts of town—a foreigner in the front seat is the best way to avoid a routine police stop. (Remember that expatriate immunity I talked about?) And if you were one of the fortunate ones, "they" would just dump you someplace near the foot of the Ngong hills to try to hitch a ride back to the city.

I had heard it all before, and I wasn't afraid. In fact, I was filled with a kind of foolish bravado. After all, I was from Detroit, the inner city, the Murder Capital of the World. And throughout my high school days in suburban Grosse Pointe Woods, I constantly had had to defend the city against the stereotype of a crime-ridden netherworld where any law-abiding citizen was an automatic target.

After all, I had grown up in Detroit and had never once been mugged or even threatened. And so Nairobi—give me a break! This was a small country town by comparison. The burglars, for the most part, were still using panga knives, not the semiautomatic weapons of their American counterparts.

So I became a crusader against the fear of crime. To anyone willing to listen, I would argue that the fear of crime was exaggerated. I would say that Nairobi was a hundred times safer than New York or Washington, D.C., or Detroit or any other big American city. And I would imply, sometimes not too subtly, that the real reason they talked so much about "the crime problem" is that they were really racist. What they really feared, I argued, was black people—so many of them. White people aren't used to being in a minority, being swamped by a sea of blacks, I said. The actual statistics, the hard facts of crime, didn't really justify their concerns. And if I was losing the argument anyway, I'd start trying to guilt-trip them, telling them that the reason there was crime was that the expats, the whites, drove around town in their fancy new Range Rovers and Land Cruisers while the natives, like Reuben and George, had to walk for miles each day along dusty roads without sidewalks. How could you not expect them to come over the walls, I demanded, when you can come to their country and live in splendor, with servants whom you pay less than a hundred dollars a month? Yes, I was very adept at appealing to white guilt, at pointing out the ironies of spending hundreds of Kenyan shillings each week on fresh meat for the guard dogs, but not even rolling down your car window to acknowledge a starving child tapping on the glass for leftover change.

But the truth is that I myself was not any more into the African mind than were my expat friends and colleagues. I, too, was living sheltered and shielded from Africa and from Africans because I couldn't see them across the great cultural divide. I was also afraid of them. My house was protected by an alarm system connected to a security company, two large dogs—a German shepherd named Chui (which means "leopard" in Swahili) and a Rhodesian Ridgeback named Hank—and a rotating group of security guards who stood by the gate, sleeping mostly it seemed, every evening and all day on weekends.

I had fallen quickly into the Nairobi "scene." It was an expatriate scene, and it was almost all white. It was a scene of house parties and drunken nights at the Carnivore restaurant and disco—but only Wednesday nights, because that was the night they played classic rock-and-roll music, which the expats invariably referred to as "white night."

And usually, whether it was at the Carnivore or at someone's house, after substantial quantities of alcohol we would start debating and dissecting the problems of Africa and what was wrong with "the Africans."

I remember one dinner party when, after the plates were cleared and the cognac began to flow, a fierce debate erupted between two longtime Africa hands over which place could be classified as "Africa's dumbest country." One reporter awarded the label to Tanzania, arguing that "they've had thirty years of peace, and they look like they've had thirty years of war." No, Todd Shields chimed in with his booming baritone, Somalia was the dumbest, because look how in a few short months they've managed to reduce their own capital to rubble. Definitely the dumbest. But the Tanzania backer wouldn't be cowed. "Somalia doesn't count," he said. "Somalia is off the charts."

I recoiled at the cynicism of my colleagues. But mostly I stayed silent, since I was, of course, the newcomer and hadn't yet set foot into some of the bombed-out cities or desolate refugee camps I heard described. And I also felt uneasy, the way you do when you're a black guy in America, and you're hanging out with a bunch of white friends and someone tells a friendly "nigger" joke. You know it's a joke, you want to laugh, you want them to accept you. But you hurt. And sometimes you stay quiet.

One member of the press corps with whom I became friendly was Jeff Bartholet of *Newsweek*, a sensitive writer and reporter who actually seemed to care about the continent. He wasn't cynical, just tired. He had been there for more than three years and was eager to move on to another assignment. I remember as the eager newcomer asking him, the Africa veteran, why so many colleagues seemed so negative about the continent.

"It wears you down," he said exhaustedly. "You just keep running and running to one shithole after another. And after a while, you feel like a rat on a treadmill."

Maybe I would get tired out too, like Neil Henry, like Jeff Bartholet. But right now I was new, I was excited about being in a new place, and I wanted desperately to avoid being infected with the same rampant cynicism.

I wanted to discover Africa on my own, see it on its own terms, without what I self-righteously saw as the preconceived notions and the baggage of others who had gone before me. I knew that this meant I immediately had to get out of my sheltered surroundings, to go beyond the fence, even out of Kenya, where it was too easy to be sucked into a comfortable world of good restaurants and dinner parties. I would spent most of my time on the road, I decided, exploring, discovering Africa.

What I didn't realize at the time was that it would end up being an exploration, and a discovery, of myself.

3

No Man's Land

> "Somalia has ceased to exist. And right now, nobody cares."
>
> —A U.S. INTELLIGENCE OFFICIAL,
> Washington, D.C., November 1991

I GOT MY FIRST EXPERIENCE with a mortar shell while interviewing the president of a country that no longer existed.

It was in Mogadishu, in January 1992, at the height of the shelling war that had already devastated what was once Somalia's gracious seaside capital. Ali Mahdi Mohamed, who at the time was calling himself the interim president, was holed up in his presidential compound—a bomb-scarred whitewashed old Italian villa on the city's north side. His domain extended for a couple of square miles around him, and his back was to the sea. His rival across town, Gen. Mohamed Farah Aideed, was determined to drive Ali Mahdi from his fortified enclave, and the artillery shells had rained down pretty steadily since November. It was a largely invisible civil war, way off the front pages and the nightly news broadcasts, with thousands of casualties—mostly civilians caught in the crossfire.

Ali Mahdi was holding court in a small room laid out with a red Persian carpet that seemed oddly out of place in a city looted of almost every necessity. He was definitely in charge in Somalia, he insisted lamely, but the war had left his country in ruins. "There is no economic entity prevailing in this country. Everything has collapsed," he said. "Anarchy is prevailing also. With no police or military, it is very difficult to run the country." Outside, the thuds of the artillery shells seemed to be coming closer. And just as Ali Mahdi finished speaking, a mortar shell slammed against the building like an exclamation mark to his concluding sentence, followed by a burst of automatic weapons fire. We all dove to the floor as plaster rained down from the ceiling.

The self-declared president was nonplussed, but only momentarily. He pulled himself up, quickly regained his composure, and grinned sheepishly. An aide next to him offered what was supposed to be a reassuring analysis of what had just occurred: "I think it was outgoing."

That was to be just the first of many close calls in Somalia over the next two years and two months. And that single episode provided in a few seconds some valuable lessons that I would find myself coming back to again and again in other bizarre situations, close encounters, and near misses.

The first rule, of course, was to always be alert for the sound of the artillery and to remember that when it sounded like it was getting closer, it probably was. But more than that, I realized how absolutely essential it was to keep a sense of humor in the face of the absurd, because that's what the Somalis themselves did. I was starting on an almost surreal odyssey into never-never land, walking into a place where all codes of what I thought constituted civilized behavior between human beings had completely broken down. All bets were off in Somalia. Here, the social pecking order was determined by the size and range of the firepower. And no one—not foreign journalists, not aid workers, and, eventually, not even the U.S. Marines or the UN peace-keepers—was exempt.

When I first saw Mogadishu in 1992, the capital looked like a transplanted set from the old "Mad Max" movies, about a surreal postnuclear world where scavengers survive by slapping together debris and bits of scrap metal. Mogadishu hadn't gone through a nuclear inferno—but it seemed about as close as you could come in an urban setting.

Not a section of the city was untouched by the devastation of the civil war. The boy soldiers who formed the guerrilla militias were fond of using heavy antiaircraft guns leveled horizontally, and their huge shells can be particularly devastating when fired into cement buildings. The old downtown section of the city was largely reduced to rubble; it was now considered the impassable "no-man's-land" between the north and south sections of the capital inhabited by the warring subclans of Ali Mahdi and Aideed. Somalis sometimes referred to this area as "the Green Line," a term borrowed, appropriately enough, from Beirut. Later on, as Somalis continued to try to find humor in their predicament, a particularly violent section of town came to be called Bosnia.

But the war destruction doesn't tell half the story, for what was left untouched by the shells and the bullets usually got ripped apart by the successive waves of looters and scavengers, for whom anything—a piece of scrap metal, a pipe, electrical cable—might eventually be bartered for a piece of meat or a handful of rice. The streets were ripped up and the water pipes removed. Electrical wires were torn from poles, and eventually even the poles themselves disappeared. Buildings were stripped bare of everything imaginable— doorknobs, window frames, toilets, even the molding around the floor and ceilings. Everything in Mogadishu might have some intrinsic value, now or in the future, and everyone was reduced to scavenging for a share of the debris.

In those days, just getting to Somalia was a chore, as the country was nearly cut off from the outside world. The journalists based in

Nairobi had to either charter a small plane and find one of the Kenyan-based cowboy pilots willing to fly into a war zone, or else rely on the few aid agencies working in the country that still had periodic flights loaded with food or medical supplies. Every trip inside usually required several hours of shopping beforehand: bottled water, canned food, peanuts to eat between meals. In Mogadishu itself, the aid agencies were generous enough to provide reporters whatever accommodation they had, which was often floor space in their own cramped compounds. I always carried a sleeping bag and mosquito netting.

With all semblance of civil administration gone, Mogadishu's seaside international airport had been taken over by one of the clan militia groups that lived in the surrounding neighborhood. When you stepped off a plane in Mogadishu, a horde of young kids— sometimes no more than twelve or thirteen years old—instantly surrounded you and the plane, leveling their AK-47 assault weapons and grenade launchers at your chest. They were usually shouting incomprehensibly, at you and at each other, as they demanded what often amounted to hundreds of dollars in bribes—landing fee, airport tax, baggage handling fee, security for the plane, even "entry" fee into the country. And you paid, willingly. I never traveled to Somalia with less than three thousand dollars in cash, always in small bills, tens and twenties, rolled up and concealed in various pockets and pouches and tucked away in a hidden money belt. Money was power in Somalia; a hundred-dollar bill pulled out at the right time could keep you from getting killed when a dispute over costs turned heated. But display too much cash all at once, and you could get killed anyway. You just learned how to operate in Somalia.

With little in the city left to loot, the militia gunmen discovered a new occupation, which might best be called "escort duty," or security service for visiting foreigners like me. To leave the gates of the airport, you needed armed protection or you probably wouldn't make it more than a block—particularly if you were carrying a backpack laden with water and food in a city with basically nothing. So I hired my own armed guards, and I learned how to negotiate the daily fee with gunmen holding assault weapons at my head. Typically, the fee was a hundred-dollar bill for a car and a couple of gunmen for the day, with time off for lunch.

Friends back home would invariably ask me, how did you know you could trust the gunmen you hired? The answer is, quite simply, I didn't. You took a guess and prayed that you were right. Invariably there were arguments at the end of the trip, when the guards suddenly increased their fee. But I quickly discovered that the Somali gunmen liked nothing more than a good argument, and you could challenge them and shout back and wave your arms at the outrageous attempts at extortion—to a point. There was an old proverb in Somali, which roughly translates as: "He who has warned you has not killed you, as yet." It seemed to me a good operating rule. As long as you were still shouting at each other, you at least were still alive.

As my trips became increasingly frequent, I began to recognize some of the gunmen, and an odd kind of professional loyalty developed. Most of the time, I couldn't even remember their names but could recognize their faces, their Ray-Ban sunglasses, or sometimes the T-shirts they wore. For them, I suppose, the cash I kept bringing in as a live correspondent was a far more secure source of revenue than the few hundred dollars they could get off of me if they killed me on the spot. A kind of forward economic planning, I guess, and, for me, a rather handy sense of mutual self-interest.

After several months traveling in and out of Somalia, I finally settled on a reliable duo who would become my constant companions through several tight spots. The translator was a small, wiry young Somali named Rashid Abdullahi, and the driver, a quiet fellow with a full beard who almost always seemed to have a mouthful of *khat*, the foul-tasting narcotic leaf that seems a part of the Somali national diet. Appropriate for a driver, his name was Gass, which I always thought ironic since he was constantly rushing off to buy more fuel for the battered white Toyota. Occasionally they were accompanied by one or two additional gunslingers, depending on their sense of danger in the city. For Somalis, being able to discern where the fighting was on any particular day became as essential and as commonplace as predicting the weather.

I inherited the duo from Liz Sly, the *Chicago Tribune* reporter, and I immediately found Rashid, who spoke decent English, to be a good analyst of local militia activity and an uncannily accurate barometer of the mood on the streets. One thing I learned pretty quickly working in Mogadishu was that you had to trust your driver and translator—they invariably had a better sense than any foreigner could for predicting potential trouble. When their internal street radar said there was trouble in a certain neighborhood, I listened to them and stayed well clear.

The weird thing about Somalia was that not only did the local inhabitants learn to adapt, but so did we, the foreigners who moved in and out frequently. It's strange looking back, or trying to describe to friends later what it was like negotiating with gunmen, traveling around a war-torn city in the backseat of a beat-up car next to a guy holding a grenade launcher. At the time it all seemed so normal— normal, that is, for Somalia. It was just what you did to get to the story.

A lot of the other Nairobi-based journalists had closer calls and brushes with danger in those early days than I ever did—and that goes especially for the television crews who were far more conspicuous moving around the streets with all their expensive equipment. Stealing cameras and then ransoming them back to TV camera crews became something of a cottage industry in Mogadishu; dozens of TV cameras got stolen and then resold on what became kind of an unofficial black market. The TV crews, usually flush with cash, seemed to look at the ransom as a kind of insurance, the price of doing business on Mogadishu's mean streets.

My friend Sam Kiley of the *London Times* recounted a particularly close call he had when he went to do a story on arms trading at a notorious gun market on Mogadishu's south side. While he was standing there chatting with a gun merchant about the price of arms and ammo, some vendor decided to have some fun with the foreigner—he tossed Sam a hand grenade. Sam caught it one-handed and tossed it back, so the vendor pitched him another one. Sam caught that one too. Soon, Sam was in a hand-grenade-juggling contest with the Somali, tossing grenades back and forth between them, faster and faster. It must have been quite a sight—Sam, with his shaved head and bandanna, tossing and catching grenades, and a Somali crowd roaring with laughter. After he told me the story, I lost my enthusiasm for the gun-trading story I had been planning to do myself.

Todd Shields knew when he had been in Mogadishu far too long for his own good. He was riding in a car with his own gunslinging bodyguards when one of them got into an argument with a Somali gunman from another group. The argument became heated, voices were raised, and the two feuding Somalis began leveling their AK-47s at each other. So Todd, impatient to end the argument and move on, stepped between the two shouting gunmen, held up his hands to block the gun barrels, and raised his own radio-baritone voice over the shouting Somalis: "Wait a minute! Hold on! Just wait a minute!" He paused, then thought for a second, "Hey, what am I doing? I'm standing between two guys with AK-47s trying to get them to listen to reason!" Todd told me this story as he was heading for the airport; he knew he had been there so long it was all starting to seem normal and not so dangerous—which is precisely when foreigners let down their guard and are most at risk.

One of the few journalists who was safely able to navigate Mogadishu's mean streets on the sheer force of his personality and good humor was Dan Eldon, the kid photographer. Somalis seemed to love Dan for his easygoing manner and his willingness to accept them on their own terms. He could sit down on a stoop and chew *khat* with them and wear a sarong and actually become one of their group. It helped his photography, since he was able to coax Somali gunmen into ridiculous macho poses, like holding up their AK-47s in the bombed-out Mogadishu cathedral. Some of his best shots he made into colorful postcards, which he printed up and sold in packets. As the Somalia story got bigger, Dan also started a booming business printing up Somalia T-shirts in Nairobi and selling them to the growing number of reporters and aid workers inside.

The Somalis affectionately nicknamed Dan "the Mayor of Mogadishu," a mark of their respect for him and for their appreciation of the time he spent in the city. The drivers and translators actually came up with nicknames for most of the foreign journalists in Somalia—and not all of them were quite as flattering. A first-class photographer named Alexandra Avakian was called "the girl with the gap in her teeth." Another photographer, Liz Gilbert, was known simply as "the thin one." Sam was, of course, "the bald one." I never had a nickname—or, more accurately, I never knew if I had a nickname, since my own driver and translator were always way too polite to ever tell me.

Was I ever scared? Certainly. Almost all the time, really. Mostly at night, when the bursts of automatic weapons fire sometimes came eerily close to where I slept. I never knew whether this was it, the one time they would come tumbling over the wall of the guarded aid agency compound because they knew I was there with a few hundred-dollar bills rolled up in my money belt. But I learned to put the fear aside when I was trying to do my job; otherwise it would have become paralyzing.

Once I went to the airport with a UNICEF team to hitch a ride back to Nairobi on the small plane they had left waiting at the runway. When we got there, a man with an AK-47 was sitting on the lowered steps of the plane. He had been "guarding" the plane, he said through an interpreter, and now he was demanding payment before any of us could leave. Negotiations ensued through various intermediaries—mostly ragged young kids brandishing their own assault weapons. But the man, the one claiming to be guarding the plane, wouldn't budge, and eventually he began aiming his weapon menacingly at us. He stood, he circled us in wide arcs, never lowering his weapon. The entire time—and the whole scene must have lasted just a few minutes—I couldn't take my eyes off the gunman's finger; it was wrapped around the trigger. I remember thinking that it would take only one squeeze, one spasm of his right finger, to send a burst

47

of automatic weapon fire heading straight in my direction.

Finally, some of the other young militiamen snuck up behind him and wrestled his weapon away. I'm not sure how close we came, but it was one of the few times I remember being absolutely terrified. The violence in Mogadishu was as random as it was irrational; I could have easily been felled by a stray bullet during the struggle.

A few of the reporters and photographers in Mogadishu started carrying around their own firearms, handguns, usually, which they kept hidden beneath their shirts or under the backseat of the car at their feet. I remember one morning when my own car was missing—Gass was out looking for gas or something—and I hitched a ride with an American radio reporter. The radio guy and I climbed into the backseat, and his translator and bodyguard sat in the front. As we started out, the radio guy opened the seat pocket in front of him, pulled out a nine-millimeter handgun, and loaded a fresh clip. "What the hell is that for?" I asked him. He pointed to his bodyguard and translator in front and replied, "In case anything happens to those two, I want to have one last fighting chance." I made my own decision never to carry a gun myself. As a journalist, I thought perhaps my own last best chance was to rely on persuasion—and maybe if I stayed unarmed, I would seem less of a threat. Also, I always thought that when covering a story got so dangerous that reporters had to become combatants themselves and carry weapons, it was time for us to leave the story and go home.

The rather bizarre state of affairs that defined Somalia has usually been described as anarchy; I used the term often enough in my stories. In the broadest sense of the term, Somalia seemed about as close as you could come to Hobbes's classic definition, where the life of man was truly "nasty, brutish and short."

But "anarchy" may be too simplistic a term, for in reality there was some kind of social order, with established power centers. In Mogadishu, rival street gangs had carved up the turf and staked it out with makeshift barricades and roadblocks. It was kind of a parallel universe, an alternative world with its own norms and rules and codes of conduct. We reporters called this state of affairs "anarchy" because it excused us from getting too close, from trying to understand and explain. But much of the violence did have reasons, reasons perfectly valid according to the rules of this parallel reality. A car was stolen, someone shot someone else's brother. That death had to be avenged, then the avenger himself was slain, and the next thing you knew the extended families and subclans of all the victims were lobbing artillery shells across the city at each other — usually inaccurately, and with civilians caught in the crossfire. Senseless, yes. And certainly destructive. But anarchy? Once I started reporting from the place and trying to figure out what triggered various skirmishes, I could never really be sure what to call it.

The Somalis themselves—the ordinary, everyday people who had been schoolteachers, government bureaucrats, secretaries, shop owners—adjusted to the new reality of chaos and violence and rule by gun by keeping an amazingly good humor and an attitude of *Inshallah*, or God's will. Sometimes, especially in the beginning, their fatalism struck me as callous or coldhearted. I remember interviewing people who would describe to me how everyone in their immediate family was dead—either killed in the civil war or dead of starvation. And they would tell it to me without tears, without any outward sign of despair, really. Just a shrug, and an *"In-shallah."*

They also survived by adapting. I discovered not only in Somalia but elsewhere across the continent that human beings possess inside an uncanny survival instinct and an ability to transform themselves to meet their circumstances. I learned that lesson firsthand from a schoolteacher named Abdi Mohammoud Afrah.

When I met Abdi, he was working as a security guard for the International Medical Corps, or IMC, a Los Angeles–based outfit that sent doctors and nurses into Third World battle zones. I was staying at the IMC house, on a dusty little alleyway in a neighborhood where several of the foreign-aid agencies were clustered. I wanted to walk the few yards to the office of another charity, but Abdi, who was working at the IMC front gate, suggested even that short distance

49

would be too treacherous to make alone on foot. He volunteered to walk with me.

I was immediately impressed by Abdi's excellent command of English—this was no ordinary gunslinger. I struck up a conversation with him and discovered that he had actually been a schoolteacher before the civil war, and that he had worked as a translator and a clerk in the offices of several big foreign companies in Mogadishu.

Like most other people in Somalia, Abdi found his world turned upside down in late 1990, when the fighting first reached the capital. He sent his family away to the countryside and hid in his house, eating only bread and bananas. He could hear outside the nonstop artillery barrages and rocket attacks that marked the final onslaught on Mogadishu.

Siad Barre fled, the foreigners were evacuated, and the rebels entered the city in January 1991. It was supposed to be the end of the war. But as Abdi and everyone else learned pretty quickly, it was just the beginning. The "liberating" army turned out to be nothing more than a ragtag bunch of kids from the bush—teenagers, really, and younger—toting grenade launchers and AK-47s and half the time high out of their minds from chewing *khat*. These young kids started carving up the territory, throwing up roadblocks all over the city, and celebrating their victory with an orgy of looting. Mogadishu became an urban free-fire zone. Abdi's family came back, but he soon regretted it; his four-year-old son was shot and badly hurt by a neighbor kid carelessly playing with a loaded automatic weapon.

Abdi needed to try to eke out a living from the ruins, so he started selling bottled gasoline along the roadside. He made enough money to buy some food in the marketplace, which he resold again on the street. Business was okay until the random sniper fire around the city became too intense. Finally he ran into a friend who had found a pretty lucrative job as a security guard for the IMC, and the friend was able to get Abdi hired. Abdi had never used a gun before—in fact, he had never picked one up in his life. As he related the story to me, he still managed a smile at the irony of his own transformation. "Now the teacher has a gun," he said, grinning.

There was something ingenious about the survival instinct, I concluded. People who had once been bank tellers were now making and selling tea on the streets. Women learned how to make charcoal by compressing dirt and mud and rock together. Some kids came up with a lucrative business collecting old Coke bottles from foreign-aid workers, smashing them up, and then reselling the shards to use atop the high cement walls for security. Where else but Somalia?

Figuring out how people survived was relatively easy. The harder question—and one that I could never fully answer—was why I went there myself.

I could give you the easy explanation, the one that says I'm a journalist, I follow "The Story." And Somalia in 1992, a nation in meltdown, was certainly an incredible story. That's true enough, but it's only part of the reason.

Maybe you could call it racial pride. Or better still just call it my own negative reaction to what I felt was the overcoverage, the inundation of news, about the civil war raging in the former Yugoslavia. The war in Bosnia was and is a tragedy, no doubt. But I had started to see things a little differently from my perspective in black Africa, as a black correspondent in black Africa. When it came to human suffering, to violence, to the spectacle of refugees streaming out of a war zone for cover, quite frankly Bosnia had nothing on the Africans.

Somalia by early 1992 was by almost any measure an equal if not greater humanitarian catastrophe than the former Yugoslavia. The shelling war in Mogadishu had already killed an estimated five thousand people. Hospitals on both sides of the Green Line were reporting hundreds of casualties each day, from shrapnel wounds, stray bullets, kids playing with unexploded grenades. I saw it myself at the Benadir Hospital in south Mogadishu—kids walking around the dingy hallways with their arms blown off, women with their stomachs ripped open by the fragments from exploding shells. And on top of it all was the threat of impending famine. You could see it as early as January—the emaciated people showing up from the countryside, jamming the few relief feeding centers set up around town. And it was going to get worse. Food stocks had been looted from warehouses, and little else was able to get in, despite the best effort of private relief agencies and charities, because the airport and port were under regular bombardment from across the Green Line as rival factions battled to expand their turf. The famine was a time bomb waiting to go off.

And yet there was hardly a mention on the American network news programs or in the morning papers. But those same programs, those same papers, were blanketed with daily Bosnia coverage. Why? It was a question I asked everyone I could.

There was no shortage of explanations. A "Eurocentric bias" in the American media. The novelty of a brutal conflict in the heart of Europe, an hour's plane ride away from Rome. The chance the conflict could spread, and even engage the West against the Russians if the latter chose to support their Serb cousins. The UN secretary-general, Boutros Boutros-Ghali, was deluged with daily phone calls from European heads of government about the Bosnia crisis, but on Somalia, the phones were largely silent. Boutros-Ghali himself touched on the disparity, perhaps a bit undiplomatically, when he challenged a Security Council decision to step up costly peace-keeping operations in the former Yugoslavia while relief operations in Africa were left underfunded. Yugoslavia, Boutros-Ghali said, was "a rich man's war."

For me, that criticism stung. But it also pierced straight to the heart of my early obsession with Somalia. These were black Africans, being neglected by the world community that was rushing thousands of peace-keepers into Bosnia, the "rich man's war." If ever there was a place where being a journalist could make a difference, this sure seemed like it. If ever there was a reason for being in Africa—for being a black journalist in Africa—this seemed like one. The world, and Washington policy makers specifically, may not have cared about Somalia in early 1992. But I could force them to care by rubbing their faces in it every day, by shoving the pictures of starving kids in front of people's noses as often as I could, in the newspaper seen daily by the White House and members of Congress. And fortunately my editors at the *Washington Post* agreed, and my dispatches ran regularly on the front page.

I also became fixated on the Somalia story because of what Somalia symbolized about Africa and the world. Somalia to me became post–Cold War Africa writ large, with all of the problems and pitfalls magnified on a grand scale. As Somalia went, so might go a host of other African countries teetering between strongman rule and violent anarchy. Africa was, in that sense, a series of Somalias waiting to happen: in Zaire, in Sudan, in Nigeria, maybe even Kenya if the tribal tensions erupted enough to loosen Moi's grip. The outcome on the streets of Mogadishu could provide some valuable clues to what was in store for some other shaky regimes across the continent. And for the world—the United States, the United Nations, the Europeans, the Organization of African Unity—Somalia represented a unique opportunity to try jointly to solve a local conflict outside the shadow of the U.S.-Soviet rivalry. If the world community could succeed in putting Somalia back together again and managing its volatile mix of clan politics, historical rivalries, and modern-day firepower, then just maybe this desolate corner of Africa could become a kind of model for how to keep other countries from splitting apart.

Somalia, then, became the prism through which I came to view the rest of Africa. It was to become the metaphor for my own disillusionment.

Food was becoming scarce. The rival armies had crisscrossed Somalia's heartland and pretty much destroyed everything in their wake. Livestock was either looted or killed. Crops were burned. The villagers of Baidoa town in south-central Somalia told how the retreating troops of the old dictator, Mohamed Siad Barre, had thrown bodies of the dead down the wells. It was one of those apocryphal stories, one of those African stories, that you could never be sure was fact or fiction.

There were some early warning signs in the capital that the situation in the countryside was becoming desperate. Emaciated stick figures in rags were trekking in from the outlying towns and villages, jamming the relief-agency feeding centers. The aid agencies started sounding the alarm bells; with the loss of an entire season's harvest, they said, Somalia soon would be in the grips of a devastating famine, with hundreds of thousands at risk.

Some of the earliest dispatches about the severity of the famine came from my colleagues Jane Perlez of the *New York Times* and the indefatigable Julian Ozanne of the *Financial Times*. They were among the first journalists to venture to Baidoa, which was already being called Somalia's "city of death." They reported that starving people were actually dropping dead in the line waiting for food handouts.

I set out to Merca, an old colonial town of whitewashed villas along the coast, on the way to the large southern port town of Kismayo on the Indian Ocean. I took a carload of gunmen for what was to be a treacherous three-hour journey along fifty miles of a crater-marked highway long ago abandoned to roaming bandits. As we got closer to the town, we passed villagers in scraps of clothing trudging barefoot along the roadside, moving slowly and often holding themselves up with walking sticks made from tree branches. Some would never make it; we were forced to swerve around the dead bodies that littered the roadside.

A transit camp had been set up just outside the town limits, a kind of "tent city" for the dead and dying. There I met a twenty-seven-year-old woman named Yaray Adem who had just walked for thirteen days barefoot from her village near Jelib, further south along the coast. Thirteen days, eating only tea leaves and branches. And in three weeks, she had lost her entire family—first her husband, then her mother, then her three children, all dead of starvation.

The town itself was how I imagine hell must look. There were starving people everywhere. Thousands of them. They crowded the few feeding centers, mostly set up in abandoned school courtyards. Sometimes they just sat on the sandy road. For the first time since my brother Mel died twenty-five years before, I was confronted with death, close up; the dead and dying were all around me, and I was looking into their faces.

And my first thought was: They look just like me.

That could be me, I said to myself, were it not for the grace of God. And I at once found the thought so disgusting, so self-centered, so conceited, that I immediately banished it from my consciousness.

And yet it returned. It returned every time I set foot in one of Somalia's hellholes of human suffering. It's not a thought I'm particularly proud to admit having. In fact, it's embarrassing, shameful even now, to confess it. But I've gotten away from my narrative.

By late summer, the famine had reached staggering proportions. Mohamed Sahnoun, the UN special envoy in Mogadishu, was estimating that some four million of the six million people left in the country were probably in need of some emergency food assistance. Relief agencies, including the Red Cross, said more than a million and a half people were in imminent danger of starvation. In Baidoa hundreds of people were dying every day, so many in fact that they were running out of room to bury them. Every morning a "death truck" would rumble through the streets collecting the corpses of those who had died during the night; after a couple hours, the truck was stacked high. The town literally smelled like death.

I'm sure these images are depressing. I understand, because they were for me, too—and I was there, not reading it, but seeing it, smelling it, walking among the dead. This was my reality. But it wasn't my reality. Even though I looked like them, and might have at some point been mistaken for one of them, I was not like them. I was always on the outside looking in, like a stranger who had wandered aimlessly onto a movie set and ended up in the middle of the film. Or maybe like a cardboard cutout pasted against the real-life images, looking somewhat like them but not quite, somehow standing apart, as if lifted from another scene and placed there artificially.

It was in another town, Bardhere, a dusty little outpost over by Somalia's border with Kenya, that it hit home to me that Somalia's tragedy was really a story of the powerful against the weak. Aideed, who by now was being called a "warlord," had made Bardhere his temporary headquarters after ousting the remnants of Siad Barre's troops. There he held court for visiting journalists, resplendent in a pinstriped shirt and gray slacks, relaxing on pillows and a Persian carpet. Outside, in the streets and at the feeding centers, hundreds of people were dropping dead from starvation every day. So many people were dying that local Red Crescent workers had run out of shrouds to wrap the bodies; instead, they were using empty food sacks. At one feeding center, thousands of skeletal people would gather outside the gates, only to be told there wasn't enough food. And when some would try desperately to push their way inside, the militia thugs serving as "guards" to the centers would beat them with tree branches and sometimes rifle butts.

The inside of the feeding centers wasn't much better. Starving people were forced to line up in front of a metal pot cooking a mixture of beans and soup. Each person got one ladleful, and that was it. If they took too long at the pot or argued over their portions, the guards delighted in thrashing them over the head and face with the branches. One old woman begged for a bit more for her family members who were too sick to stand in line; for her troubles, she got a beating. A small boy jumped up too quickly when it was announced the food was ready. Sorry, but pregnant women go first, and the boy was beaten on the head for his impertinence.

What was happening in Somalia wasn't about food, even though this was a famine. This was about power and control in a country where security had broken down. The food was coming in, tons of it, by ship and airlift. But it was falling into the hands of these thugs with the AK-47s slung over their shoulders who used tree branches to beat the weak and the elderly while hoarding most of the booty for themselves. More than once I stood on the congested road outside Mogadishu's main port, watching trucks loaded with bags of relief food turn left instead of right, and head straight toward the storage bins of the warlords instead of the agency feeding centers. Solving this growing crisis would require more than the world simply throwing money and food at Somalia. It would require restoring some semblance of order and control, breaking the grip of the gun-slingers and the so-called warlords who were willing to let their people starve.

Those were the thoughts racing through my mind when, on August 14, 1992, President George Bush announced an airlift.

The rather clumsily named "Operation Provide Relief" was supposed to bring 145,000 tons of food to Somalia's interior towns on U.S. Air Force C-130 cargo planes based in the Kenyan port of Mombasa. At the same time, the United Nations, heeding the aid agencies' calls for a protection force to secure Mogadishu's troubled port and airport, was arranging to ferry in five hundred troops from Pakistan. The world was slowly, reluctantly, being dragged into Somalia's civil war.

The first steps into Somalia were tentative, like a child still unsure of his footing as he first starts to walk. The Americans wanted to airlift food, but they wanted first to make sure that none of our boys was put in harm's way. The food would be put on pallets for quicker off-loading—never mind that it meant they couldn't carry nearly as much food that way. And once on the ground in Somalia, U.S. planes would keep their engines running for the possibility of a quick getaway if things got hairy. The first town chosen to be the beneficiary of this new American largess, Beledweyne, was the least likely candidate. Beledweyne, while needy, was far better off than towns like Baidoa and Bardhere.

As the airlift expanded around Somalia, so did the problems. A bullet in a fuselage during a runway skirmish between Somali workers caused a brief suspension of the airlifts to Beledweyne. Similar gun battles broke out in Kismayo and Baidoa. The pattern was unmistakable; dumping food into a country without a government or police force was only heightening the lawlessness. Similar difficulties were developing for the five hundred Pakistanis being airlifted into Mogadishu's airport as UN "peace-keepers." Their main problem was that there wasn't a peace to keep.

One event in Mogadishu was emblematic. A UN military officer from Fiji had spent days negotiating with the local subclan faction controlling the airport to allow the Pakistanis to arrive and take up their position without incident. After arduous negotiation, the Fijian finally struck a deal with the subclan to provide the outer security for the airport's perimeter during the Pakistanis' arrival. The subclan chieftain presented to the Fijian a list of 110 names of Somali guards who would be paid for their "protection."

The story gets worse. The next day, the Somali "security guard" force had expanded to more than two hundred gunmen, all claiming to be part of the airport security detail to protect the Pakistanis' arrival. And they all expected payment from the United Nations. The Fijian, exasperated, demanded a final, complete list of all the Somali "guards." And he got it a day later—a list complete with 489 names. That made nearly one Somali gunman for each of the Pakistani soldiers. And they were each demanding about twenty thousand Somali shillings a day for their labors, which translated to roughly $10,000 for the entire detail—per day. It was nothing less than extortion; the UN was effectively paying the thugs not to shoot the soldiers coming in to keep the peace.

That was Somalia—no demand too outrageous, no situation too absurd. Famine and starvation had become a growth industry, and relief agencies, including the UN, were the money tree. It was a question of resources, control of the resources, and the power that flowed from that control. And no one was exempt—not the aid agencies that found themselves being held hostage to the exorbitant pay demands of their armed drivers and bodyguards, and not the foreign reporters, myself included, who knew that ultimately the guys with the guns had the final say, no matter how "loyal" you considered them.

Mogadishu had degenerated to an urban jungle. Superior force was the only thing that the local strongmen would respect, and from what they had seen so far, there was no superior force to challenge their sway. The Somali gunmen who ran the place viewed the incoming Pakistanis with such disdain that as the poor Pakistanis landed, the Somalis simply stood lounging at the airport smirking, salivating at the thought of eventually being able to loot their U.S.-supplied equipment. "Too skinny," one Somali quipped to one of my colleagues from Reuter after eyeing the first batch of Pakistani troops.

It was clear that there would have to be a far larger, far more muscular military action to take Somalia back into the orbit of civilized nations.

Here I'll have to admit that I was among those early believers that a military intervention in Somalia could work and that the United States should lead it. After all, these were just a bunch of teenage kids with outdated, rusty weapons who were likely to scatter in terror at the first sight of a well-armed American paratrooper or marine making a helicopter landing at Mogadishu's airport. Like everyone else, I had watched the Gulf War and had marveled at the pinpoint accuracy of America's high-technology weaponry. And what better place than Africa, in the midst of a devastating famine, to raise the flag for a new kind of American interventionism, a benevolent, selfless interventionism with no American interest at stake other than the collective revulsion at violence and a desire to relieve human suffering?

It was an increasingly common sentiment at the time. Some aid agencies were openly advocating it. Well-timed opinion pieces were appearing in America's major newspapers calling for it. Many of the reporters in Nairobi had dropped all pretense of objectivity and were openly demanding it. I remember Julian Ozanne once pounding a table in anger that the UN and the world were doing so little to help Somalia when it was clear a major military intervention was needed. And I was nodding in full agreement.

The only prominent voice against an American intervention into Somalia came from Smith Hempstone, the crusty U.S. ambassador in Nairobi. In an opinion piece in the *Washington Post*, Hempstone warned, "If you liked Beirut, you'll love Mogadishu."

4

The Wrong Place

"We fed them, they got strong, they killed us."
—MAJ. DAVID STOCKWELL, U.S. Army,
UN military spokesman

I SHOULD HAVE KNOWN something was wrong when I saw the burning tire barricades on the streets.

That there would be trouble that day was obvious—there was always trouble of some sort in Mogadishu. Random shootings. Carjackings. Maybe a sniper attack on the UN troops who had replaced the American marines in positions around the city. But this was different—more dangerous, somehow. You could feel it in the air.

It started over breakfast in the Al-Sahafi, the bullet-scarred three-story hotel that had become the home away from home for foreign journalists covering the Somalia story. It was Saturday, June 5, 1993, and only a handful of us were there that day; most of the U.S. troops had recently departed after a five-month intervention, and despite predictions of an immediate slide into violence, Mogadishu had remained surprisingly calm. The famine was over, farmers were slowly starting to trickle back to their fields, even the notorious warlords had remained strangely quiet. Good news is often no news, and Somalia had largely receded from the front pages.

I, too, had for the most part given up on the Somalia story. I had come in from Nairobi with a bundle of cash for what was supposed to be a few days' stay, a quick in-and-out, to close down the *Post*'s temporary office at the Al-Sahafi and pay off Rashid and Gass.

Then over breakfast we heard the shots.

It wasn't unusual to hear gunfire in Mogadishu, but this time, the sound of automatic weapons fire in the distance gave me an uneasy feeling. I was going to try to hitch a seat on the UN flight back to Nairobi that afternoon, to spend at least part of a rare weekend at home, probably have dinner at one of my favorite Indian restaurants, maybe catch up with Julian and Sam and the others over at the Carnivore disco. I was damned if I was going to be held back by some inconsequential clan mix-up in Mogadishu. These brief flare-ups were happening all the time now, and the U.S. military spokesman in his daily briefings called it "Somali-on-Somali" violence. No foreign troops involved, no report on casualties, no story.

But somehow today seemed different. Things had been too quiet here for too long. We all suspected that the warlords and their militias had just been lying low, biding their time, waiting for their chance to put the United Nations "blue helmets" to the test. Maybe this was the test we'd all been waiting for.

I had an appointment that morning with an American officer over at the UN military headquarters compound, so I slurped down a cup of bad instant coffee and headed from the dining room to the hotel's enclosed parking lot to find Rashid and Gass. That day, Rashid's ever-accurate internal street radar was on high alert. He even brought along two extra gunmen, just in case.

There was big trouble, Rashid told me as I climbed into the backseat of the battered old white Toyota with a gunman on either side of me. The word on the street was that there had been an attack on the Pakistani UN contingent. Rashid didn't know the details—he rarely did, because his street radar didn't extend to eliciting hard facts. But the word was that some Pakistanis may have been killed.

We pulled out of the guarded front gates of the hotel, and I could immediately see smoke rising from burning tire barricades a few blocks away. Rashid suggested we take the back roads to the UN headquarters.

Rashid then told Gass to stop, and he ran back inside the hotel gate for a few seconds; one of the bodyguards wanted an extra ammunition clip for his AK-47. It was a bad sign.

The UN compound stood on the sprawling site of the old American embassy grounds, and when we arrived, the front gates were closed off with coiled razor wire. And the Pakistani troops manning the sentry positions around the high protective wall seemed more edgy than usual, setting off my own rudimentary Mogadishu street radar. I was always a bit wary when approaching the Pakistani soldiers in Mogadishu, always conscious, I suppose, that many of the Pakistanis probably couldn't distinguish a black American reporter in a car filled with bodyguards from a band of potential Somali terrorists on a suicide run at their position. Whenever I had to approach the Pakistanis at their base camp or in one of their sandbagged bunkers to interview an officer or perhaps just to set up an appointment for later, I always made a habit of telling Gass to stop the car at least a half-block away. I would get out and approach the Pakistanis alone, on foot, usually waving my powder blue UN-issued press card wildly with one hand and keeping the other hand visible at all times. I'd usually remove my sunglasses—less sinister-looking, I guessed—and I'd shout at them from a distance in the thickest midwestern twang I could muster.

For the most part, it worked, although on more than one occasion I could see the machine gunners taking aim at me from behind the sandbags, and I could hear the unmistakable clacking sounds of a clip being locked and a machine-gun bolt being pulled back. That's when I usually scurried back to my car, interview or not.

This time I was lucky enough to find a Pakistani officer at the back gates to the UN compound. Unlike the ordinary soldiers, the Pakistani officers were always overly courteous and spoke in crisp and courtly British-accented English. The Pakistani used his radio to somehow track down the American officer I had come to see. And the American, a female major, looked positively shocked to see me standing there.

"I can't believe you made it!" she said. "Don't you know what's happening out there?" I told her I had heard some shots and seen the burning tires blocking some intersections. But I had no clue what was going on.

Some Pakistani soldiers on patrol in the city that morning had come under attack, she told me. The details were still sketchy, but it appeared to be an orchestrated ambush, somewhere in the vicinity of Radio Mogadishu, the radio station used by Mohamed Farah Aideed's faction. There were some confirmed casualties, but she didn't know how many—and some American soldiers also had been hit. The American army's heliborne "quick reaction force" had been activated. And the fighting was still raging at various points around the city.

I ran back to the car and headed straight for Radio Mogadishu.

An angry Somali crowd was gathered outside the radio station when I arrived. Pretty soon I was swept up in it, caught in the middle, being jostled and shoved from all directions as each member of the crowd tried to shout his own version of events to me. In all my time in Somalia, I found nothing quite so terrifying as being caught at the center of a Somali crowd, never knowing which way the pack might turn. I kept Rashid close at my side. He had an easygoing manner and a way of engaging in the shouted banter while letting the mob know that although I was an American, I was really on their side. For those occasions when persuasion didn't quite cut it, he also kept a small pistol tucked in his waistband, underneath his loose-fitting T-shirt. My bodyguards, as usual, had stayed with the car, the vehicle being a possession far more valuable than the journalist.

According to some of those in the crowd, the Pakistani troops had come early that morning to the radio station, presumably on a spot inspection for heavy weapons, which had been declared illegal in the city under the UN intervention rules. A mob quickly gathered outside, believing the UN troops were there to take over the radio station, which had become the anti-UN mouthpiece for General Aideed and his Somali National Alliance militia. The Pakistanis panicked, fired some shots in the air to clear the crowd, and a young Somali man had been killed.

This account was actually complete nonsense, but it would be at least a day before another, more accurate rendition of events that morning would emerge. Pakistani troops had indeed gone to the radio station that day as part of a hastily announced UN inspection for arms caches, but Aideed's guerrillas had chosen that moment to launch an ambush against the Pakistanis at the radio station, at a feeding center, and at three other points around the city. The Pakistanis were caught unawares and completely unprepared; they had been riding around the city in vulnerable, open-sided or "soft-skinned" Jeeps instead of heavy armored vehicles, and the soldiers at the feeding centers weren't even carrying extra ammunition. The massacre was ugly, too; dead Pakistani soldiers were disemboweled and some had their eyes gorged out. It was a type of attack particularly vicious for Moslems: mutilate the body, leave it unburied, violate one of the basic tenets of Islam.

I didn't fully grasp it at the time, but the bloody attacks of June 5 marked the turning point for the entire U.S.-led military operation in Somalia. It was also the beginning of a turning point in my own mind, the start of a bitter wake-up call that would forever alter my view of Africa and how the continent could—or could not—be saved from itself.

In the first days of the intervention, I was rather proud of myself for having been one of those who had pounded the drumbeat for an American military involvement. My stories about Somalia's deterioration had made it onto page one of the *Post* throughout the summer and fall of 1992, often with some huge photograph I'd shot of a lifeless stick-figure child or a bent-over old woman pleading for a few more scoops of gruel from a steaming metal caldron. The subtext was always the same—this is a humanitarian crisis that the world, and particularly the United States, can and should do something about. I remember joking with the other reporters about how the Somali teenage thugs with their rusted weapons and flip-flops weren't nearly as tough as they liked to think. "One Washington, D.C., crack gang could come in and clean out this whole city in about two hours," I used to boast.

But Somalia's a pretty cruel place, really, and particularly so to those who come armed with noble intentions. It's a hard, often brutal land, no place for dreamers. Somalis will take what you've got, chew you up, and spit you right back out again. My notebooks are filled with the names and stories and quotes of people who came to help—people who flew into the darkness to bring a little bit of light—and a good many of them ended up turning coldly cynical, or being flown out wrapped in a body bag. They were good and caring people like Valerie Place, a nurse for the Irish charity Concern. She was an endlessly cheerful woman, the kind who always finds the silver lining. I talked to her on Christmas Eve at a Concern feeding center she was running at the edge of town, and she was excited about the progress the kids were making, some of them brought back from near starvation and actually smiling and playing again. And a few weeks later, Valerie was shot dead, ambushed in her car along a deserted stretch of road.

And then there was Sean Devereaux, who ran the local office for UNICEF in the southern port town of Kismayo. He was a fiery-tempered Irishman with a keen sense of fair play, well loved by almost everyone in the community. But he also made some enemies—maybe because of contracts on rented cars, something to do with Somali workers wanting more money, who knows? What is known is that a guy with a gun walked up behind him on the little dirt road he used to walk home and shot him point-blank in the back of the head.

It was, I often mused, one of Somalia's strangest paradoxes. When no one comes to help, they cry that the world is indifferent to their suffering. And when people do come, what do the Somalis do? They shoot them in the back of the head, drag the naked bodies through the streets, beat them to death with bricks. It would take me a little while longer after the events of June 5 to figure that out—five more weeks to be exact. The American military would learn the lesson, too, after a bloody street battle that would leave eighteen soldiers dead, one of them with his corpse trussed up and dragged through the streets like a chicken. Seventy soldiers would be wounded that day, a Black Hawk helicopter pilot would be taken prisoner, and a chastened President Clinton would call the whole thing off and order the troops home. The United Nations, after spending $3 billion trying to save Somalia, would fold its tent and go home about a year later.

And as far as I know, those young thugs with the sunglasses and the AK-47s still rule the streets. And the weak and the innocent still die.

At its ending, the global operation to rescue Somalia went so horribly wrong that it's easy to forget the upbeat, feel-good atmosphere that surrounded those first days of America's high-profile, televised intervention into a remote corner of Africa.

When the first marines and navy SEALs landed, they were met not with the sharp crackle of Somali sniper fire from rooftops but with bursts of light from the camera flashes from the horde of journalists lined up along the beaches to record the event. It had to be one of the oddest military operations on record—big pumped-up marines in combat gear roaring ashore in their amphibious landing vehicles, only to be greeted by swarms of reporters from around the world, toting their laptop computers and satellite phones and transmitting equipment, all into the middle of what was supposed to be a famine.

The "intervasion" was bizarre from the start, launched with some rather comic scenes. Like the squad of young marines at Mogadishu's port racing one after another toward an old warehouse building to search it for hidden Somali gunmen—and one of the marines getting tangled up and tripping over a television camera cord. Or the chaotic scene at the airport, when the first marines on shore spotted a group of Somalis who had been sleeping in some abandoned cars parked near the airport fence; the marines pulled the Somalis out one by one at gunpoint and shouted at them—in English, which the Somalis did not understand—to lie down on their stomachs. And there were the camera crews and photographers shouting at the Somalis to roll over onto their backs so they could get pictures of the terrified expressions on their faces.

In the beginning, though, the vast majority of Somalis really did seem to welcome the arrival of the troops, if only because they offered some respite from the gunplay and anarchy on the streets. They lined the streets outside the port and the airport to wave at the incoming marines. Kids would run alongside the open-sided "humvees" to slap five with the burly Americans—and maybe try to steal their wristwatches. And the name of the operation—"Restore Hope," or *Rajo* in Somali—began popping up everywhere. There was a new "Rajo" restaurant that opened on the main drag. "Rajo" and "Hope" were spelled out in Christmas lights over what had to be the city's only functioning electronics store. Everywhere, it was thumbs up to the new American saviors.

For me, it all seemed a bit surreal. First, there was the sight of these American marines—white guys, mostly—incredibly pasty-looking dudes in this desolate corner of black Africa, sweating profusely under their helmets and flak jackets and loaded down with all their gear under the brutal equatorial sun. They were all young and bright and they had obviously read their brief on the way over, because they would all speak in generalities about the clan situation and factional breakdown as if it were common knowledge. "See, these are Moslems," I remember one marine explaining to me in a kind of southern drawl that seemed really out of place here, "but these here are the Sunni Moslems. They aren't the bad ones, like the Shi'ites, like you got over in Iran." And they were always starved for news from home—college football scores, anything. I used to pass on my old copies of *Newsweek* whenever I passed a marine checkpoint.

The marines moved on to the old abandoned American embassy compound, which looked more like the sprawling campus of a small community college than a one-time diplomatic outpost. And they proceeded to erect from the looted debris of the old compound a new Potemkin village that grew and spread with every passing day. Traffic signs went up to direct the continuous flow of military vehicles inside the compound. Abandoned and burned-out buildings were surrounded by sandbags and converted into workspaces. They set up generators to get electricity turned on, they laid piping to get some water flowing. A post office came in, and soon I could mail letters directly back to the States, using U.S. stamps. A PX soon popped up, and I could buy Doritos and Pringles potato chips and Chips Ahoy and all the American junk food you couldn't find anywhere else on the African continent. They had carved a little slice of America out of the ruins of Somalia. It made life more comfortable for the boys, but it seemed utterly preposterous given the squalor just on the opposite side of the compound's high fence.

This is totally insane, I thought to myself.

Then the United Nations bureaucrats started arriving, dozens every day, some fresh from desk jobs in New York, others coming from war zones around the world—from Cambodia, from the West Bank and Gaza, from Angola and Mozambique, and from the mess in the former Yugoslavia. Somalia had become the "in" place to be, a chance for the UN to finally get one right, and they were flooding in from everywhere, all young and eager to have a hand in rebuilding a shattered country from scratch.

They started moving into the old colonial villas along the road to the airport and the dusty side streets beyond, giving them names like House One and House Two, and so on. They hurried around the UN's Potemkin village with clipboards in hand and walkie-talkies hitched to their belts. They divided themselves into sectors and divisions and departments dealing with things like "local governments" and "justice" and "humanitarian relief" and "liaison" with the other private relief agencies. And of course "logistics," in charge of allocating the houses and the walkie-talkies and the clipboards and the vehicles for all the hundreds of new UN bureaucrats pouring in.

How much, I wondered, is all this costing?

I started using the Mogadishu airport to measure the extent of the foreign buildup in Somalia. When I first flew into Mogadishu, well before the marines came, the airport was a microcosm of the factional feuding on the streets outside—just a bunch of raggedy guys with AK-47s all trying to stiff you for bucks when you flew in on a little prop plane. Then the airport was taken over by the marines, and the tarmac became a deafening roar of activity, with huge American cargo planes, their engines still running, bringing in fresh men and supplies. Then the UN bureaucrats arrived, and they installed a check-in counter. After a while, reporters like myself— who used to go to the airport to hitchhike rides back to Nairobi— were suddenly told that the airport was under UN control and that we needed "approval" to fly on the aircraft. And they set up a new air travel office and a complex procedure for getting approval for plane travel that required filling out several forms, getting the forms signed by several different people, and getting your name on a manifest.

I knew the UN bureaucracy had finally crossed the line into the ridiculous when I arrived once in Mogadishu and we were met at the plane by a little minibus to shuttle us the few hundred feet from the plane steps to the "terminal building." I had come in on a Kenyan Airways plane that had been chartered by the UN to bring in still more bureaucrats and soldiers back from weekend leave. Before we landed, a stewardess got on the microphone and said, "We have just landed in Mogadishu. We hope you have a pleasant stay."

Rashid and Gass were always there waiting for me at the airport. But now they had to "check" their AK-47s with a soldier stationed at the front gate. Once I was in the car, we'd exit the airport, Rashid would hop out and present his tag, and he'd collect his guns and the ammo clips again. Rashid and Gass even had new yellow UN-issued identity cards, with their photos, authorizing them to carry automatic weapons.

This place, I thought, has become a total mind warp.

Looking back, I see now that this was all part of a grand deception, a kind of self-delusion on the part of these foreigners flocking in who desperately needed to impose some semblance of normalcy on what was otherwise a completely abnormal—and still very dangerous—place. And of course, we journalists played our part, too. Pretending it was all normal, and trying to replicate the familiar and the comfortable, was simply one way we all coped. These collective attempts sometimes crossed the line into the absurd.

For a while, there were almost nightly parties among the aid workers, the journalists, and the foreign troops. There was a party for the opening of a new American embassy building, with a marine guard playing disc jockey while Black Hawk helicopters hovered protectively overhead. UNOSOM—the acronym for the UN Operation in Somalia—held a formal-dress benefit banquet and ball to raise money for a refugee settlement just behind the UN's headquarters compound. Pakistani military officers were there in stiff tunics and plumes, older women wore evening gowns, and younger ones donned miniskirts and heels, and they all hovered around tables lined with Pakistani buffet food while rock music blared in a courtyard below. And outside, Somali drivers, street children, and refugees from the countryside climbed trees or onto nearby walls just for a glimpse of what must have seemed a very weird foreign tribal ritual.

The scene became just as bizarre at the Al-Sahafi Hotel, our rather familiar redoubt. The hotel had advanced from its rather spartan beginnings—a few mattresses on the floor were initially the only amenity—to offering hot water for showers, cold soft drinks sold at the reception desk, and, eventually, even a television set in the lobby that was hooked into a rooftop satellite for CNN. The rooftop became the site for our own regular nightly party sessions, which usually began with Paul Alexander, the Associated Press reporter, mixing up his particularly wicked batch of whisky sours, using lemon Kool-Aid bought from the U.S. military PX. Sometimes we could get the American military officers who conducted the daily press briefings to stop by. The marines and airmen and soldiers in Somalia were under orders to stay "dry," but the rooftop was always the one area of the city where everything was strictly "off the record."

One of the strangest evenings was when we had a few marines and soldiers on the roof for a blowout party. The music was blasting, the whisky sours were flowing, and then from somewhere in the darkness came the unmistakable "crack" of a bullet being fired. We heard it all the time on the rooftop, and usually ignored it; you could generally tell when a shot was close by, and directed at you, versus the routine and lonely burst in the night. But at this shot, all the marines were suddenly flat out on their stomachs, shouting at each other. "Sniper! Sniper!" And the journalists stood there puzzled, still holding plastic cups of booze, peering out into the night and saying, "Where? Where is he?"

An even weirder evening came soon after a little outdoor movie theater opened just across the traffic circle from the Al-Sahafi. The theater "screen" was the side wall of an abandoned, bomb-damaged building, and the larger-than-life image was clearly visible from our hotel rooftop, although we couldn't make out the sound. That night, the little theater was playing the old movie *Patton*, with George C. Scott. I remember the absurdity of watching the huge towering figure of Patton in his opening monologue, standing in front of the massive American flag—and I remember wondering to myself: What on earth could the Somalis watching this be thinking?

Once, I decided to liven up the usual evening rooftop session by bringing my small compact-disk player and portable speakers. We balanced the speakers on the ledge of the roof, and I selected Bruce Springsteen's "Born in the U.S.A." to blast across the darkened city streets. We all found it hilarious and played it over and over until a sniper from somewhere in the darkness fired a bullet that came whizzing over our heads, sending us all diving onto our stomachs for cover. "Guess he didn't like the music," I remember someone quipping in the darkness.

Alexander Joe, the Zimbabwean photographer for Agence France Presse, nicknamed the hidden sniper "our friend." Every night, after we had consumed a few cold beers on the roof and engaged in our usual loud discussion about which way Somalia was heading, our friend would fire one or two shots in our direction, sending us scrambling. "Okay, our friend is tired," Joe would say. "It must be time for bed."

For a while, the UN posted a small contingent of Nigerian soldiers on the roof of the Al-Sahafi Hotel. This was partly because of our strategic position overlooking the Kilometer Four traffic circle where the roads leading to the port and the airport converged. It was also partly—or so we liked to think—to provide some protection for the journalists, the largest group of foreigners in a single place outside the heavily fortified UN compound and the "secure" zone around the airport road. We presumably offered a tempting target to any fanatic Somali terrorist or unemployed militiamen with a grudge, and—another presumption here—the American and UN military commanders, while finding us a cynical and meddlesome bunch, would find it even more annoying to have reporters killed or kidnapped on their watch.

I always imagined our Nigerian protectors found us a rather odd bunch, these foreign journalists with their expensive computers and satellite transmitting equipment, our rooftop beer bashes with stereos blasting away into the cool night air, while they, the Nigerians, lived a pretty spartan existence, sleeping on thin army mats on the hard cement roof, with all their belongings in their rucksacks. I tried a few times to speak with them, but found few had more than a superficial grasp of English beyond "hello" and "thank you," and I had even less idea what language they spoke when I heard them laughing together in the darkness on the rooftop. Sometimes I would offer them my old magazines and newspapers, particularly if I found somewhere a story on Nigeria that I thought might interest them. They gratefully accepted the small handouts with a flash of a smile and a "thank you," and that was it, really; they went back to their world, and I to mine.

Two worlds. Just as I had found in Nairobi, with the distance between myself and my own Kenyan staff members. This gap was too wide between the Africans and myself, and I found that no matter how hard I tried, I could never cross it.

Even while this rapidly growing foreign community stayed busy constructing its parallel universe on the Al-Sahafi rooftop and in the UN compounds, all of us, I think, had the same nagging feeling that this noble Somalia rescue mission could go terribly wrong. It had all been too easy from the start—the beach landing, the waving Somalis lining the streets. But they weren't waving anymore. Now they were throwing stones and taking potshots from rooftops.

The raggedy guys with the guns and the flip-flops who had been terrorizing the population had the good sense to disappear when the marines first showed up. They recognized a superior force on the ground. Somali gunmen may be a lot of things, but they're generally not suicidal. A lot of them just buried their weapons someplace, waiting to fight another day. Many got jobs working as construction workers or drivers or translators for the huge number of reporters flooding in, and even on the UN compound itself. That was the nature of the oddball fantasyland called Mogadishu; the guys working for the UN during the day could be the same ones taking sniper shots at marine positions at night.

One who understood the potential danger, and had warned about it, was Maj. Gen. Charles Wilhelm, the marine commander in Mogadishu. Wilhelm was one of those tough, no-nonsense marines, the kind you'd expect to be played by Clint Eastwood in the movies. Wilhelm had been there in Beirut, and he'd seen firsthand what could happen if you let your troops get sucked into a factional conflict. I found him surprisingly candid about the hidden dangers facing his young marines.

"Do I see us running the risk of getting drawn in more deeply through prolonged involvement? The answer to that is, quite frankly, yes I do," he told me. Recounting what he called his own "mental milestones" from Beirut, Wilhelm warned, "We could be drawn into it. Through a flood of events, we could be drawn in, and we've seen that before. That's one of the lessons history has taught us."

That had to be the most sane—and most prescient—analysis I'd gotten from anyone involved in the entire intervention. I found myself recalling his warning as America did get drawn ever deeper into the Somali quagmire. And of course I remembered the similar warning from Smith Hempstone, "If you liked Beirut, you'll love Mogadishu."

But with all due respect to the general, he was slightly off on one thing: History hadn't taught us anything at all. Because when the flood of events did happen, we repeated the exact same mistakes as before. And so what started out as a touchy-feely humanitarian mission to feed starving people ended as an embarrassing manhunt for an egotistical baldheaded warlord.

When I met Mohamed Farah Aideed for the first time, I thought he was crazy. He seemed neurotic, edgy, his wild eyes constantly shifting, unable to focus. I saw him a second time in Bardhere, holed up in a compound sitting on cushions and twirling his walking stick, with piping-hot food laid out on a long table while a few yards away people were dropping dead of starvation. That second time I thought he was not only crazy, but evil.

I would meet Aideed many times over the years I covered Somalia, but my first impressions were lasting ones; he was a ruthless man who cared little about human life and suffering. He was a first-class liar, a cynical role-player, and a wily guerrilla fighter who understood, among other things, the importance of an inflated body count in what was essentially a television war. He was a master spin doctor who could reinvent himself as circumstances required—one day he was embracing Islam, beginning his press conferences with a prayer to Allah, the next day he was the diplomat-statesman, racing to regional meetings in dark pinstripes and crisp white shirt, and the next day still he was the underground resistance leader, coldly calculating his next bloody ambush while exhorting his followers through clandestine radio broadcasts.

Aideed was a disastrous public speaker, especially when he insisted on talking to reporters in English. His press conferences would always start (after the prayer to Allah when he was in heavy Moslem mode) with Aideed reading a prepared statement in a high-pitched voice that broke in odd places and with painfully tortured syntax. He would rest a pair of eyeglasses at the very end of his nose, hold the paper right in front of his face, and read slowly, deliberately, syllable by syllable, with stresses in all the wrong places. Sometimes he would thrust one finger into the air for emphasis, but he was always a syllable or two off beat.

Aideed's hopeless attempts to speak in English became the butt of jokes among the press corps. I myself developed a pretty wicked imitation of the old warlord by holding a piece of paper in front of my face, letting my glasses slide down to the very tip of my nose, and then taking an exaggeratedly long time to spit out every syllable. It was a performance usually reserved for the end of the evenings, on the roof of the Al-Sahafi, and I'd have my colleagues rolling with laughter. Once, after a few of Paul Alexander's lethal whisky sours, a friend from Worldwide Television News brought up his camera and recorded a session, with me playing Aideed to perfection. I even took questions from the reporters, answering each, as Aideed always did, by first thrusting a finger into the air for emphasis. It was a hilarious routine, I thought—that is, until a few days later, when I was told that someone had played a copy of the performance for One-Eyed Abdi.

One-Eyed Abdi was kind of an unofficial Aideed spokesman, in an organization without real titles; he used to pop in at the journalists' hotel to give us updates on the latest clash with UN troops or to hand out the most recent SNA statement. He seemed to enjoy his role as intermediary to the foreign press, and would abuse that position by making sure we kept him well plied with cold drinks and whatever latest newspapers and magazines we happened to have had shipped in from Nairobi. But I had little doubt that he was fairly close to the old man and that he even knew Aideed's whereabouts when he was in hiding. And when my colleagues told me that One-Eyed Abdi had taken a copy of the video of my rooftop performance to play for Aideed, I had more than a few nervous nights—and got up more than once to recheck the lock on my door. I never knew if my friends were just pulling my leg; on the other hand, this was Mogadishu, and I wasn't going to take any chances, just in case Aideed didn't share my sense of humor.

If I was frightened of Aideed, it was because I knew he was a cold-blooded killer. He of course had orchestrated the attack on the Pakistani soldiers on June 5. And he showed over and again that even the lives of his own followers meant nothing to him; one of his favorite techniques was to use women and children as "human shields" to draw the fire of UN and American troops and conceal his own snipers hidden in the crowds.

Aideed would also resort to outright assassination when it suited him. In May 1993, he blurted out in a meeting of his top aides that he would have an American killed because the United States was trying to strip him of his power. What he didn't know was that one of his aides in the room at the time was an informant for the Americans, who promptly reported the threat before it could be carried out.

But while I knew Aideed and understood his penchant for ruthlessness, I made a key mistake in assessing him—I underestimated him. And it was the same mistake America's military planners made when they launched the disastrous operation to have the old man arrested.

It was an operation worthy of the Keystone Kops—army Rangers snaking down ropes from helicopters asking baldheaded Somalis: "Are you Aideed?" There was even a "WANTED" poster, Wild West style, and an offer of a $25,000 reward for Aideed's apprehension. Here was the supreme irony, I thought. Aideed had made the city streets so unsafe that the only place they could tack up their "WANTED" posters was inside the walls of the fortified embassy compound itself.

The lunacy of the botched "search" came clear to me one day when I paid a visit to the spacious Mogadishu home of Osman Ato, or "Osman the Thin," one of Aideed's key henchmen and the warlord's principal financier. Ato had become one of my regular contacts in the SNA organization. Before the marines landed, he had taken me to a small garage area across from his house where young men were busy assembling "technical" vehicles, battle wagons mounted with heavy machine guns. Then we walked to an old rusted, Chinese-made field artillery gun, where we stopped, he patted the relic, and brushed aside all my questions about its accuracy. It was a warning, Ato said, if the American marines try to come in and disarm the SNA and the warlords.

Ato was ostensibly one of those top Aideed lieutenants on the UN's arrest list. But apparently not on that day, when I found myself sitting comfortably at home in his living room, watching CNN thanks to a satellite dish on his roof. He ushered me in to a seat next to him on the sofa, had a servant girl bring sweet, piping-hot Somali tea, and then, noticing it was ten o'clock, the top of the hour, hushed me to silence for a few minutes so we could watch the latest CNN news bulletin. The big news that day, the announcer said, was a raid on a hideout of suspected top members of the Aideed militia. The film footage, being beamed live, showed helicopters in the air encircling a villa while a reporter breathlessly told of a major American military operation under way. Ato looked at first serious, then mildly amused. "Wonder where that could be?" he said with a wink as we watched another futile operation, brought live into the SNA living room.

And so Aideed was never captured or even forced into retreat; rather, it was the U.S. Army and the United Nations that threw in the towel. All those fresh-faced young kids with heady ideas of "nation building" all packed their bags and went home. The sprawling embassy compound that they had paved and manicured enough to look like a college campus was abandoned and overrun by Somali looters. No one knows for certain, but the whole thing cost more than $3 billion and thousands of lives, on both sides.

And for what? So we could stop people from starving to death. So we could help them rebuild their country. So we could save Somalis from themselves.

No one ever calculated what you do next if the people you come to help have no interest in being saved.

I can pinpoint fairly precisely the beginning of my own disillusionment about Somalia ever being saved; it was July 12, 1993, at ten o'clock in the morning. That was the day four of my friends were beaten to death by a Somali mob outside of a packed house that had just been blown to bits, along with everyone inside, by American helicopter gunships.

I was in Nairobi when I heard the news, taking a rare weekend break back home after a long stretch in Somalia. My plans to close up the *Post*'s shop in Mogadishu had been put on hold after the June 5 attacks, for there was obviously still a lot of news to report in Somalia. Before leaving the Al-Sahafi Hotel, I had said good-bye to Dan Eldon and Hos Maina, both there for Reuters; Anthony Macharia, a soundman for Reuter television; and Hansi Kraus, a German photographer working for the Associated Press who had come to Somalia to get a break from covering the wartime atrocities in the Balkans. Dan owed me one of his Somalia T-shirts, and I told him not to worry; I'd pick it up when I came back to Mogadishu in a few days.

When the main force of U.S. Marines withdrew from Somalia in May, they left behind a smaller contingent of about two thousand American soldiers who were operating under the United Nations flag. The marines earlier had steadfastly avoided being drawn into playing the role of street cops and sorting out Somalia's internecine clan feuds. But the UN came in with a different idea of its mission—they called it "nation building," which in practice meant stripping the guns away from the warring factions and trying to set up "neutral" institutions like a police force and a judicial system. Problem was that there was no such thing as a "neutral" Somali—you'd be more likely to find a Somali with blond hair and freckles—and the UN, with its well-meaning but overly ambitious agenda, allowed itself to be sucked into a tit-for-tat war of attrition against Aideed.

For a while, the UN planners thought they could solve the problem by making Aideed the object of a military manhunt around the city; instead, they simply pissed him off. Aideed would send a mortar round into the American or UN base, and the Americans—supposedly there only in a "support" role but who more and more became the frontline troops—would respond by sending up Cobra helicopters to fire their cannons or TOW antitank missiles into one of the warlord's supposed strongholds. Then Aideed upped the ante, sending his thugs to kidnap and kill a half-dozen Somalis who were working for the United Nations helping distribute the UN's propaganda newspaper, *Maanta*.

The murder of the Somali staffers badly rattled Jonathan T. Howe, the retired American admiral and onetime submarine commander who was the top UN man in Somalia. Howe was much derided by the military men and even by some of his own UN staffers for his "aw, shucks" demeanor, his Boy Scout enthusiasm for this messy job, and because with his ghostly complexion he was the only white guy in Somalia who never seemed to get a suntan even under the scorching sun. "Too much time on a submarine," one UN official used to quip off the record. But when Aideed upped the stakes, Howe, like any good military man, knew he had to respond in kind, or the battle against Aideed for hearts and minds on the streets would be lost. He agonized for a while, then finally approved a long-standing American military plan to strike at the senior members of Aideed's Somali National Alliance faction, and his Habre Gedir clan, while they were meeting at the house of the warlord's self-described "defense minister," Abdi Qaaybdid. It was, to anyone's knowledge, the United Nations' first-ever officially authorized assassination.

The attack was a messy affair. In fact, it was a slaughter. A half-dozen Cobras pumped sixteen TOW missiles and two thousand rounds of cannon fire into the house with deadly accuracy. First they blew away the stairwell to prevent anyone from escaping. Then they blasted their missiles and cannon fire directly into the top floor of the house where the meeting was taking place. A video taken just after the attack showed the mangled bodies literally blown apart in the attack—the religious leaders, the elders, even the women in their colorful wrap dresses who were always on hand to serve the tea. American soldiers dropped in and took pictures of the carnage, just to confirm that it was a job well done.

No call for those inside to come out and surrender. No warning to vacate the premises. Just a straight-out, bloody massacre.

No one knows exactly how many people died in the Qaaybdid house that morning. The International Red Cross estimated at least seventy people were killed. The Americans, after insisting for weeks that the figure was far, far lower—probably only two dozen or so—later admitted that the Red Cross had probably been right. The number of dead Somalis never seemed to matter to anyone, especially not to U.S. military officials who insisted they were not going to be drawn into a Vietnam-style "body count."

For me, that policy always seemed a backhanded way of saying that when the bodies were black and African, no one would bother trying to count. Whenever I wrote a story from Somalia, I always insisted on some estimate of the Somali dead.

Dan, Hos, and their two colleagues showed up a short time later at the Qaaybdid house slaughter, after the helicopters had left and just as an angry Somali crowd had formed. I wasn't there, but I can picture the scene—I'd seen many crowds like it before, like the one outside Radio Mogadishu on June 5. There would have been a lot of pushing, shoving, shouting, finger-pointing. Rocks were thrown. And then the knives came out. And the guns.

My friends were beaten to death, mostly. Their faces were smashed in with stones. When Dan's body was plucked up by a helicopter and taken to the U.S. Army field hospital, the commander there, Col. Artie Shelton, who had met Dan just a few days earlier, couldn't recognize him. He said Dan's face was just a mass of blood.

The others didn't fare any better—beaten, stoned, stabbed. Hos, the Kenyan journalist who had so generously let me use his photos of that long-ago beauty pageant, was found a few blocks from the carnage. Anthony almost made it back to the Al-Sahafi Hotel, running from the mob, but he was felled by a knife to the back. And

Hansi's body went missing for a few days, the Somali attackers apparently thinking they could possibly get some ransom for it.

I didn't cry when my friends died; I became obsessed.

When I returned to Somalia, I tried to interview everyone involved in making the decision to bomb the Qaaybdid house that day—as if finding a flaw in the decision itself might somehow allow me to fix the blame for the death of my colleagues. I talked to the military officers who planned the operation, who called it "a good hit" and the people inside "punks" and "gangsters." I talked to a State Department officer who told me, "Maybe we killed some people we wouldn't have wanted to kill, but we also got the guys we were after." And I interviewed Howe, repeatedly, on the July 12 attack, and his "gee-whiz" all-American shoulder shrugging never wavered; he insisted that the meeting in the house that day was a "military planning cell" and the people inside were "plotting and planning for their terrorist attacks."

With each interview, with each American justification for the attack, I grew more and more angry; after a few weeks, I was seething. My own moral universe had just been turned completely upside down. We were the United States of America, and my country, I believed, did not go around assassinating people in houses and using the convenient cover of the UN flag to get away with it. We were supposed to be the good guys, the ones who always surrounded the house and told everybody inside to come out with their hands up. We read people their rights, gave them the chance to defend themselves in a court of law. But something had happened to the United States in this first postwar military expedition in Africa—we were behaving like they were. We had come into the jungle (or in this case, the desert) and adopted their survival-of-the-fittest rules. We had lost our moral high ground.

I couldn't bring back my dead friends, but I felt that perhaps I could make their deaths carry some larger meaning if I could use the tragedy at the Qaaybdid house to point out the dangers of falling into Somalia's moral abyss and adopting, as the Somalis had, the age-old law of the desert to survive.

Of course, I also interviewed those on the other side, Aideed's guerrillas and henchmen, since it was their supporters, after all, who had actually murdered my friends. They offered some pathetic explanations, excuses really. The crowd was enraged after the slaughter in the Qaaybdid house and set upon any foreigners in sight, they said. At least one of the photographers had been wearing those camouflage "chocolate chip" military pants, and the angry mob may have mistaken these foreigners with cameras for foreign soldiers, one told me. And another of Aideed's sycophants even suggested that when the mostly illiterate Somalis saw the foreigners with their fancy camera equipment, they might have misunderstood and believed that these gadgets were being used to direct the helicopter air strikes. This was nonsense, like so much of what Aideed's thugs tried to tell me. Any Somali camel herder could tell the difference between a journalist with a camera and a soldier with a walkie-talkie or radar tracking device. And Dan, of all of those killed, was well known in the neighborhood, the "Mayor of Mogadishu."

Looking back on it, there were several competing emotions that drove me to keep digging deeper, to put some meaning and pin some blame for the slaughter of July 12. The first was guilt.

I wasn't there the day my friends were killed. But I might have been.

If I had stayed a few extra days in Mogadishu instead of opting for a weekend back home, I am certain I would have been right out the front door of the hotel when the first missiles were fired. We would have all been there, together, surrounded by the same mob. Maybe Rashid's street radar would have told him something was wrong, and I could have warned the others that it was time to leave quickly before the crowd turned too nasty. Or maybe as we were all racing out the door after breakfast, I might have been there to offer a note of caution—"Hey, let's wait a while first," or, "Hold up, my guys tell me the crowds are pretty nasty out there."

Maybe I should consider myself lucky. I don't remember now what was so important that weekend that caused me to leave Mogadishu—a dinner date, something. But when I did return, I wasn't exactly thankful for my good fortune. I felt sort of like a guy walking past a train wreck who would have been one of the mangled bodies on the tracks if he hadn't missed the last whistle and been left stranded on the platform.

The second emotion driving me was fear.

As reporters covering violent situations, we often cloak ourselves in the myth of our own invincibility. It's not a macho thing at all. We're not playing God, or even playing the odds. Rather, it's our only defense mechanism against paralyzing fear that would otherwise prevent us from doing our job. We cover ourselves in a protective shell, believing that our impartiality is our immunity. And when one of our own is killed, violently and deliberately, it shatters that shield and leaves us standing there exposed. And that's what the deaths of my colleagues did to me, left me naked and exposed. And for the first time, I was terrified.

But trying to explain what happened that day, being able to rationalize it and pin the blame, seemed like what I needed at the time to put some order back into our protected little journalistic universe. If I could write off that tragedy as the result of a series of very specific, bad decisions, a confluence of specific conditions and circumstances, then it suddenly became a fluke, an aberration—and something that of course could never happen again. And then I could exhale, nod knowingly, and get on with the job.

I visited and revisited the Qaaybdid house—not just in my mind, but physically. Often when I was in the back of the battered old white Toyota, riding along the familiar and dusty streets clogged with wartime debris, and I was returning to the Al-Sahafi Hotel from an interview with some clan leader or religious elder, or after getting the updated casualty figures from nearby Digfer Hospital, I'd tell Rashid and Gass to swing by the Qaaybdid house. Just to give me one more look.

And I would walk there amid the rubble, letting my anger give way to an intense sadness that would wash quickly over me, then recede, letting the anger roil up again. The house was basically a skeleton now, the walls mostly gone, the parts that remained charred black from the fire of the missile explosions. And the demolished stairwell was clearly visible, too—just debris, really, arching grotesquely upward, in the place where steps should be. And there was some graffiti now painted on the shell of the old house, denouncing Howe and American imperialism in English, and in Somali mockingly telling the world that this shambles of brick and wood and bullet fragments and missile debris constituted American "foreign aid" to the Somali people. I didn't read Somali, but I had Rashid translate the words so many times that I could recite them by heart.

I would walk down the narrow alleyway of a path that led from the street, where the car was parked, to what was left of the demolished villa. And here I would see the images of my friends, trapped there at the far end of the alley near the house, with the crowds forming quickly, angrily, swarming into the path, blocking the way back to the street. And I could see the rocks being thrown, and my friends falling down, and the crowd swarming around them.

And I knew that buried there in the burned-out rubble of the Qaaybdid house were a lot of my own preconceived notions about Somalia, about the United Nations and about my own country, about what was possible in the world and what was not—indeed, what would later become many of my perceptions about the entire continent. Much of my anger had been misdirected, I now realized; I was angry at myself. I had been one of the early advocates of the tough-cop approach to Somalia. I had been first on the bandwagon for intervention. I was the one telling anyone who would listen, screaming it, really, that we had to do something—anything—to save Somalia from dying, because as Somalia went, so went the rest of Africa. And some of those who died here had been there with me, arguing the same; they had produced some of the most moving images of the famine that had jarred public opinion back home, forcing the world to take notice. And now they were dead, killed by the very people they had tried, through the lenses of their cameras, to help.

And now here I was, standing in the debris of my own long-held assumptions. Those bullets and missiles had blasted away my illusions. All that was left was an ugly shell.

Somalia dashed the world's hopes—and mine—that Africa might somehow become the testing ground for the New World Order and the idea of benign military intervention. But the effect on me was perhaps even more profound because it was in Somalia that I first learned what it was like to be a black reporter covering a major story in Africa.

It was, I decided, a distinct disadvantage.

In Kenya, I had already figured out that being black in Africa could mean putting up with all the petty slights and inconveniences. In Somalia, I realized, it could be fatal.

Early on I had learned that when I approached any of the foreign troops on Somalia's streets, I had to do so making it pretty clear I was an American, and a reporter, in case they decided to shoot first and check passports later. What I never counted on was that troops from my own country, American soldiers and marines, might also mistake me for the enemy.

Once, after finishing an interview in a particularly dicey part of town near Checkpoint Pasta (the Italian checkpoint at the site of an abandoned pasta factory), Rashid and Gass were bringing me back to the UN compound. We didn't have the usual extra bodyguard that day—I think he had called in sick—and it was Rashid riding shotgun in front with his own rusted AK-47. Gass carried a pistol under his shirt.

Suddenly, without warning, they pulled the battered old Toyota off to the side of the dusty street.

"What's the matter?" I asked, noticing dusk was falling—a dangerous time to be stopping on Mogadishu's streets.

"Flat tire," Rashid said.

"Okay, let's hurry. You do have a spare, right?" I paused, and saw Rashid's eyes drop slightly. "Shit," I said. "You mean we don't have a spare?"

What do you do when you're on a deserted street in the world's most dangerous capital in a car with a flat tire, no spare, and only one gunslinger? You hitchhike, of course.

Rashid and Gass wanted to stay with the car—an obviously more valuable commodity than me. So I stood there in the middle of the road, with darkness falling, and the first vehicle I spotted in the distance was a U.S. Army humvee—two of them actually—in a convoy heading my way, and obviously going straight to the UN compound. I waved my press card furiously with one hand and my passport with the other. And as the Americans approached, they picked up speed and plowed right past me, leaving me shouting, furiously, in their dust. One of the soldiers in the front car—a white guy—stared right at me as they whipped past. I know he was looking at me because I saw his head turn and face me, just a few feet from where I was shouting and waving my arms.

Goddammit! I thought. This is like trying to find a taxicab in Washington, D.C., at night!

I did manage to get a ride, about an hour later, after it was dark and I was shaking with fright, from a truckload of Indian soldiers who passed by. How ironic, I thought. My own countrymen left me standing in the dust because all they saw was a black guy—to them a dark-skinned Somali, a potential assassin. Thank God for the Indians!

Being black in Somalia I suppose did occasionally have its advantages—particularly when anti-Americanism was running strong and when, if I kept my mouth shut and stayed crunched down in the backseat of the old Toyota, I could pretty much pass for a Somali. With sunglasses on and my Somali-style checkered scarf slung over my shoulder, I was often able to venture undetected into some of Mogadishu's most dangerous back alleys and neighborhoods. That helped me get some of my best firsthand reporting details.

Once, after a U.S. helicopter attack someplace, my AP colleague Paul Alexander (of the rooftop whisky sour fame) decided we needed to get into one of the main city hospitals for a more accurate casualty count. But anti-American sentiment was at fever pitch, and we weren't sure how we'd be received walking into an emergency ward taking a body count. So I wore my cleanest white shirt, and Alexander trailed behind me with a notepad like an obedient underling. We strode purposefully up the steps of the main hospital, and I started barking orders and questions as if I owned the place.

"Okay, how many wounded we got here?" I demanded from the first person in the hospital who looked like he was in a position to know. "What's the extent of the injuries?" And to add that extra air of authenticity, I inquired, "Okay, now what do you need in terms of medicine? Supplies? Enough bandages?" All the while, Alexander was furiously scribbling, and I would snap my fingers at him occasionally and bark, "Get that down!"

I assumed they thought I was some medical worker, maybe an African volunteer doctor. And later we laughed about how the Somalis seemed positively tickled watching the white guy take orders from an authoritarian black guy. Kind of a role reversal, I guess.

Mostly, though, it wasn't fun and games; being black in Somalia meant I was constantly at risk.

That came home to me in late 1993 when I was one of the reporters on hand at the first public rally Aideed held in Mogadishu after emerging from hiding. The arrest order had been lifted, and the Clinton administration had called off the humiliatingly futile manhunt. The mood at the rally was predictably euphoric. A group of us were hustled through the crowd and allowed to wait on the far side of the stage for what we knew would be the Old Man's grand entrance.

Suddenly, one of the Somali gunmen guarding the stage raced up to me and shoved me hard in the chest with the flat of his hand, sending me hurling down on my back. I looked up, stunned, into his wild eyes as he pulled his AK-47 off his shoulder and seemed to take aim at me. He was shouting wildly in Somali, and I couldn't understand a word. A crowd gathered and there was more shouting and shoving until eventually somebody wrestled the madman's gun away from him.

One of Aideed's aides rushed over and helped me to my feet. "I apologize," he told me. "You look like a Somali. He thought you were someone else."

Being black in Africa. I felt the tears welling up in my eyes, but I fought hard to keep from bursting out crying right there on that stage. It dawned on me then how close I came to being just another statistic. A few seconds, really—the time it took him to get the machine gun off his shoulder, and before the crowd gathered around him. And it would have been over for me, just like that. An error. A case of mistaken identity.

All because I was a black man in the wrong place, a black man in Africa.

If the "intervasion" began as a comedy, it ended as a tragedy. Edgy UN soldiers on patrol opened fire on a hidden sniper and ended up killing an elderly unarmed security guard working for a UN agency. American army "snipers" saw a kid holding a pistol at an Egyptian troop position and shot the kid dead—only to discover later he was holding a toy pistol the Egyptians had given him. Newly arrived U.S. soldiers, we were told, would "take back the streets" from the militia gunmen; they stayed hunkered down in their barracks trying hard to avoid any more casualties. When the Americans finally did go home, they slipped out the back door, by ship, because commanders feared that planes might be a tempting target for a Somali with a rocket-propelled grenade.

In one of my last dispatches, I called the American withdrawal a "retreat." The U.S. commander, Maj. Gen. Thomas Montgomery, was so angry he refused my request for a final interview.

And so I left Somalia feeling angry, frightened, vulnerable, exposed. I had been so sure at first; Africa's problems—its passions, its furies, its penchant for self-destruction—were all right there, writ large, in the sands of Somalia. And the remedies were all there as well—$3 billion, the most powerful military force on the earth, the weight and prestige of the United Nations, the attention of the entire world.

And it was all there for me, too, the whole reason for being a reporter in Africa—a black reporter in Africa. To expose the suffering, to make the world pay attention. Then suddenly my friends are dead, some two dozen American soldiers and marines are dead, billions have been spent and wasted, the world has turned out the lights and closed the door, and I've got a guy leveling a machine gun at me because I'm black and he thinks I'm an African.

And I'm left naked, shorn of all my truths and certainties, no longer sure what I believe. And I'm hating them, the Somalis. Hating them because they betrayed me. Hating myself for having been so wrong, for setting myself up for the betrayal.

I saw that I would have to arm myself with a new set of truths if I were to survive in Africa. But another crisis was brewing, and there was no time now for me to sit back and take stock.

5

Thy Neighbor's Killer

"There are no devils left in Hell. They are all in Rwanda."

—A MISSIONARY,
quoted in *Time* magazine, May 16, 1994

THE YOUNG MEN with the machetes and the pistols had beer on their breath and murder in their eyes. But it was the dried bloodstains splattered across their filthy T-shirts that sent a cold shiver of fear slicing straight through to my gut. It was the blood of their last victims.

We were at a militia checkpoint in southwestern Rwanda at the height of an ongoing campaign of genocide that had already claimed untold hundreds of thousands of lives. Most of the victims were from the Tutsi tribe, but the bodies piling up by the roadsides and on the riverbanks also included a fair number of Hutu tribesmen considered Tutsi "sympathizers." For a Hutu, simply sheltering a frightened Tutsi neighbor from the rampaging mobs and militiamen was enough to warrant a machete blow to the head. And the other victims were Belgians, hated chiefly because Belgium was the former colonial power here. And that's what these crazed young men at the checkpoint were on the lookout for that day—Tutsi, Tutsi sympathizers, and Belgians.

These were hard-looking young men, and though they had a dazed, faraway look in their eyes, they conducted their search of our car with deadly efficiency—opening backpacks, checking under the seats, even peering inside the gasoline tank. One wore a red, black, and green beret, affixed at the top with a small button bearing the smiling likeness of Juvenal Habyarimana, the Hutu president who had organized these young killers and whose plane, days earlier, had mysteriously exploded in the night sky over the capital city, Kigali. I looked around while our car was being stripped apart, and I found Habyarimana's likeness everywhere—on buttons, and on the dirty T-shirts splashed with blood.

What I also noticed were the weapons—crude farming tools, really. Machetes and long panga knives, more typically used for clearing brush and chopping firewood than for severing human limbs. There were also clubs. Big, flat wooden clubs, smaller at the handle end and rounded at the top. They reminded me of the all-purpose clubs Fred Flintstone and Barney Rubble used to carry in the old TV cartoon. But with one small difference: To make the clubs more deadly on impact, the Hutu militiamen drove long nails into the end. That's what Rwanda has become, I thought. The country has reverted to prehistoric times, to a kind of sick version of Bedrock. And could these be fully evolved humans carrying clubs and machetes and panga knives and smashing in their neighbors' skulls and chopping off their limbs, and piling up the legs in one pile, and the arms in another, and lumping the bodies all together and sometimes forcing new victims to sit atop the heap while they clubbed them to death too? No, I realized, fully evolved human beings in the twentieth century don't do things like that. Not for any reason, not tribe, not religion, not territory. These must be cavemen.

We have no business being here, I thought. We have to get the hell out.

I was traveling with my friend and colleague Ruth Burnett, a loquacious and fiery-haired British producer for the German television station ZDF, along with her crew. It seemed like we'd all be safe here, and I, the only black person in the group, would be most at risk—which is why I kept my blue American passport clutched tightly in my hand. I had heard of other black American journalists being harassed in Rwanda, mistaken for Tutsi, almost killed. Ron Allen, from ABC's London bureau, a tall, photogenic black American, barely escaped when he was mistaken for a Tutsi by a mob just like this one.

From the start, the Rwanda crisis of 1994 had been something of a personal and professional dilemma for me. I wanted to be right there, on top of the story, like any other journalist based in Africa. But at the same time, I knew the risks for a black reporter were even greater in Rwanda than they had ever been in Somalia. The dangers were so real that the United Nations office in Nairobi flatly refused to transport "people of color" into Kigali on its food airlift flights. No blacks and no Belgians was the order. And no apologies. They were discriminating for reasons of personal safety.

My editors in Washington issued a similar edict: Do not set foot in Kigali while the massacres are going on, and go into the other parts of Rwanda only with explicit approval, and only then once I was certain it was absolutely safe.

I couldn't blame them. But still it made me seethe with anger and resentment. The massacre under way in Kigali was the biggest story in Africa, indeed in the world at the time. And I couldn't go inside for much of it because I was the wrong color, the same color as the victims.

Dipping a toe over the border from Burundi did seem absolutely safe at the time—or so I thought. But I was nervous that day as Ruth and I and the others crossed into Rwanda, into the darkness.

I told the others that at the first sign of trouble, we turn tail and head as fast as we can back to the safety of the Burundi border. They weren't as worried as I was, though; Ruth carried a British passport, and the rest in her group were Germans.

What I didn't know at the time was that Ruth's passport had been issued not in Great Britain but in Brussels, where her parents were living at the time. At the bottom of one page in her passport, a small line in tiny print read, innocently enough, "Issued at British Embassy, Brussels, Belgium." Ruth had realized the potential problem and cleverly tried to conceal that small fact with a tiny strip of masking tape.

It didn't work.

When we arrived at the first checkpoint, just across Rwanda's southwestern border with Burundi, we were hustled into the small building that still served as the immigration headquarters. The Rwandans crowded around us, taking turns inspecting our passports and the visas we managed to obtain from the Rwandan embassy in Bujumbura, the Burundian capital. It never ceased to amaze me that even countries in the midst of collapse—countries gripped by civil war and anarchy, with machete-wielding militiamen outside chopping the limbs off people—still insisted on preserving the familiar bureaucratic and exhaustively time-consuming formalities, like checking for valid visas at border crossing points. In Rwanda; in Liberia, where the central government was reduced to controlling only the capital city and not much else; even in Goma, the Zairean border town choking under the influx of a million Rwandan refugees, there was always, invariably, some self-important immigration official wearing sunglasses and a cheap imitation silk shirt, sitting in a dark, windowless, and stiflingly hot cement hut demanding to check visas and requiring an inexplicable series of stamps, forms, and photographs before allowing a foreign journalist to enter to cover the carnage. But that was Africa, I had decided. Or, more accurately, that was what Africa was on the road to becoming: a series of feuding fiefdoms, designated by artificial boundaries where nation-states used to exist, and the only thing left to mark the old colonial delineation of the continent would be a series of little cement huts occupied by immigration bureaucrats with sunglasses, fake silk shirts, and the all-important rubber stamp. And these bureaucrats would continue to take their jobs seriously because they knew that in them resided all that was left of their nation's fictitious claim to sovereignty.

That was what was going through my head when the immigration officer in the sunglasses and silk shirt asked Ruth, "What's under this tape?"

He pulled it off, and there for all to see was Ruth Burnett's darkest secret—that her passport had been issued in Brussels.

"You are Belgian!" he said, a proclamation, not a question. No, she explained, she was British, but her passport was issued in Brussels because that's where her parents live.

"Why do your parents live in Brussels if they are not Belgian?" he demanded suspiciously.

Rather than explaining the nuances of Western employment patterns and the staffing practices of multinational corporations like Procter & Gamble, she simply opted to plead that she was indeed British, the passport was indeed a British passport, and her parents just happened to be living in Belgium at the time the passport was issued.

"I think you are Belgian and you are lying about your nationality," the little man in the sunglasses and fake silk shirt persisted.

This went on for some time, until the interrogation turned very weird. "Are you married to a Belgian?" he asked her. Told she was single, the little man in the sunglasses then asked, "Do you like African men, or do you want to marry a Belgian?"

By this time, I—or rather my passport—had already passed the crowd's inspection, and they were satisfied that I was not a Tutsi. In fact, several of the young thugs with the machetes and berets and the bloodstained Habyarimana T-shirts seemed positively tickled to see a black man, an African in their view, with an American passport. "*Noir Americain*," they said, touching their own skin, and then my exposed arm. "Like you," I replied in English. "Same like you." And this would bring a roar of laughter from the crowd. And then I decided to go and help rescue Ruth.

I identified one of the young men who appeared to be some kind of a leader, if anyone in such a rabble can be said to look in control. "That woman is my wife," I said, thinking of the first lie to come to mind; my first lesson in Africa, lie. And lie big. "She's not Belgian, she's my wife." I spoke in English, and again in French, to make sure "the leader," or at least someone else in the crowd, would understand. "She is okay," I said. "She is married to an African, she is one of us."

The crowd seemed to accept this new knowledge, and in fact they delighted in it. The self-important immigration officer also had grown weary of his little interrogation. We were allowed to go forward, on to the next checkpoint, which we were told was at a bridge just a few miles down the road.

A Rwandan government soldier was lounging idly outside the little cement immigration house. We asked him if he could accompany us in our car for safety reasons. We also thought having a soldier with us might provide some form of official protection against the young militiamen manning the roadblocks. "No, no," the soldier said, waving us off. "You're on your own. Very dangerous."

We did venture on, past a few more militia roadblocks and more crazed young men with blood on their shirts and the cold stare of death in their eyes. More searches. More inspections of our passports. More heart-stopping moments as the killers determined whether I was really a Tutsi, or whether Ruth was really a Belgian. And eventually we panicked—I panicked—and we reversed course and headed out of Rwanda as fast as the car would take us back to the border, back to Burundi and the security of the Novotel Hotel in Bujumbura.

That one brief trip over the border in Rwanda was the closest I came during three years in Africa to being overwhelmed by my own fear. I had been frightened before in Somalia, many times, lying flat on the roof of the Al-Sahafi while mortar shells exploded nearby, being shoved in the chest to the ground by that crazed gunman holding an AK-47 at my head. But all those instances were different somehow, quick and isolated moments of fear, a few seconds really, flash points made larger by the memory. And most of the time in Somalia, the fear was of what was random and unseen—a stray shell slamming into my bedroom while I tried to sleep, or a sniper's bullet picking me off in the crowd gathered for rooftop cocktails at the Al-Sahafi.

When I ran into Sam Kiley in Bujumbura, the veteran *Times* man who had juggled hand grenades in Mogadishu looked more shaken than I had ever seen him. I had not yet been in Rwanda, and Sam had just come out, and it was the first time I ever knew Sam to be rattled in Africa. I asked him what was the matter, how could Rwanda be that much worse than what we had gone through together in Mogadishu. "Oh, man," Sam said, shaking his head at the demons in his mind, "Rwanda makes Somalia look like a picnic in the Queen's garden!"

If Rwanda was different, it was because the violence, the death, was up close and personal, and unprecedented on the scale of savagery. Here, the militias wouldn't shoot you in the head, Somali style. They would carve off your arm first and watch you bleed and scream in pain. Then, if you didn't pass out, they would chop off one of your legs, or maybe just a foot. If you were lucky, they might finish you off with a machete blow to the back of the head. Otherwise, they might carve off your ears, your nose, and toss your limbless torso atop the pile of dead bodies, where you could slowly bleed to death. That is, of course, unless you happened to be rescued soon afterward by the Tutsi guerrillas of the Rwandan Patriotic Front, who would then take what was left of your near lifeless body to some dirty field hospital with no anesthesia set up in an abandoned church or schoolyard behind their lines, where a French or Belgian doctor with an international charity might patch you up, just so you could live with your own nightmares.

I must admit, I too found it hard at first to believe the scope of the horror, not even when the initial stories of the atrocities started filtering back to Nairobi. Like the story of bodies piled up six feet high outside Kigali's main hospital. Or the story of the ten Belgian paratroopers who were executed while trying to protect Rwanda's prime minister; first they had their Achilles tendons cut to prevent them from escaping, then they were castrated and the severed organs shoved into their mouths. These were the stories, repeated over and over again, and I didn't believe them. But now I was seeing it with my own eyes. It could no longer be denied.

A tour of Rwanda's horror show might begin in Byumba town, in the rebel-controlled section of northern Rwanda not far from the border with Uganda. A man named Amiable Kaberuka is there, lying on a cot in a makeshift rebel field hospital. He might be considered lucky, since luck is a relative term here; he survived with only a gunshot in the shoulder. The Hutu militia entered the school building where he and thousands of others had taken refuge. The attackers told Kaberuka that he must die because he was a Tutsi, and then they used machetes and pangas to hack and club to death his wife and three of his four children. Kaberuka they simply shot, then left him for dead amid the pile of corpses.

Angelique Umutesi is there too. He is only nine years old, and he survived by running hard and fast. The Hutu militia entered his house and killed his parents and his six brothers and sisters. Then they started on Angelique, first chopping off his left hand with a machete, then taking a chunk out of his right leg. Another machete blow opened a gaping hole in the back of the little boy's head, but he still managed to run to his grandparents' house nearby. Of course, the militia had already been there, and Angelique found everyone in that house dead, too. So he lay down to die, right there, next to the corpses of his grandparents and others. And he stayed there like that, with the corpses, for four days and four nights, almost bleeding to death until he was rescued by the advancing Tutsi guerrilla soldiers.

And over there is Hassan Twizezimana. He is a Hutu, but even so the madness did not pass him by. His crime is that he was not a card-carrying member of Juvenal Habyarimana's ruling political party. That means, of course, that he must be a secret Tutsi sympathizer, and for that, the Hutu militiamen used their machetes and panga knives to hack to death Twizezimana's father, his brother, and his brother's wife. Twizezimana himself got the back of his head cracked open with a garden hoe, and he, too, lay bleeding to death

97

until he was found and brought to this haven in northern Rwanda. Shocking? Yes. Disgusting. Impossible to read without flinching, wanting to turn the page. But this is just a small sampling of it, a few random snapshots, individual faces and stories lifted from the entire grotesque tapestry. Press on, because there's much, much more.

Like the three little girls, ages six to eight, whose heads and eyes are swollen because they have been buried alive up to their necks in a mass grave that contained the mutilated bodies of their parents. I find them in Byumba, still dazed, unable to speak or walk properly, still vomiting dirt.

And there's the old woman who was hiding in a church in Butare, in western Rwanda, when the militiamen burst in and killed nine people in her family, including all but one of her children. They chopped off all the fingers of the old woman's hand. And just for spite they slashed her across her face. She made it out to a refugee camp in Burundi, across the border.

There's another stop on our grisly tour, the Catholic church in the town of Gafunzo, in Rwanda's far southwest, near Lake Kivu. The large crucifix bears silent witness to the atrocities committed here; the life-size figure of Christ is framed with bullet holes, the altar awash with blood. Some ten thousand people packed into this church and the surrounding buildings, the schoolhouse, the rectory. They fled here in April when the massacres began—the church, after all, being the final and most sacred place of refuge. But this once-holy place now screams out with the souls of those who died in the search and slaughter. Handprints of dried blood along the wall give witness to the struggle; blood trails from the ceiling tiles where some, in vain, sought to hide before the panels were ripped away. Two mass graves flank the church on either side.

Nobody knows how many were killed and wounded in Rwanda's bloodbath. Estimates range as high as a million people killed; at the very least, from the numbers unearthed in mass graves, from the skeletons found in churchyards, from the bodies found floating in the river, there were hundreds of thousands, Tutsi mainly, but also an untold number of Hutu "sympathizers." The Khmer Rouge killed more perhaps, but it took them three and a half years, and most of their victims died from starvation, disease, and forced labor. The Hutu militia accomplished as much in three months, using decidedly more low-tech methods of extermination.

How does one find the adjectives to describe this senseless orgy of violence? Mine were worn out; I had used them up already in Somalia. It was easier in Rwanda not to believe. But I had to believe. I talked to the ones who survived. I also saw the bodies.

I first saw the bodies floating down the Kagera River from Rwanda into Tanzania. They floated down the river and over the Rusumo Falls.

I am standing now on a three-hundred-foot-long yellow metal bridge, looking down over the falls. And the bodies are coming by, sometimes singly, sometimes in bunches of two or even three. They are badly bloated, and white now, which surprises me a little; black bodies quickly become discolored. They move slowly, in eerie procession through the river's murky water, twisting in the current, sometimes banging against rocks. One is wearing bright red underpants. Another has green pants. Many have their hands tied behind their backs. Some, if not most, are missing limbs, or a head. And when they reach the top of the falls, they pick up speed and hurtle over, crashing down on the rocks below.

At the foot of the falls is a collection of craggy rocks, and several of the bodies have gotten stuck there. They seem to be struggling with the current, trying to break free; their limbs flap and turn in distorted movements. And the body of a baby is there, atop one of the rocks. I watch each successive wave roll in and crash atop the rock, waiting to see which one, if any, will be high enough to catch the baby's body and send it floating free.

Who are these people?

I think that to myself. What are their names? Do they have families? What were they doing when they were killed and dumped into the river? What were they thinking as they died? I remember my first training as a reporter, when I was a summer intern covering the night police beat. If a body—a single body—was discovered in the city, there would be a full-scale investigation. The police would find a name, contact a family, determine a cause of death. I remember one story of a murder victim whose corpse was discovered with a severed limb, an arm I think it was, and that's how the police report phrased it, and that's how I called it in to the city desk. But I immediately got a call back from the alert night editor, Gene Bachinski, shouting at me in his characteristic baritone: "Which arm was severed?" Which arm? Right or left? I had no idea. But I went back to the police and found out, because it mattered. But that was Washington, D.C., where every murder victim had a name, an identity, and it mattered how they died and which limb was severed. This is Africa. These are just bodies dumped into a river. Hundreds. Thousands. No one will ever count. No one will ever try to check an identity, contact a family, find out which limb was severed. Because this is Africa, and they don't count the bodies in Africa.

This is what I find the most difficult to accept and comprehend. It's not the death itself, although that is bad enough. It's the anonymity of death in Africa, the anonymity of mass death. I had the same troubling feeling in the sprawling refugee camps inside Somalia, where I watched people starving to death: Does anyone care about their names? Does anyone at least try to count them, to record the fact that a human being has passed away from the earth and someone may be searching for him? Or is life so tenuous here that death scarcely matters?

As I stare down from the bridge at the bodies collected in the crag, I imagine myself now falling over the railing. Falling, and crashing onto the rocks, my own body now just another lifeless form struggling against the current. Will anyone notice that I have fallen? Will the Rwandan Tutsi soldier make note of the fact that I was standing next to him on the bridge and then fell over? Will he report the fact of my death anywhere? Will he care? Why should he care, with so many of his own people floating by, unaccounted for? What makes me any different from the others?

Here I check my watch. One minute goes by. And a corpse.

Another minute, another body. Two more minutes, another, and on it goes like that. A body every minute or two. And I stand there for an hour, counting, watching, waiting. Thirty bodies an hour, they tell me. Seven hundred each day. And it has been this way for several days.

These are not memories I like to keep. No, I would rather keep them filed away, buried deep in the recesses of my mind. But I am pulling them out again now, hoping that perhaps those who read this will understand.

Standing on this bridge with me is a Tutsi officer of the Rwandan Patriotic Front, the guerrilla army that is slowly advancing through the country and unfolding new evidence each day of the atrocities within. I am here because the Rwandan "story" has become a refugee crisis; some 250,000 Rwandans have just crossed over this very same narrow yellow bridge—a quarter of a million people crossing a single bridge in a single twenty-four-hour period. The UN High Commissioner for Refugees is calling this an unprecedented catastrophe, one of the largest mass movements on a single day in recorded history. And here I am with a notebook in hand, and I find it hard to take a single note. I've simply run out of adjectives. Instead I watch, and I count.

I walk the quarter mile or so back up the dusty road to the main camp where the refugees have gathered. It is, indeed, an incredible mass of humanity; I've never seen anything quite like it. An entirely new city has been created, literally overnight, here in this little dusty crossroads in a desolate section of northwestern Tanzania. The stench from tens of thousands of cooking fires makes a thick haze in the air. It stings my eyes and makes me cough, and I curse myself for not bringing a scarf of some sort to cover my face. And now I'm walking among vinyl suitcases, plastic blue mats, cooking pots, goats wandering aimlessly, women and men walking with firewood balanced precariously on their heads, women carrying jerry cans filled with water dipped from the same river where I've seen dead bodies floating past.

I walk amid this human torrent and figure, yes, this truly is, at this moment, the world's worst humanitarian crisis. But I can't find any sympathy for the refugees here. I look at them and I think, yes, this is what you deserve. That's because these are not the victims but the killers. These are the Hutu, forced to flee Rwanda as the Tutsi rebels advanced and as the evidence of the Hutu's atrocities was revealed. They have fled here to this remote corner of Tanzania because they are escaping whatever justice is in store for them at the hands of the Tutsi army rapidly taking over the country. They fled here and left the tools of their genocide gathered in a huge pile at the foot of the Rusumo Falls bridge—machetes, panga knives, and spears, collected by the Tanzanian troops who disarmed the Hutu masses before allowing them to cross the border.

I search their eyes, looking, I suppose, for any sign, any hint that might help me understand what makes an ordinary person, a peasant farmer, one day become his neighbor's killer. What I get instead are cold, hard, blank stares. Hostile stares. I know that they were egged on by the vituperative radio broadcasts of the Radio Mille Colline, owned by Habyarimana's brother-in-law Seraphim Rwabukumba—radio messages that exhorted the Hutu to "clear the brush," a euphemism for killing Tutsi. I know too that the militia was organized into small, village-based cells, and every cell leader had a list with the names of all the Tutsi in the village, making the executions simple and systematic. That much I have already learned from my reporting. But that explains only the mechanics of how it was done; for me, it still doesn't answer the key question: Why?

This mountainous, picturesque little country hidden in central Africa on the eastern shore of Lake Kivu is probably better known to the outside world as the home to Dian Fossey's famed mountain gorillas than as Africa's latest killing ground. The land was originally inhabited by the Twa people, pygmylike hunter-gatherers, until the arrival several hundred years ago of the Hutu, a Bantu migrant people who settled on small plots of land and became farmers.

Sometime in the fifteenth century, the Tutsi arrived. They were a Nilotic tribe from the northern part of Africa, a tall people, fierce, cattle herders mostly, with aquiline features and angular noses that made them closer in physical appearance to the Ethiopians and Somalis than to the shorter Bantu tribes of the south. They soon established their dominance over the Hutu, as well as the Twa, the pygmy tribe whose number soon diminished. The Tutsi imposed their own monarch, taking the Hutu name Mwami, and the Hutu were reduced to little more than feudal servants.

The Europeans came to the area much later, in the nineteenth century, first the Germans and then, during the First World War, the Belgians. But the Belgian colonizers were never very interested in the area now comprising Rwanda and Burundi; their main interest was the mineral-rich Belgian Congo to the west. So they decided to rule indirectly, using the Tutsi as their local administrators to collect taxes, settle disputes, and otherwise act as the enforcers of the Belgian king's sovereignty. And the missionaries came, too, similarly relying on the Tutsi as the area's natural rulers, providing them with education and training that was denied the Hutu. Thus, colonization reinforced the centuries-old ethnic and social division and laid the seeds for the upheavals that would come later.

The first explosion came in 1959, when the Hutu rebelled and overthrew the Tutsi aristocracy. Some one hundred thousand Tutsi were killed in the Hutu uprising, and hundreds of thousands more fled to the neighboring countries: Tanzania, Zaire, and Uganda. It was the displaced Tutsi in Uganda who would later form the nucleus of the guerrilla army that installed Yoweri Museveni as Uganda's president, ousting Milton Obote in 1986. Museveni then returned the favor, allowing the Ugandan Tutsi to form their own guerrilla army, the Rwandan Patriotic Front, with the aim of waging a war against the Hutu regime in Rwanda. The RPF invaded Rwanda from Uganda in 1990 and a guerrilla war raged until a shaky cease-fire took hold in 1993.

After the 1959 uprising, the Belgians withdrew and the Hutu expanded their control of the new state, replacing Tutsi in all the layers of administration. The job was made easier by the fact that the Hutu represented about 85 percent of the population (and the Twa pygmy people a negligible 1 percent). It was the same ethnic mix as in neighboring Burundi, but there the political situation was reversed, with the minority Tutsi clinging to power through continued control of the armed forces. In Rwanda, Juvenal Habyarimana came to power in a 1973 coup that replaced the existing southern-based Hutu elite with a new group of northern Hutu hard-liners. And Habyarimana emerged as one of the continent's most ruthless and corrupt tyrants, surrounding himself with a coterie of loyal family members, friends, and military officers whose main purpose seemed to be to enrich themselves.

As his ruling instrument, Habyarimana formed the National Republican Movement for Development, known by its French initials MRND. Under outside pressure to allow for more pluralistic politics, he allowed the formation of the more extremist companion party CDR, the Coalition for the Defense of the Republic. But the true power—the power of terror—rested not with the parties but with their militias. The MRND militia was called Interahamwe, which loosely translates as either "Those who stand together" or "Those who kill together." The CDR's militia arm was the Impuza Mugambi—"the Single-Minded Ones." The two Hutu militias received military training at Rwandan army base camps, and according to U.S.-based human rights groups, they also received arms from the military.

All African strongmen find it convenient to play on ethnic fear—the tribal card—to remain in power; in Habyarimana's case, the fear of a Tutsi return to dominance became the regime's perverse ideological glue. Playing on this historic hatred and jealousy found a ready audience among the mostly illiterate, rural Hutu population as the social division between Hutu and Tutsi, reinforced by ethnic stereotyping, had managed to persist long after independence. And the stereotype was based on the Tutsi's perceived good looks and privilege, and the Hutu's perceived ugliness and backwardness.

If there was one thing I learned traveling around Africa, it was that the tribe remains the defining feature of almost every African society. Old tribal mistrusts and stereotypes linger, and the potential for a violent implosion is never very far from the surface.

Even in the supposedly more sophisticated or developed countries like Kenya, thirty years of independence and "nation building" had still failed to create any real sense of national identity that could transcend the tribe. In Kenya, the Kikuyu still think the Luo are inferior and that they, the Kikuyu, have the right to rule. The Luo don't trust the Kikuyu, who they think look down on them. And both tribes look down on the Luhya. It goes on and on.

In Kenya I also saw the devastating effects of what can happen when politicians, like Daniel arap Moi and his cronies, are willing to play the "tribal card" and stoke the flames of ethnic animosity for political advantage. I walked through the burned-out town of Enosupukio, after it was raided by Masai warriors driving out Kikuyu who they believed had settled on traditional Masai grazing land. It looked like a war zone after a major battle, which, in a way, I suppose it was. Not a single house or shop was left standing. Even two churches were stripped of everything except a few pews. And when I spoke to the Kikuyu refugees who had fled the town, they told me how the Masai who had once been their neighbors suddenly swooped down on the town with guns and machetes and spears. One woman named Loyce Majiru told me how she had to flee with her nine children, and how she looked back and saw the body of a neighbor on the side of the road, naked, with his head chopped off.

And this was Kenya, a major tourist destination and a country long considered one of the more "stable" in Africa.

These things, though, are not too popular to discuss outside of Africa, particularly among the Africanists and Western academics for whom the very term "tribe" is anathema. The preferred term is "ethnic group" because it's considered less racially laden. But Africans themselves talk of their "tribes," and they warn of the potential for tribal explosion.

It's long been the argument of the old African strongmen that authoritarian rule is needed to prevent just those types of tribal blowups. Multiparty politics, according to this theory, inevitably leads to tribal violence, because pluralism encourages people to seek protective refuge in their familiar tribal units. It's virtually inevitable that political parties will be organized along ethnic, meaning tribal, lines. And that's not too different from tribal voting patterns in American big cities, where you can count on the black vote, the Irish vote, the Polish vote, the Italian vote, the Jewish vote. But in America, we don't reach for our pangas if our tribe loses the election.

Another thing I learned from traveling around Africa is that the notion of skin color, facial features, and the sense of attractiveness and identity are also very real, and in many ways closely related to tribe. One of the first articles I wrote after setting foot in Africa was a simple feature story about a beauty contest to pick a Miss Kenya to represent the country in international pageants. (This was the story for which Hos Maina helped me get a photograph.) But there was a debate raging because the local beauty picked by the judges, a twenty-one-year-old business student named Karimi Nkirote M'Mbijjiwe, was not so local at all; she had light skin, high cheekbones, a narrow straight nose, soft hair, and something approaching a perfect 36–24–36 figure. She was, in fact, more Somali looking than Kenyan. And her crowning ignited a storm of controversy about whether there was such a thing as an "African standard of beauty."

Some pageant judges said they thought Miss Kenya had to conform to internationally accepted standards of beauty if she was to have any chance at all in global competitions. But others argued that finding a Miss Kenya who conformed to international standards meant essentially finding a representative who "looked white" and was essentially not a true Kenyan at all.

"When our African women go into the international arena, because the Western standard is vigorously used, it becomes difficult for them to make an impact," said Stephen Mwangi, a group manager at Eastman Kodak Co., who was one of that year's judges. As a pageant judge, he said, "It is very difficult for me. It is not easy. You always have to be careful that you don't send a girl all the way to London or Puerto Rico just to embarrass her because she's black."

He added, "There is a saying in this part of the world—a really common saying—that if you really want to see beautiful African women, go to Ethiopia."

"The ones who win are almost always mixed," a woman named Susan Oloo-Oruya told me. She herself was a strikingly tall, dark-skinned beauty working as a public relations officer at the Inter-Continental Hotel. "You've got to be fair—you can't be like me," she said. "They consider the fairer you are, the more beautiful you are. 'Oh, she's so fair, she's so beautiful.' It's because she's light that she's beautiful. I know men who will go out with a woman just because she's light-skinned. Some men just like their meat white."

Back in Byumba, behind the Tutsi rebel lines, there is the hospital, where we have met some of the survivors of the ongoing massacre. There is the orphanage. And there is a woman named Rose Kayumba.

She is tall, very tall, and thin, a quite striking woman really, particularly out here in the middle of nowhere in the African bush. She looks positively out of place because she is so well kept, obviously a woman from the city in tight blue jeans and neatly arranged corn rows. She is very beautiful, and she tells me about ethnic attitudes and about growing up as a Tutsi in Rwanda.

With their narrow noses and sharp features, the Tutsi were considered the more physically attractive tribe, even long after they had lost political power in Hutu-controlled Rwanda. Even with growing wealth and power, what the Hutu really aspired to was to look like a Tutsi, to actually become a Tutsi. There were even earlier provisions for it in law; a Hutu with enough wealth could literally go to the local government office and apply to be reclassified as a Tutsi. The modern version of the same was for a Hutu who had obtained a measure of wealth and status to immediately marry a Tutsi woman. An old Rwandan joke asks, What's the first thing a Hutu gets when he becomes wealthy? The answer is a Mercedes-Benz. What's the second thing? A Tutsi wife.

Rose, who is about my age, remembers growing up in Rwanda, before she became a refugee, and her elderly grandmother admonishing her never to play with the small, dark, and flat-nosed Hutu children in the neighborhood because they were beneath her. Rose also had relatives from the countryside, Tutsi relatives, but because they were not from the city, because they lived a harsher life, they dressed poorly, they were smaller in size, and their complexions had been darkened by exposure to the sun. And before these relatives would come to visit, Rose's parents would calmly explain to her not to be frightened by the appearance of these strangers, that they are indeed Tutsi, not Hutu, that it's not their fault they look so dark and so ugly.

And when the violence started, the killing was sparked by anger over Habyarimana's death in a plane crash and was orchestrated by the militia cells in the villages that systematically went door to door. But on a deeper level, many Hutu did not need to be egged on too strongly to pick up the machete they normally use for chopping firewood and to cross the road and slash to death the Tutsi family living in the hut across the road. Because the Hutu who participated in the killings were slashing at centuries of stereotypes and discrimination. They were slashing at these images of physical beauty they had affixed in their own mind. They were slashing at their own perceived ugliness, as if destroying this thing of beauty, this thing they could never really attain, removing it from the earth forever.

As Rose explains all this to me in a remote town in northern Rwanda, in an abandoned churchyard under the moonlight, I am taken back to a place at once very different from this one, but also eerily, sadly familiar. I am no longer in Byumba but in Detroit. I am the small child, and it is not a grandmother but my own father and my relatives I am hearing. The place is different, the voices are different, but what I'm hearing is very much the same.

"Don't you go out there playing with those black kids down the street. They're no good."

They were "no good" because they didn't own their home; they rented. Because they stayed out on their porch until all hours of the night playing the radio too loud and disturbing the peace of the neighborhood. Because when they walk down the block to Fred's party store on the corner, they wear their worn-out house shoes and have curlers in their hair, and they shout loudly over their shoulder, saying, "What you want, girl? You better bring yo' ass on and git it yo'self!" Because the boys shout "Yo', motherfucka'" at each other from well on the opposite side of the street, and you can hear them from a block away on summer evenings when you have only the screen door closed. Because they are black—dark black, just-up-from-the-South black, backwoods-country black, and that makes them no good.

My mother came home once and told me a story about how she had just ridden the Grand River bus back from downtown. And at one stop, a group of loud teenagers got on, cursing loudly, using "bad language" as my mother would say. And she and some of the older people on the bus looked up and were surprised. Shocked, she said. Because the loudest member of the young group was a light-skinned boy. "You know, you never expect to see a light-skinned boy talking loud like that," she said. And it really perplexed her. "Usually, when you hear all that cussin', you know it's some dark, ugly one," she said. But this was a light-skinned boy. Nice looking, too. The order of the universe was shifting.

That was how black people in Detroit in the 1960s, even the 1970s, described each other. Light skinned. Brown skinned. Dark skinned. And there were more subtle gradations of complexion—a "high yellow nigger" and a "redbone." The terms might sound odd, particularly to a white person looking into our universe and seeing basically a bunch of black people. But these distinctions mattered. We all not only appreciated them but lived for them. Those were the days when, as my father more recently recalled, "If you called somebody black, you had to be ready to fight him." Blacks in those days, good black people, called themselves "colored."

This was black Detroit. Or, to be more precise, one of the two black Detroits, at least as perceived by the good colored people I grew up around. The dividing line was Woodward Avenue, which separated the city's east and west sides, sort of our own version of Beirut's notorious Green Line. But the line was more psychological than geographic, centering on our own caste system and where you could place your roots in the South. Roughly put, the South Carolina blacks were on the west side, the Alabama blacks on the east side. And the divisions were as real as the divisions between the Hutu and Tutsi tribes in Rwanda.

And so my parents drummed it into me, much the same way Rose's parents and grandparents drummed it into her, that black people like us—we were the South Carolina, west-side blacks—were different from the blacks over on the east side. South Carolina blacks owned homes and rarely rented. They had neat little patches of lawn in front yards delineated by little fences. They came from Charleston, Anderson, Greenville, sometimes Columbia, places where whites were never quite so oppressive, and blacks never quite so hardened and bitter. They worked hard, saved their money, went to church on Sunday, bought new clothes for Easter and for the start of the school year. They kept their hair cut close, very close, to avoid even the appearance of nappiness. They ate turkey and ham and grits and sweet potato pie. They were well-heeled, well brought up, and they expected their children to be, too.

Don't go across Woodward Avenue, we were warned. The blacks over there are hard. They're Alabama blacks, hard and bitter. They cuss loud in public. They don't own, they rent. And because they rent, they let their places go down. They don't mend their fences when they get broken, and they let the grass in front run down to dirt. They eat pigs' feet and more often than not have a dozen relatives all "just up from Alabama" packed into a few tiny rooms. They were dark, from working in the cotton fields under the hot sun all day. They were, in a word, "niggers," or so the good colored people from South Carolina called them. And the gravest insult was; "He ain't nothin'—he just came up here from Alabama!"

Sure, these were all stereotypes, based not on reality but on the psyches of those who told the stories. But for me, a black man growing up in America, these divisions were once very, very real—as real as the tribal divisions Rose Kayumba described for me there in that abandoned church complex under the moonlight in Byumba.

In Africa, you belong to a tribe; without a tribe, you don't belong. Black Americans were torn from Africa four hundred or more years ago, torn from their tribe, torn from any sense of where they belong. And without belonging—without any real identifiable group, without an African identity—you are constantly held under suspicion from all sides, particularly when Africa's tribes are at war with each other. Black Americans are constantly being asked to choose sides. Even more dangerous, black Americans are likely to be mistaken by one tribe as a member of another. Anyone who is unknown, a stranger, is potentially the enemy—you can be targeted for something as innocuous as the shape of your head, the width of your nose, your height, even the fact that you wear glasses or speak English or French. To be black and American in Africa is to constantly try to hide behind the false shield of protection of that blue American passport—hoping that the guy pointing the AK-47 or holding the machete at your throat can at least recognize the eagle emblazoned on the front, even if he is illiterate and unable to read the words "United States of America."

Linda Thomas-Greenfield found all this out in Rwanda. She's a strikingly big woman, tall, from Louisiana. She was almost killed in Rwanda because she was mistaken for a Tutsi.

It happened on April 7, 1994, the morning after Habyarimana's plane exploded in the sky and the Rwandan capital, Kigali, erupted into violence. Thomas-Greenfield was a refugee affairs officer at the U.S. embassy in Nairobi, and she had gone to Kigali just two days earlier to look into the refugee situation in Rwanda. She decided to stay at the home of a longtime friend, Joyce Leader, the deputy chief of mission at the American embassy in Kigali.

In those first bloody hours after the crash, Leader and Thomas-Greenfield knew exactly what to do. They packed up a few belongings in case of a swift evacuation, and they retreated behind a sealed door, away from the windows. Theirs was a particularly vulnerable location; Leader's house was next door to the Rwandan prime minister's official residence.

The prime minister at the time was Agathe Uwilingiyimana, a woman appointed as part of the compromise the international community forced on Habyarimana in an effort to broaden his hard-line

Hutu government. And as the death squads roamed the city that morning, Uwilingiyimana was at the top of their list.

The prime minister was up early, desperately phoning for help, calling friends, neighbors, the small United Nations force in Kigali at the time to enforce the earlier peace agreement between Habyarimana and the Tutsi rebels. Her house was surrounded by a high wall, meant for security—but ultimately it became her prison.

The American diplomats tried moving furniture into the yard, but nothing was high enough to reach the top of the prime minister's wall. At one point, one of Uwilingiyimana's unarmed protectors tried lowering a board over the wall as a kind of makeshift ladder, but this attracted the attention of the rampaging troops outside, who fired warning shots in their direction. The prime minister ultimately found an escape over a different wall and took temporary refuge in the compound of the UN Development Program. When the soldiers burst in to take her away, Uwilingiyimana was already gone.

That's when they came to Leader's house, believing the prime minister had fled there. But when they burst in, instead of the prime minister, they found Linda Thomas-Greenfield—tall, statuesque. An obvious Tutsi.

"Tutsi!" they shouted at once. "Tutsi!" She recognized them from their beret caps as members of the elite presidential guard unit.

"I whipped out my passport," Thomas-Greenfield said later. And she pleaded with them in the thickest American accent she could muster. "Please," she begged them, "I don't have anything to do with this! I'm not Rwandan! I'm an American! I don't have anything to do with this!"

"I was a whimpering, scared fool, begging for my life," she recalled.

The killers were unconvinced. They held her there at gunpoint while they searched the house. They did find a Tutsi, a gardener who was cowering in a kitchen cabinet. They dragged him out and killed him in cold blood while the horrified diplomats looked on helplessly. "They took the butt of the gun and hit him in the head," Thomas-Greenfield recalled. "They hit him in the side." And finally, one of them announced, "*Il est mort*,"—he's dead.

Outside the house came a raucous cheer and the sound of shooting in the air. It was a celebration; the prime minister had been discovered at the UN compound and was being dragged back to the street where she lived. That's when Agathe Uwilingiyimana was executed. And that is likely when ten Belgian troops arrived to protect her. Following an instruction radioed from the UN headquarters in Kigali, the Belgians laid down their arms, hoping to avoid a confrontation with the crowd; they too were brutally tortured and executed.

The Hutu troops did eventually believe Thomas-Greenfield, and she was allowed to leave with the rest of the American citizens who were evacuated to Burundi in an overland convoy a few days later. It was a Saturday morning, and they first had to go to designated assembly points from the U.S. embassy about three blocks from the deputy's house.

And at one roadblock, her car was stopped. A soldier with the distinctive black beret of the presidential guard, reeking of whisky, leaned into the car. Thomas-Greenfield braced, thinking again this might be the end. Then the soldier broke into a broad smile. "*Ah, mon amie!*" the soldier said. She took a second look at him and saw it was the same soldier who had held her at gunpoint at Leader's house.

"My friend?!" she said, outraged. "You held a gun on me for thirty minutes! If I had a gun, I'd shoot you myself!" Fortunately for her, the soldier did not appear to understand English.

In the convoy, Thomas-Greenfield was assigned to a car along with a Rwandan woman—an American dependent—and three small children. The woman's husband worked for the Africa Development Foundation, and the children all had been born in the United States. Thomas-Greenfield was both angry and afraid. "This is another thing about being a black American in Africa," she said. "I was put in a vehicle with a Rwandan woman. I was terribly annoyed with the embassy. I thought it was insensitive. But I had my protection—I had my black diplomatic passport. And I used my worst Louisiana drawl, so there was no doubt I was an American."

Sitting a few months later in the serene surroundings on the terrace of the Inter-Continental Hotel in Nairobi, Thomas-Greenfield related to me what had happened to her in Rwanda and how, she said, it had come to change her view of the continent. "I think it's an absolute disadvantage" being black in Africa, she said. "Here, as anywhere else in Africa, the cleavages are not racial, they are ethnic. People think they can tell what ethnic group you are by looking at you. If there's any conflict going on between the ethnic groups, you need to let them know you're an American."

Rwanda's nightmare, and mine, didn't end with the massacre. As the Tutsi rebels advanced throughout the country and the government army collapsed, more than a million Hutu fled across the border. But not to Tanzania, which was already reeling under the weight of the first mass exodus. The second wave fled west, into Zaire, swarming a remote mountain resort town called Goma on the shores of Lake Kivu. A million people. Maybe a few more. A population larger than Washington, D.C.—a million men, women, young children, and infants, carrying bedrolls and yellow jerry cans, leading goats and a few cows, with cooking pots and firewood balanced on their heads. And carrying their panga knives and machetes and sometimes their firearms.

Many of those who came were the killers, the militiamen and the soldiers of the routed government army, still in uniform, still seething with the anger of the defeat, which of course they blamed on an arms embargo imposed by the United States and the international community. And these militiamen and soldiers quickly established their sinister control inside the refugee camps that sprang up around Goma; they terrorized the refugees, they seized control of the food distribution system in the camps, and they intimidated, and sometimes physically chased away, the foreign relief workers who flooded into the area to help.

The camps, of course, became breeding grounds for disease, so it was inevitable that an epidemic would sweep through the refugee population. There was little water in Goma, and the refugee camps were far from the town because that's where the local Zairean authorities wanted them. And when cholera did strike, it came with a vengeance.

Most of the victims died at night; you'd find their bodies laid out by the roadsides, wrapped in their own blankets and straw mats, or sometimes just laid out uncovered on their backs, with only a small scarf around the faces. When driving from the town center to the camps, down the narrow and winding roads, I became fairly deft at weaving around the bodies. You tried not to run over the legs.

Sometimes the bodies weren't neatly laid out at all. Sometimes they just lay there stiff, in the same position as when they collapsed, or when they stretched out for a rest from the heat and the thirst. Maybe a head gently resting in the crook of an arm. Maybe the arms outstretched, as if the person had been trying to crawl to the road-side from the field when they died.

I saw a small kid screaming and crying furiously—I think it was a girl, but it was hard to tell since boys and girls both wore the same torn clothing made from a single piece of cloth, the color of the earth. This particular kid was beating with both tiny fists on her mother's chest. The mother was obviously dead. I slowed for a few seconds, considered picking the kid up, not quite sure what I'd do with her if I did. But I knew UNICEF had an orphan truck that made the rounds every morning picking up kids just like this one. I pressed on ahead.

I waited once outside a relief group's tent to get a quick word from a doctor about the latest count in his camp. While waiting, I watched the medical workers using a stretcher to carry out the body of a woman who had just died inside the tent. From her face, I could tell that she was a young woman, maybe just in her late teens. Her eyes were still open. And I watched two men carry her just past me on the stretcher to a pile of about two dozen or so bodies just a few feet from where I was standing. When they got there, they tipped the stretcher to one side, and the young woman with her eyes open tumbled off, arms flailing, onto the top of the pile. Her head landed so that it was slightly upturned, facing my direction. She looked right into my eyes. She seemed to want to say something to me, trying to tell me her story, to relate to me, somehow, her pain. I stood there staring at her for what seemed like a very long time, trying to hear her.

Funny, the little things you notice under conditions like that. In the middle of mass death, bodies all around me, and I remember just one face, one body, one kid pounding on her mother's chest. I think it's the little images that make the whole less overwhelming, more comprehensible somehow. I couldn't focus on the pile of bodies, just the one who's looking right at me. And I tried to imagine what her last few days had been like. What she was thinking before she died. Whether if, under other circumstances, she might have been a happy young woman, maybe married with a child, or maybe going out on dates. I tried to imagine what she was like when she was alive, maybe guess what her name was, whether she had many friends, whether anyone would miss her, whether anyone here in this godforsaken hellhole of a refugee camp with bodies lying around everywhere even knew her name.

The ground was hard around Goma, volcanic rock that made digging impossible. So for several days, the bodies just piled up. The French troops stationed in Goma managed to dig a huge pit at the site of an old plantation. I went there and watched a line of a dozen dump trucks piled high with bodies waiting for their turn to drop their loads into the open pit. In all of the trucks, the bodies made a huge mound that came to a kind of a peak, far higher than the top of the trucks. And one by one, the trucks would back up to the pit and tip their loads inside. And I stood and watched the bodies tumbling down anonymously into the waiting earth.

Who are these people?

Once I went to interview a Canadian nurse working in one of the medical tents at a refugee camp. She asked to step outside, behind the tent, so she could have a cigarette while we talked. And as I stood there taking notes while she explained to me the various stages of cholera, I glanced down and suddenly realized that we were standing in a field of corpses. They were dragging the dead from the tent and depositing them directly outside, and there we were, bodies all around us, coldly discussing the statistics, the number of cases, the various treatments.

I'm not sure how many dead bodies I saw there in Goma during the cholera epidemic. Estimates are that some fifty thousand people died, but even that is just a guess. No one was ever really counting, because this was Africa, and you don't count the bodies in Africa.

Even as I retell it here, I can't quite put my finger on what it was that was going through my head, standing there amid such misery and death. And in truth, I'm not sure I can really answer, because my thoughts were so confused at the time.

I was repulsed at this waste of human life, that much is for sure. At the same time, though, I was also strangely ambivalent because I knew that many of these people dying around me were the Hutu, the killers, the perpetrators of Rwanda's genocide. And if they weren't killers, then almost certainly they knew what was happening, and it's likely they did nothing. Maybe, I thought, this was some form of divine justice.

But it was the anonymity of it all that troubled me most.

I can't describe it here, really—a terrible admission on my part, to be sure, since I make my living with words and descriptions and adjectives. I stood there, counting the bodies as best I could, and then I would go back to my dingy hotel room or to a tent where I had a sleeping bag and try to think of new adjectives, new turns of phrase, to describe for readers half a world away what it looked like. And the bodies ceased to be people anymore, just more victims, more appalling statistics. And then the face of that one woman in a pile of bodies would come back into my mind, and she was looking directly at me, peering into my soul, and saying: I, too, have a name. I, like you, have an identity. I'm not just another statistic, so please don't let me be forgotten that way.

The problem is, this is Africa, and there is nobody counting, nobody taking names. You just bury the dead and move on.

6

Enemies Unseen

> "Diseases crucify the soul of man, attenuate our bodies,
> dry them, wither them, shrivel them up like old apples,
> make them so many anatomies."
>
> —ROBERT BURTON,
> 1577–1640

ESTHER IS AN ATTRACTIVE young woman, somewhere in her early twenties, who favors long braids, tight jeans, and white high-top sneakers. I met her in a down-and-dirty Nairobi bar called Buffalo Bill's, where she used to hang around the horseshoe-shaped bar or in one of the side booths shaped like stagecoach wagons, waiting for someone to buy her a large bottle of Tusker White Cap, the cheapest of Kenya's local beers.

Sometimes, if the scene was slow, she'd ask for a lift downtown to the Florida 2000 disco, or maybe its companion bar, the circular-shaped New Florida nightclub, which was perched precariously on a narrow stem of a pillar right above a gasoline station. The two Florida bars were almost always guaranteed to be packed with hot, sweaty bodies, Africans mainly, but also European and American men out jamming to the pulsating disco beats and checking out Nairobi's local action.

Esther is definitely considered hot local action on the Nairobi nightlife circuit and is very much in demand by the resident expat set. That's because Esther is a full-time prostitute.

I met Esther fairly early on after my arrival in Kenya, and I found her absolutely fascinating—a weird kind of visceral attraction that men are occasionally supposed to feel for whores, I suppose, the kind that Graham Greene wrote about in *The Honorary Consul*. Well, Nairobi often seemed like a Graham Greene novel to me, so I suppose Esther was the rough equivalent of the woman of Dr. Eduardo Plarr's fixation. So I'd keep Esther well plied with Tusker White Caps at Buffalo Bill's, then maybe give her a lift over to the Florida in my banged-up cream-colored Peugeot. Our meetings were always just by chance, never arranged beforehand since I was frequently traveling, and always just for conversation, whether sitting in one of the stagecoach booths or just parked in the alleyway behind the Florida, where she'd want to smoke "bang"—a marijuana joint— before going upstairs to troll for customers. Once I even took her home, let her take a hot shower, gave her a bed with clean sheets for the night and a full breakfast the next morning. I never took advantage, though, of what no doubt was her considerable experience in bed—but it's not that I wasn't tempted, just self-controlled. The truth is, I was downright terrified that Esther might have AIDS.

A Nairobi hooker is probably in the highest of high-risk groups, and I figured that Esther was no exception. She was a Kikuyu, having moved to the big city from her family *shamba* up-country, but now she was a thoroughly urban young woman, "de-tribed" so to speak, devoid of any real sense of tribal loyalty and cut off from the traditional African support system of family, clan, and village. Alone, fending for herself, Esther lived in a squalid little shack of a room out near the Nairobi airport. And for money, she slept with men—almost exclusively white men, or so she told me—Europeans, and the occasional American, tourists passing through, but mostly the local expat "regulars"—the aid workers, the journalists, the bush pilots, the adventurers, the oddball down-and-outs whose world travels, like their cash and their luck, had run out at the horseshoe-shaped bar at Buffalo Bill's.

Through our conversations, Esther became my private window into the seedy underside of Nairobi's gritty urban scene. I asked her once, before she stopped showing up at the bar and I lost track of her, whether she ever worried about catching AIDS from her high-risk employment. She immediately produced for me a tattered, probably forged health certificate to show that she had passed her last AIDS exam. She said she always insisted on making her customers use condoms—and if she thought the man a likely HIV carrier, she would sometimes insist that he wear two.

I was never sure if I believed Esther. Whenever I asked, all the African hookers I ever met insisted that they used condoms. But in a pinch—and if the customer balked at the discomfort of that little piece of latex protection—then almost certainly the girls would be more than willing to go "live," as they say in local street jargon. For these working women, the driving force was their desperate need for money, not common sense, even if that meant risking their lives. And some did. Esther would sit next to me at that horseshoe-shaped bar and point out to me some of the regular girls who were rail thin, with sad, sunken eyes, and she would say the girl is "very sick," and I would know what she meant. These were the girls I'd see sometimes in the bar every time I was there, and then they would disappear for long stretches, unexplained absences chalked up to a cold or fever.

And what amazed me most was that Western men, and Africans too, would still sleep with these women! Nairobi hookers never seemed to want for customers, and Esther herself was a prime example; she would often leave my side, even in mid-conversation and with her Tusker barely touched, whenever one of her paying customers showed up and was willing to fill her with more than just free booze and conversation. When she stood up to leave with her man, she'd sometimes wink at me conspiratorially from across the crowded bar.

Were these guys crazy? Didn't they realize the risk? Apparently so, but most just seemed not to care—or had convinced themselves that they were playing the odds correctly in their own favor. When I asked one of the expat regulars at Buffalo Bill's whether he was frightened of catching AIDS, he replied, "Sometimes, man, you just gotta go for it!"

One friend of mine, an American who had been posted in Nairobi as a journalist a few years before I arrived, had given me the rundown on the dos and don'ts of sleeping with the "locals." Nairobi is a great city for sex, he said, but you have to take a few basic precautions. First, it helps to find one and stick with her, take her to a hospital and make sure she checks clean, then keep her under lock and key as best you can. Always use a condom. And if you want to perform oral sex, it's best to stretch a piece of cellophane across your mouth first. And if you want to perform it "live," make sure not to brush your teeth beforehand, since the bristles of the brush can leave tiny puncture marks on your gums, giving the opportunistic HIV virus more handy routes to your bloodstream.

Wow, I thought. These guys have really got this one figured out—or so they were willing to believe. But my attitude was, no thanks, I'll pass all the same; all that advice just convinced me that the local scene was probably more trouble than it was worth. My objections weren't simply moral; I was also scared to death.

It was a powerful fear of mine, this fear of contracting AIDS, and one that I was always mindful of in Africa. The bullets, the militia guys with machetes, the random mortar shells—that was one thing. I couldn't really do anything about it if an artillery shell or a stray bullet was going to rip my head off while I was tying my shoelaces. If it happened, then with any luck death would come quickly and painlessly. But AIDS was different. Death would come slowly, painfully. And it was also something that I knew I could prevent.

I never considered my fear irrational. I knew enough about the disease to know that you couldn't get it from casual contact, shaking hands, even kissing, that kind of thing. But I did know that you could get it from blood—and I saw an awful lot of blood in Africa, and that's what frightened me. I saw blood on the T-shirts of those young militia thugs at the checkpoint in southwestern Rwanda when they stopped the car Ruth and I were traveling in. I saw blood every time I stepped into an African hospital, whether at the field hospital in Byumba town, where I saw the carnage wrought by the Hutu militiamen, or the Benadir hospital in Mogadishu where Paul Alexander and I masqueraded as health officials to count up the latest casualty figures. There were bloody sheets piled up in the corners and in the corridors. There was blood on the white coats of the hospital staffers. There was blood on the walls and blood on the floor; whenever I stepped into an African hospital, in a war zone or a refugee camp, I was literally walking through blood. And yet I would see hospital staffers, doctors and nurses and orderlies, lifting bloody patients, rolling up bloody sheets, all without taking the most rudimentary precautions, like using rubber gloves. Didn't they understand the risk?

I carried my own set of needles with me whenever I traveled in Africa, just in case I got sick and needed an injection. (Fortunately I never had occasion to use them.) I also tried to avoid, when I could, shaking hands with hospital staffers who had just finished turning over a patient bathed in blood or had touched a bloody gunshot wound; I would sometimes awkwardly and unnaturally balance my pen and notebook and camera in my hands and pretend not to have a hand free. Once, in Rwanda, I was interviewing a young man who was helping to bury the bodies of cholera victims. He was wearing rubber gloves as he pulled the fresh corpses one after another from a pile on a flatbed truck. I asked him a few questions about how he coped with his grisly task, and then I asked him for the spelling of his name. Before I could say anything, the young man grabbed the pen from my hand, took my notebook, and, with the gloves still on, wrote his name out for me to ensure that I got the correct spelling. When he handed the notebook back, smiling at me, I hesitated at first, and then took it for fear of appearing rude. But a few yards down the road, I tossed the pen and the notebook into a ditch and made sure not to touch anything, not to scratch, not to roll back my sleeve to look at my watch, until I made it back to my hotel and running water. Then for a good thirty minutes I soaked the hand that had touched the notebook.

If I convinced myself that this terror of mine was real, then I justified my fear by the statistics. There are currently about 21.8 million people in the world infected with the HIV virus that causes AIDS, but the pandemic is most prevalent here, in sub-Saharan Africa, where a whopping 13.3 million adults are HIV-positive—over 60 percent of the global total—and that on a continent that holds just 10 percent of the world's population. Whereas AIDS infections in the United States and Western Europe are largely concentrated in the so-called high-risk groups—homosexuals and intravenous drug users—the disease in Africa is found almost exclusively in the heterosexual population, and infected women outnumber infected men by a six-to-five margin. The main cause of infection here is not dirty needles, not blood transfusions, not anal intercourse, but heterosexual vaginal sex. And the impact in Africa is immediately visible; I could see it in entire villages in Uganda, where old people take care of young children because the parents in the middle-age group have died off. And I saw it in some of the major cities, where AIDS has taken the lives of some of the best and brightest of Africa's "yuppies," urban intellectuals, armed forces officers, local entrepreneurs. Whenever I picked up a Kenyan newspaper, or any local paper from Lusaka to Lagos, I was always stunned to see the obituary pages and how many young people, in their late twenties and thirties, were prematurely dead. "After a long illness," the reports always cryptically said, and I knew what that phrase meant.

One of the obvious reasons the pandemic has spread so far and so fast in Africa is the rampant prostitution and the Africans' free-and-easy attitude toward sex. Sex with prostitutes and sex with neighbors, co-workers, or almost anyone else is almost a way of life, especially in many of Africa's sprawling urban centers. African men come from a recent past where polygamy was the norm, and siring dozens of children was the only way of insuring that at least a few would survive past infancy. So today, monogamy still seems an alien concept. And the same is true for those hardy white expat adventurers who have been on the continent so long that they've "gone native." The runaway sex also means that other kinds of venereal diseases are rife—gonorrhea, syphilis, herpes, warts, all kinds of ailments that might leave open sores on the genitals. Western researchers long ago concluded that the presence of other venereal diseases makes it far easier for the opportunistic AIDS virus to find an entry point and make a home.

Almost everywhere in Africa, prostitution is rampant, from the Florida bar in Nairobi to the disco at the mezzanine floor of the Inter-Continental Hotel in Kinshasa, from the seedy bars of Kigali and Kampala to the lobby of the posh Lagos Sheraton, where girls with long, fake braids wink and smile at newcomers collapsing at the lobby bar for a beer after the treacherous ride in from the airport. It's a breakdown of Africa's more conservative social tradition, these young women from the countryside making their way to the cities to sell their bodies for cash. To get a glimpse of the scope of prostitution in Africa, one need only travel part of the truck route from the Kenyan coast inland, around Lake Victoria, into Uganda, and on into Zaire and central Africa. Along the way are innumerable brothels where the truckers stop for a quick night of sex before hitting the road again. It's no wonder that Africa today has most of the world's AIDS cases.

And not all the prostitutes are women, either. Travel to Mombasa, the tourist town on Kenya's Indian Ocean coast, and you'll find the Kenyan "beach boys," male prostitutes by another name, who make their living having sex with the hordes of European women who make Mombasa their vacation retreat. I could never figure out what these white women must have been thinking, other than trying to live out some "mandingo" fantasy. And I was never sure the poor "beach boys" realized the risk they were taking, since they were just as likely to contract AIDS or other diseases.

Of course the widespread prostitution isn't the only reason AIDS has taken off here. The infection rate has been helped along by African sexual practices, too, like what they call "dry" sex, meaning immediate sex without lubricants, rough and hard sex that cracks the skin and makes sores. I once asked Esther about this, about whether she liked to use lotion or oil for smoother sex. At first she looked at me as if I were crazy, and then she asked what the oil would do. I gave her a bottle of Johnson's baby lotion, and she promised to try it next time.

Polygamy, the common practice of men taking more than one wife, is another reason why sexually transmitted diseases spread so rapidly here. I often thought about George, my office assistant, and his own lifestyle, which seemed so strange to me, and how every time I gave him a pay raise, he seemed to take a new wife or girlfriend. Even then, I was never certain that George was all that faithful to the "wives" he did have. My phone was always ringing with various women asking for him, and on pay day, once a month, a steady stream of women would come in with their hands extended for a portion of George's meager earnings.

Part of the reason for the polygamy, I guessed, was that the desperate poverty and the search for employment had separated so many African families. One of the first things that struck me about Nairobi was the imbalance between men and women in the town. Men held many of the jobs that I was accustomed to seeing women hold— waiting tables in restaurants, working as switchboard operators and receptionists, cleaning rooms and making beds in hotels—even my own "secretary," George, and my housekeeper, Hezekiah, were men. In most cases, the men married early while still living in the countryside, then left their family to come to the city for work. Once in town, maybe feeling lonely or perhaps just more affluent, they ended up taking another wife and siring another brood of kids in the urban shantytowns where they lived.

One traditional tribal custom still very much in practice in some rural areas also contributes to AIDS's rapid spread. In some societies, if a man in the village dies prematurely, it is customary for the next eldest brother in line to marry the widow. It was a historic practice meant to keep the widow in the family's protected cocoon and the deceased's property in familiar, meaning patriarchal, hands. The problem arises when traditional practice collides with modern-day reality: If the man has died of AIDS, there's a good chance that he has passed it on to his wife through unprotected sex, and when the surviving brother consummates the new marriage, he is also passing the death sentence on to himself.

Another hindrance to fighting the disease is that many Africans who do think about the AIDS problem tend to become defensive. There's still a large school of thought that AIDS and HIV are a "Western" phenomenon that has been foisted upon unsuspecting Africans. There is a widespread belief in a Great White Western Conspiracy to keep Africans down by unleashing deadly plagues, and more than once I picked up a Kenyan newspaper with some ridiculous commentary or editorial decrying the West over AIDS or claiming—in total disregard of the statistics—that Africans were being unfairly singled out as the largest group of carriers. And when they weren't denying the scope of the problem, many Africans were often out promoting some snake-oil cures that were as dangerous as they were ludicrous if only because they fed into popular myths and the collective denial. In Kenya, for example, the newspapers for a while were filled with stories about a group of young prostitutes who supposedly were "immune" to AIDS. There were also stories about doctors who had allegedly—and wrongly—claimed to have discovered an African "cure" for the disease.

Compounding the ignorance, though, was the problem of sheer poverty. In Kinshasa, I met a physician named Dr. Eugene Nzila, who was in charge of what was once an internationally respected AIDS research center for central Africa. Nzila also ran his own small walk-in clinic for Zairean prostitutes in a seedy section of the sprawling city close to what would be considered the red light district. Dr. Nzila kept a chart of all the young women patients who came back for repeat visits, and he dutifully recorded the results of their tests. He also sold condoms to the girls for the equivalent of about two cents each. He could have given the condoms away, he said, but he was trying to instill in the Kinshasa prostitutes some sense of responsibility. He believed—reasonably enough, it seemed to me—that if the girls had to pay a token amount for the condoms, they would not view them as a worthless handout but something actually to be used; condoms for free, Nzila said, are condoms easily thrown away.

Sadly, though, when I went with Nzila to visit his clinic, he introduced me to several young hookers in the waiting area who had not been using their condoms—and who were HIV-positive. Nzila was trying to explain to them why they had to come in off the streets, why this invisible disease in their bodies was killing them. But he knew he wouldn't have much luck. These girls would continue to work, and would continue to infect others, because not turning tricks meant not eating, even though they knew they might be passing on a fatal disease to their unsuspecting partners. All Nzila could do was try to convince them that if they did continue to work, then please—for the sake of their customers—use the condoms.

Maybe one of the reasons for the relative nonchalance about AIDS across Africa is that so many other, more immediate, fatal diseases are ravaging the continent as well. Africa is a breeding ground for myriad viruses, germs, plagues, parasites, bacteria, and infections that most people in the West probably never knew existed—or that were thought to have been eradicated long ago. In Kinshasa once, I talked to foreign doctors who told me that they were growing alarmed about a new outbreak of sleeping sickness in some remote villages in the interior. Sleeping sickness! Entire villages just lying down, falling asleep, and dying. I found it amazing that this could still be going on in the 1990s; the reports seemed to be something out of the nineteenth century. More amazing still was that except for a few doctors in Kinshasa getting scattered reports, very little attention was being paid to the problem. In Africa, a few isolated villages falling asleep and dying would rank as a minor health irritant, not a medical crisis.

The greatest killer in Africa, though, is not AIDS or sleeping sickness but malaria. According to the World Health Organization, some 88 million Africans have the disease. (Of the four types of malaria, the most common three are chronic, which means they can recur over decades, while the fourth, which does not recur, can be fatal.) Another 171 million Africans have TB in some stage. Malaria, TB, measles, and diarrhea together account for most of the deaths in Africa. Malaria alone kills an estimated 2 million children each year. The World Bank estimates that the cost of lost productivity in Africa because of malaria exceeds Africa's total expenditure on health care. This state of affairs is not surprising, given the dilapidated state of most publicly funded African hospitals, which usually do not even have enough bandages and needles, let alone prescription medicines. It often occurred to me that my yearly bill for dog food and veterinary bills probably exceeded what most African governments spend on health care.

The dismal condition of most African public hospitals is sad testament to the abysmal state of health care. Hospitals, more than anything else, are the main breeding ground of disease and infections. I walked through hospitals in almost every country I visited because I found them a fairly good gauge of how well a government invested in its own people. In almost every place, conditions were, to put it mildly, disgusting. Stiflingly hot, windowless rooms, with flies swarming through fetid air. Patients stacked up almost on top of one another in crowded wards. Blood everywhere. Sick people, most likely with TB, coughing uncontrollably in the open wards. Family members lining the hallways and packing the courtyards, cooking meals for patients inside who might not otherwise eat. If you weren't sick before you went into an African hospital, I always mused, you most certainly would be by the time you emerged. It's no secret, for example, how the Ebola virus briefly flared up as an "epidemic" in Zaire in 1995. There had been Ebola outbreaks before in isolated Zairean villages, but on that one occasion in 1995, an Ebola patient made the mistake of going to a hospital and checking himself in for treatment. Because of unsanitary and unsafe conditions, the lack of rubber gloves, and the lack of common sense in dealing with blood, the Ebola quickly spread to the health-care workers, and a new epidemic was born.

One of the main problems afflicting Africa's health-care system is corruption. Most African hospitals are desperately short of medicine. But on the streets outside, any type and variety of medicine is readily for sale, most of it pilfered from the hospital pharmacies or diverted before it even makes it that far. Those with money can afford to buy medicines privately; those without—and that means the vast majority of Africans—simply suffer until they die.

Before I first set out for Africa, I went to the traveler's clinic at Georgetown University Hospital in Washington and subjected myself to a dizzying array of injections for almost every conceivable ailment—hepatitis, tetanus, typhoid, even rabies. I was told there were a lot of stray dogs roaming the streets, and having some of the initial rabies shots in Washington before I left might save me the series of painful shots in the stomach later on if I were unfortunate enough to cross the path of a stray canine.

I also started out my tour with a yearlong supply of malaria tablets, which were supposed to be taken once each week. I took them religiously for the first few months, but then dropped the routine. It was better to take my chances with mosquito netting and repellent, I reasoned, than stick to that regimen over three years and perhaps only lower my resistance. Also, the pills were useless against the most deadly kind of malaria—the cerebral malaria that attacks the brain and can kill within days if not quickly treated. My worst nightmare was catching cerebral malaria and being caught somewhere in the bush, days away from a doctor or hospital, and having the parasites eat away my brain. I never caught it, but several friends did, including a colleague from the *New York Times,* a reporter from the British *Daily Telegraph,* and a BBC television reporter who had flown out to Africa from London during the Rwanda crisis. Of course, they went for medical checkups immediately after suffering the first symptoms, and all were cured in time.

Daily living in Africa is also a constant battle to ward off possible disease and infection from the water you drink, cook with, and bathe in. Neil Henry, my predecessor, had given me the basic rules—don't drink the tap water, and make sure Hezekiah kept a supply of boiled water in the refrigerator at all times. I also learned a few things on my own, like steering clear of meals that included uncooked vegetables, like lettuce, since you never know what kind of water was used to wash them.

I considered Neil something of an expert; he told me how he had recently just recovered from a bad bout of conjunctivitis—"red eye," the Africans call it—which is a painful inflammation of the eyes. Neil got the disease in both eyes, catching it, he realized, on his last trip to West Africa. He explained that the traditional friendly handshake greeting in West Africa involves grabbing one's hand, shaking firmly, and pulling the first finger between the greeter's thumb and index finger, to make a quick snapping sound; Neil reckoned that after a few West African handshakes, he must have inadvertently rubbed or touched his eyes—and the result was that he ended up using eyedrops until the conjunctivitis healed.

Even something as simple as brushing your teeth—an act that an American takes for granted every day—can result in a nasty bout of diarrhea or worse. It can also become a rather cumbersome procedure in a place like Somalia or Rwanda, or sometimes in the countless hotel rooms where there was no running water. On those trips, I always made sure to carry an adequate supply of bottled water— sometimes a boxful, if I suspected I might be on the road for a long haul. To brush my teeth, I'd first dip the bristles into the water, apply the toothpaste, and then rinse my mouth and the toothbrush with the bottled water. I was always mindful not to waste too much, since bottled water was a precious and often costly commodity.

Even while taking precautions, though, I knew it was impossible to wrap myself in a protective bubble. I often ended up just plunging in and taking a chance—like sitting down for tea with Somali elders in Baidoa town, not knowing how they managed to wash the little teacups, or sharing my water bottle with a Rwandan

Tutsi soldier in Byumba because it was the polite thing to do.

I was never seriously sick in Africa, despite all the sickness and disease around me every day. But serious, I suppose, depends on one's definition; diarrhea and occasional stomach pains were kind of a constant. Most of the expat reporters I knew suffered from bowel illnesses for at least part of their time on the continent. Ruth Burnett, the fiery redhead, became so ill and lost so much weight in covering the Rwanda crisis that when she finally went back to London her doctors put her on a strict diet to kill all the amoebas that their sophisticated tests found floating in her system. As Sam Kiley of the *London Times* used to put it, in his own crude but endearing way, "Farting with confidence is a rare luxury in Africa."

Whenever I thought of all the sickness and disease—and that was pretty often, when I was walking through some rundown up-country clinic, watching refugees in Goma dropping dead from cholera, making my way through an overcrowded TB ward in Merca trying not to breathe too deeply—I would feel a great weight of sadness wash over me, as thick as the stale air of death that hangs over so much of Africa. So many Africans died needlessly, it seemed to me, from infections and diseases that could be cured so easily with a simple injection or a weeklong supply of antibiotics. It seemed like such a tragic waste, always, that as an American, I would take an aspirin or cold tablet at the first hint of a scratchy throat or runny nose, that at the slightest appearance of a hitherto unseen rash I would rush immediately to a doctor for a complete physical.

And yet in Africa, people would walk around for weeks, years, a lifetime, without ever setting foot in a hospital. Sometimes treatment was simply too expensive, and other times—as in Mogadishu—just getting to the hospital could be more dangerous than the ailment, especially if it meant crossing the no-man's-land during an artillery barrage. In Somalia I met scores of people who would show me bullet wounds that had gone untreated for weeks; they typically just wrapped old rags across the wound and let it fester.

I also thought that perhaps these Africans thought the same way

I did—that there was no use in going to a disease-filled African hospital because in many places the hospital was simply a place to die.

Mostly, though, I just felt angry about the entire situation. Angry that there was so little I, or anyone, could do to help. Angry that even when medicine was available, it was pilfered and sold in black-market street stalls. Angry that governments around the continent made sure that the soldiers had new boots and rifles, while the hospitals sometimes had no working electricity, to say nothing of bandages and disposable syringes.

I thought of Esther, and wondered whether she was now another African AIDS statistic.

And I thought of Hezekiah and Reuben, and even George with his free-spending lifestyle, and how I had wanted to fire him for ripping me off. And I thought of how every day their lives were a constant battle not only against the ordinary deprivations of Africa but also against the health problems that we in the West can safely assume we'll never come in contact with.

Those feelings all just reinforced for me my own sense of my good fortune in life. I had been born in a country where the health-care system, flawed and as costly as it is, does not produce hospitals that are breeding grounds for disease. In America, we debate questions about health insurance and Medicaid and abortion and HMOs; for most Africans, basic health care isn't even an option.

And so I watched my step, checked my supply of water, and said a silent word of thanks.

7

Homecomings

"We need to stop airing our differences in front of the
white man, put the white man out of our meetings, and
then sit down and talk shop with each other."

—MALCOLM X,
Detroit speech, 1963

ON A STICKY HOT November morning in 1992, I found myself at
the foot of the Po River Bridge, on the outskirts of Monrovia, the
besieged capital city of war-torn Liberia. I was interviewing soldiers
from the Alligator Battalion, and the boys (none of them looked
older than twenty-one) were passing around a particularly pungent
marijuana cigarette while keeping a vigil here against rebel incursions into the city from the surrounding swampland.

The battalion commander, Captain Jungle Jabba, was dressed in
an Operation Desert Storm T-shirt and gold-rimmed sunglasses.
His deputy commander, distinguishable mostly by his tennis shoes

and thick dreadlocks, identified himself as Captain Pepper-and-Salt—"because I will peppa' the enemy," he explained, waving his AK-47. And further down the road, at the very foot of the bridge, the soldier inspecting cars was decked out in a flowing ash blond woman's wig, held down by a black plastic shower cap pinned on his head. At his side was a twelve-year-old boy named Abraham, who called himself a member of the "special forces" and claimed to have been fighting in Liberia's jungles since he was ten. Abraham wore camouflage pants and had two grenades fastened to his belt on either side.

Welcome to Liberia, scene of one of the wackiest, and most ruthless, of Africa's uncivil wars. It's a war with a general named Mosquito, a war where soldiers get high on dope and paint their fingernails bright red before heading off to battle. It's a war where combatants sometimes don women's wigs, pantyhose, even Donald Duck Halloween masks before committing some of the world's most unspeakable atrocities against their enemies. It's the only war that hosts a unit of soldiers who strip off their clothes before going into battle and calls itself "the Butt Naked Brigade." It's a war where young child soldiers carry teddy bears and plastic baby dolls in one hand and AK-47s in the other. It's a war where fighters smear their faces with makeup and mud in the belief that "juju," West African magic, will protect them from the enemy's bullets.

It might be easy to dismiss Liberia as an oddball case if the consequences of the continuous warfare weren't so brutal: tens of thousands killed, many more displaced, and some of the most senseless of wartime atrocities committed. I came to Liberia just a few days after five American nuns had been abducted in the bush and slain, in the area known as "Taylorland," which was under the control of a Boston gas station attendant-turned-rebel leader, Charles Taylor.

Liberia was supposed to be the most "Americanized" of African countries, a nation founded in the 1820s by freed American slaves. Liberia, whose very name means "freedom," was the dream of the American Colonization Society, whose goal was to settle black "freedmen" in Africa, the land of their roots. Funded by a grant from the U.S. Congress, the society outfitted caravans of ships that crossed the Atlantic, establishing settlements near the mouth of the Mesurado River on West Africa's Gold Coast. In 1847, when Liberia became Africa's first independent republic, the American influence was unmistakable. The capital, Monrovia, was named for the U.S. president James Monroe, and other cities and counties bore familiar names like Buchanan and Maryland and New Georgia. Liberia's flag was virtually a carbon copy of the American Stars and Stripes—though with a single star—and its national motto bespoke the hope of its founders: "The love of liberty brought us here."

And for a long time, too, Liberia seemed on the surface at least to live up to its dream; the country had one of Africa's longest periods of political stability—more than 130 years without a coup, the common affliction of modern Africa.

If I was to find any country in Africa to which I would have some immediate connection, Liberia should have been it—a country founded by freed slaves and the sons and grandsons of slaves from the American South, and myself the descendant of southern slaves. But instead of encountering some long-lost soul mates, I found myself in the only English-speaking country in the world where I have had to hire a translator, listening to dope-smoking soldiers in drag explaining how "juju" can stop bullets from going into a man's chest.

Liberia's free fall in the late 1980s and early 1990s was as rapid, and as complete, as Somalia's or Rwanda's. The rot began in 1980, when President William Tolbert, the grandson of a freed American slave, was overthrown by an illiterate, twenty-eight-year-old army sergeant named Samuel K. Doe. It was a particularly nasty ending for Tolbert, who was disemboweled while still lying in bed and buried in a mass grave along with two dozen of his security guards. That alone might seem enough to have prompted the United States—still a powerful influence in Liberian affairs—to suspend all contact with the thugs in power and bring its weight to bear to force a return to democracy and the kind of peaceful succession Liberia had known. Instead, the Reagan administration became one of Doe's partners in repression, lavishing millions of dollars in aid and taking seriously Doe's empty pledges to steer the country back to democracy.

On Christmas Eve in 1989, Charles Taylor and his rebel army invaded Liberia from the neighboring Ivory Coast. By September of the next year, Doe was brutally assassinated, the full horror of the execution captured on a videotape now for sale on Monrovia's streets. A month later, a peace-keeping force of West African states moved in and installed a soft-spoken academic from the American Midwest, Amos Sawyer, as interim president. Taylor's troops, however, controlled 90 percent of Liberia's territory, including the key rubber-producing region, and Sawyer's regime consisted of just the city of Monrovia proper and not even the suburbs past the Po River Bridge.

Liberia is on Africa's western edge, just where the coast curves to dip around into the continent's armpit. To the east is Ivory Coast, which Taylor's rebels used as the staging area for their invasion. To the west is Sierra Leone, a onetime British colony established when Her Majesty's ships intercepted slave vessels on the high seas and returned their human cargo to the African shores. Sierra Leone's capital, Freetown, was the original destination for the American freedmen's ships, but when they were refused admission, they moved further along the coast to found Liberia.

Sierra Leone is also wracked by chronic instability. A long-running civil war has made parts of the country impassable, and in 1992, another cocky, twenty-something army captain, Valentine Strasser, toppled the incumbent president and became Africa's latest, youngest dictator. I got a chance to see him close up when I went to Dakar, the capital of nearby Senegal, for the annual heads-of-state summit meeting of the Organization of African Unity.

There were so many requests to interview the twenty-seven-year-old boy-president that some OAU officials persuaded Strasser to give a press conference. When he entered the room set aside for the press meeting, he was full of a soldier's swagger. His oversized green military uniform made his body look puffed up, as if he'd been lifting weights, and he wore a black beret and those ubiquitous Ray-

Ban sunglasses favored all over Africa by dictators, security guards, and border immigration officials alike. But what struck me most was his baby face; he looked barely old enough to shave, let alone be running a country. I got the odd sense that he was actually some American teenager dressed up in combat fatigues for Halloween, playing the role of a tinpot African dictator.

Strasser presented himself as a champion of clean government and social progress. Corruption, he said, had affected every aspect of daily life in his country. "We didn't have any electricity," said Strasser. "Telephones are not working properly. The standard of living for our people was below the poverty line." So he and a small group of soldiers overthrew the government.

According to some accounts, what actually happened was a bit less dramatic than Strasser was willing to admit. The soldiers, upset that they hadn't been paid, had launched a noisy demonstration, firing off their weapons and causing a general ruckus outside the presidential palace. The government, fearing a coup attempt, packed up and fled, leaving Strasser in charge.

The circumstances of his takeover notwithstanding, young Strasser knew immediately the kind of words the world, and especially the West, wanted to hear. "We give our solid and unflinching commitment to return our country to democracy at the soonest possible time," he pledged then. What he didn't say was that as he was making his promise, his regime was engaged in the systematic arrest and execution of dissidents and officials of the previous regime. That was in 1992.

Four years later, Strasser was still the military dictator of Sierra Leone, until he too was overthrown in yet another coup by some of his own coterie of officers. This time, with Strasser in exile in London and a new civilian government elected and installed, Western diplomats were cautiously hopeful that Sierra Leone might now be on the path to democracy.

I got to see Strasser again about a year later in Libreville, the capital of the small, oil-rich central African state of Gabon. The occasion was a summit meeting between Africans and African Americans organized by the Reverend Leon Sullivan, the veteran civil rights campaigner and anti-apartheid activist who had authored the "Sullivan Principles" outlining fair employment practices for U.S. firms doing business in apartheid-era South Africa. The summit brought together some of the most prominent luminaries from the American civil rights establishment—including Coretta Scott King, former UN ambassador Andrew Young, Jesse Jackson, the comedian Dick Gregory, the Reverend Joseph Lowrey, Nation of Islam leader Louis Farrakhan, and Virginia governor Douglas Wilder. Hundreds of African diplomats and some twenty heads of government were also in attendance.

When Strasser entered the meeting hall, sporting his now-trademark sunglasses and his camouflage battle fatigues, the crowd of mostly middle- and upper-class black Americans went wild with cheering, swooning from the women, some hoots, and frenzied applause. Sitting in that hall, you might be forgiven for thinking Strasser was a music celebrity instead of a puny boy-dictator. These black Americans were obviously more impressed with the macho military image Strasser cut than with the fact that he represents all that is wrong with Africa—military thugs who take power and thwart the continent's fledgling efforts to move toward democracy. The chanting and hooting was a disgusting display, and to me it highlighted the complete ignorance about Africa among America's so-called black elite.

The reception for Strasser wasn't the only thing sickening about that summit meeting. I sat there and listened as speaker after speaker heaped a nauseating outpouring of praise on some of Africa's most brutal and corrupt strongmen and their repressive regimes. An uninitiated listener might not have noticed the farcical nature of Jesse Jackson's fulsome tribute to Nigerian strongman Ibrahim Babangida. Jackson called Babangida "one of the great leader-servants of the modern world in our time," proclaiming, "You do not stand alone as you move with a steady beat toward restoring democracy." Jackson also called on President Clinton to reward

Babangida with an official visit to the White House on what would be a "triumphant tour as we herald the restoration of democracy" in Nigeria.

The problem with Africa is that nothing is ever quite as it seems. The assembled luminaries didn't seem to realize that dictators like Babangida and Strasser don't always do what they say, particularly when it comes to things like allowing free elections. But they are pretty good at saying what they think their audiences want to hear. Good thing Clinton held off on giving Babangida that official White House visit—he might have had a pretty tough time cleaning the stench from the Lincoln Room carpet.

Babangida had learned to talk a good game when it came to African democracy. At the 1992 OAU meeting in Senegal, it was Babangida who delivered one of the most impassioned pleas for pluralism, declaring, "Africa cannot and should not be immune from the political developments taking place in the world. The quest for democracy and freedom is so universal that no amount of repression can hold it in check for too long."

Nice words. Problem is, when it came to antidemocratic repression, Babangida was a master practitioner. He tried to engineer his own lengthy and cumbersome "planned" transition to end his military rule. And he left no detail to chance; he created two political parties, wrote their platforms, provided their funding, and orchestrated a series of primaries and local elections leading up to a June 1993 presidential vote. Babangida repeatedly pledged to step down once a successor was in place. "The question of clinging on to power is something of the past," he once told me. "We have all talked about democratization. We all have to come along with it, otherwise we will get swept away."

I must admit, I was half tempted to believe him too, or at least to give him the benefit of the doubt. I went to Nigeria several times in 1992 and 1993, covering each step in the lengthy electoral process, wondering whether maybe—just maybe—Babangida was sincere about relinquishing power. His track record of repression throughout the process didn't give much cause for hope. He repeatedly

closed down critical newspapers, jailed opposition leaders and journalists, and several times had reneged on his own timetable, delaying
his exit. And sure enough, when the presidential elections were held,
Babangida showed it was all a lie—The Big Lie, African style.
When he didn't like the election result—a victory for millionaire
businessman Moshood Abiola, a member of the rival Yoruba tribe—
Babangida simply canceled the counting and annulled the election.
For all his visionary talk, he was just another African despot, a small-
minded military man who enjoyed the perks of power and had no
concept of what real democracy is all about.

But Babangida wasn't the only one singled out for effusive praise
that day in Libreville. Also in for a fair share of the plaudits was
Omar Bongo, Gabon's own corrupt little despot in platform shoes,
who at the very moment he was being applauded was busy shutting
down the country's only private radio station. Didn't matter, I guess,
since Bongo was footing much of the bill for the big gala and, in that
sense, had bought himself a measure of respect.

None of the black Americans in Gabon ever bothered to get into
a taxi and venture twenty minutes to the edge of town to talk with
Jules-Aristide Bourdes-Ogouliguende, who at the time was waging
an uphill battle to challenge Bongo for the presidency. I went to see
him at his home, and I found a very frustrated man, angry, among
other things, that these black American "leaders," as they deem
themselves, had crawled into bed with a despot like Bongo while
apparently ignoring the plight of ordinary, struggling Africans. "The
Americans came here to create a dialogue," he told me. "They need
to understand our problems of education, in health care. . . . But
they are not going around enough, to be able to see the true problems of the country, and to talk to members of the opposition."

Weird things seem to happen to a lot of American black leaders
when they venture into Africa. They go through a bizarre kind of
metamorphosis when they set foot on the continent of their ancestors. Some of the most prominent veterans of America's civil rights
wars—articulate advocates for human rights and basic freedoms for
black people in America—seem to enter a kind of moral and intel-

lectual black box when they get to Africa. Dictators are hailed as statesmen, unrepresentative governments are deemed democratic, corrupt regimes are praised for having fought off colonialism and brought about "development." Black Americans were most vocally at the forefront of calls for immediate democratic reform in South Africa, but when the subject turns to the lack of democracy and human rights elsewhere in Africa, those same black Americans become defensive, nervous, and inarticulate. They offer tortured explanations as to why America shouldn't criticize Africa, why America shouldn't impose its standards, and why reform must not be immediate but gradual, step by step.

It's as if repression comes only in white.

So I was disgusted and angry in Gabon. And to keep from venting my disgust, I decided to have some fun by asking the various black leaders at the summit about the lack of human rights and democracy in black Africa. I enjoyed watching them wrap themselves in their own contradictions when I pointed out their contrasting views on South Africa versus the rest of the continent. I found the whole affair in Gabon so distasteful, I actually liked watching them squirm.

I asked Doug Wilder, Virginia's first black governor since Reconstruction, about the problem of democracy in black Africa. "We cannot and should not force them to undergo a metamorphosis in seconds," he replied. "If they are on track and on the path and giving evidence of trying to adjust, then our job is not to interfere, and to understand that there is a difference from what they are accustomed to."

Interesting. Now imagine the conversation was about South Africa, and the year is, say, 1980, and imagine a white governor of a southern state saying of the apartheid regime, "We cannot and should not force them to undergo a metamorphosis in seconds. . . . Our job is not to interfere." I can imagine that white politician would immediately be branded a racist or worst, and probably by no less a personage than Doug Wilder.

And consider the comments of Leon Sullivan on the question of democracy in black Africa: "We must be on the side of human rights and democracy," he told me. "Many African leaders recognize it must be done and are trying to find a way to bring it about." Then he added, "I don't like to see anything stringent from America, saying you must do this or you must do that."

Really? I seem to remember Reverend Sullivan being made of stronger moral fiber. What were the Sullivan Principles, after all, if not a way to bring pressure on the morally bankrupt apartheid regime? And they worked. So is Reverend Sullivan now trying to tell me that it's okay to be stringent with despots when they are white racists, but for black despots we'll let our standards slide a bit?

Or how about this comment from the Reverend Benjamin F. Chavis, Jr., at the time the new executive director of the National Association for the Advancemepnt of Colored People: "The pace and character of democratization in Africa is different from the pace and character of democratization in Europe, or the pace and character of democratization in Latin America. We still don't have a fully participatory democracy in an advanced, industrialized country like the United States. We have to be careful how we stand in judgment of others. . . . The African American community would like to see the process of democratization continue in Africa, but not try to dictate the character or pace of that democratization. . . . We in the United States must support the emerging African democracies—the African understanding of democracy—rather than attempt to superimpose a Western standard of democracy."

That was a mouthful, and all this he told me in his hotel suite just before going off to give his keynote speech to the assembled luminaries before I could think of all the questions that his comment raised. What, after all, is "an African understanding of democracy" and how is it different from your or my understanding? Why is American democracy today not truly participatory? Why should Latin America and Europe be considered different from Africa?

And when I spoke to Jesse Jackson, he added that while Africa "has to eventually get to democracy, one cannot go blindly imposing it. Ultimately, it must be self-determination."

In fairness I do recognize the awkward position that America's black leaders find themselves in when facing tough questions about black Africa. I know that there are no simple choices, no easy positions to take, on a case as complex and with the deep historical antecedents as a Somalia or a Rwanda. In Africa, it isn't always easy to pick out the good guys—often, as in Somalia, there aren't any good guys, just varying gradations of evil. Finding a defensible position on an African crisis like Liberia is far more vexing than attacking apartheid-era South Africa, which was, literally, a question of black and white.

But there is a deeper aspect to the reluctance of black America to speak out. There is a sensitivity about publicly criticizing the black leadership of independent black countries. There is a sense, rightly or wrongly, that a measure of our self-esteem as a black race in America is somehow tied to the success or failure of independent black governments running their own shows in Africa. "There was an element of not attacking your own brothers," said C. Payne Lucas, president of the Washington-based black development group Africare. "That's not radically different from Jews in America, or Poles in America."

When I was still a toddler, way back in 1963 in Detroit, Malcolm X made much the same point when he came to my hometown to address a Northern Negro Grass Roots Leadership Conference at the King Solomon Baptist Church. "Instead of airing our differences in public," Malcolm told the cheering crowd, "we have to realize we're all the same family. And when you have a family squabble, you don't get out on the sidewalk. If you do, everybody calls you uncouth, unrefined, uncivilized, savage. If you don't make it at home, you settle it at home; you get in the closet, argue it out behind closed doors, and then when you come out on the street, you pose a common front, a united front."

I didn't hear Malcolm speak then. But his was an argument with which I would later become painfully familiar during my years as a reporter on the metropolitan staff and the national staff of the *Washington Post*. And it was an argument that trailed me as a black reporter covering black Africa. It's a dilemma that faces almost every black journalist working for the mainstream (read: "white") press, which can be succinctly summed up in a single question:

Are you black first, or a journalist first?

What the question really asks is, are you supposed to write accurately, and critically, about what you see and hear? Or are you supposed to be silently supportive of a black agenda, protecting prominent blacks from tough scrutiny and ignoring their foibles, while writing and reporting only favorably about issues of concern to America's black community?

Many of those questions were at the heart of a debate stirred up by my colleague at the *Post*, Milton Coleman, when in the midst of the 1984 presidential campaign, he reported remarks Jesse Jackson made referring to Jews as "Hymie" and New York as "Hymietown." Coleman was unfairly accused of using material that should have been off the record; just jiving between black folk, between brothers, not meant for public consumption. More troubling to me, however, was that Coleman was accused of being a traitor to his race, bringing upon himself the wrath of the black community and even some veiled threats from Louis Farrakhan's henchmen.

I remember at the time feeling empathy for Coleman. Black reporters often face that kind of intellectual condescension when we are told—in the face of an event like Jackson's candidacy, which mobilized much of black America—that our job is to become something more like cheerleaders than objective reporters, protectors rather than the professional cynics we are. If you report and write critically about black politics and politicians in Washington, D.C., which I did during my year and a half as a city hall reporter, then you are accused of "selling out" and trying to curry favor with the "white establishment." You are either in the tribe or you are out, and by working for a "mainstream" newspaper and just trying to be a hard-nosed reporter, you get accused of turning your back on your race.

Even members of my family sometimes asked me those same troubling questions, and at times it made me angry. I remember being home in Detroit one Thanksgiving or Christmas and having one of my cousins ask me, "Why do the media have to tear down our black leaders?" She cited the cocaine arrest of D.C. mayor Marion Barry and the assorted investigations of wrongdoing by Detroit mayor Coleman Young, who, it seemed, was always under an ethical cloud for something or other. She cited a couple of other examples, and each time I tried to explain that journalists who expose these scandals are only doing their job, that wrongdoing should be exposed whether the perpetrators happen to be black or white. But my cousin wasn't convinced. "But they are the only role models we have," she said.

I've heard variations of that same criticism before, from relatives, from people I interview, even from Washington taxicab drivers, who launch into their "conspiracy theory" rap the minute I'd settle into the backseat and give them the address of the *Post*'s downtown office. I've heard it so often, in fact, that I now automatically tune it out. I've become too tired to be defensive anymore.

Thinking about it now, there are a lot of compelling arguments I could have used in those conversations. I could have said that because these black politicians are indeed our role models, then they have a special responsibility to keep their noses clean. Let's call it racism, for the sake of argument, but let's also then say that blacks who assume prominent leadership positions in America should expect a closer kind of scrutiny; they should pay their taxes on time, they should keep their pants zipped, they should keep their hands out of the public treasury, and they shouldn't smoke crack, precisely because they *are* role models for the black community. White politicians are held to these standards, and black officeholders should not expect to get either a protective wall of silence around them or the conspiratorial acquiescence of the black reporters who cover them.

Those are all solid comeback points. But none of them would really do much good. It is an argument that cannot be won.

It can't be won because many blacks are firm believers in a grand white conspiracy to suppress blacks, to keep black people in America down. In the streets, in the barber shops, in the taxicabs of

Washington, Detroit, and other black communities, the conspiracy theorists have even concocted a name for it: "The Plan."

In its broadest sense, "The Plan" is supposed to involve the targeted harassment of black elected officials, celebrity entertainers, sports stars. Everything from Marion Barry's cocaine conviction to Mike Tyson's rape prosecution are all seen as part of this vast, interconnected conspiracy.

"The Plan" is the secret agenda of Washington's white business establishment, the government, and the media to maintain white domination of the nation's capital. "The Plan" is subtle, complex, and long-term. It involves allowing a limited measure of home rule for D.C. residents and the emergence of a black political class. But of course our home-rule government in Washington is deliberately shackled from the start, with congressional restrictions on taxation and a reliance on a lump-sum federal payment to fund much of the city budget. The city's black leadership is hobbled and destined to fail.

The media—and in Washington, this means the *Post*—are an integral part of "The Plan." Using brainwashed black reporters like me, who constitute a kind of racial fifth column of infiltration, the media will mount a systematic campaign to tear down the city's black leadership through investigation of scandal and wrongdoing. And come election time, the *Post*'s influential editorial page will weigh in with hard-hitting endorsements of the candidates seen as most pliable to the white establishment.

That, in essence, is "The Plan."

If it sounds ludicrous, that's because it is. The troubling part is, a lot of blacks believe it—even those who are intelligent enough to know better.

I learned pretty quickly after coming to Washington that as a journalist, especially one working for the *Post*, there's no escaping the ongoing urban race war, no way to ignore the byzantine layers of racial conspiracy theories, no way to simply do your job and be a reporter without being "a black reporter." My first beat at the *Post* was city hall, and I soon found myself confronting this "Us"-versus-

"Them" mentality. If I wrote a hard-hitting story about a black politician or a story considered favorable about a white politician—hell, even if I were seen being too friendly with some white staff person in the District Building or asking a white press secretary out to lunch—the blacks in that building laid into me thick and labeled me a traitor, working for the ubiquitous "Them."

White reporters are never forced to choose sides, I thought, but being black, I was told I had no choice. All my life, I had managed pretty well to escape just that kind of forced choice. Now here I was, a reporter in the nation's capital for one of the world's most prestigious newspapers, and I felt myself being reduced to a cog in a grand white conspiracy, viewed with racial suspicion, accused of some amorphous betrayal, essentially being told by black people that unless you're all the way with "Us," you may not be black enough.

I got so weary in Washington of hearing about the "white conspiracy" that I decided to have some fun with it. For a while, whenever I got into a cab and told the driver I was going to the *Post*, I would wait for his response. If—as was usually the case—he started up about some supposedly critical story in that morning's paper about malfeasance in the city government, I would reply, "Well, you know, brother, it's all part of The Plan. You see, I checked my copy out just yesterday, and it said right there on page 673 that it was time we move into Phase Two, which means we're right on schedule but it's time to step up the pressure on 'em. Haven't you even bothered to read The Plan, brother? It's all laid out right there. Of course, I don't see the whole thing—just the parts they let us see. The whole Plan is kept upstairs, under lock and key." And then I would just sit back, pretend to bury my head in my newspaper, and chuckle silently as the stunned driver moved on without another word.

It was quite an unexpected relief to get away from covering city politics after my first full year at the *Post*. I never expected that as a foreign correspondent in faraway countries of Africa—a job I had always wanted precisely because I could escape America's race wars, escape the pressure to choose sides—I would still be hearing about the "white conspiracy," a Western conspiracy against blacks and a master plan to keep blacks down.

"It is the West that is trying to force a solution here. The West is trying to force the president to adopt a solution."

The speaker was Kitenge Yesu, Zaire's minister of communication. He was trying to explain to me the ongoing political stalemate that had brought his country's economy crashing to a halt. President Mobutu Sese Seko was refusing to negotiate with the leader of the opposition bloc, Etienne Tshikedi. Mobutu had closed down a national conference on the country's future and had retreated to his presidential yacht, endlessly plying the Zaire river, or to his specially constructed palace at Gbadolite. In the meantime, government ministries were shut down and weeds were growing straight through the floors and walls of the buildings. Hospitals, schools, and government offices were closed. Zaireans, including the unpaid civil servants, were sinking so deep into poverty that malnutrition—always a problem in the countryside—was starting to appear among residents on the streets of the capital, Kinshasa. Even the animals in the zoo were starving to death because no one had the money to feed them. And yet Kitenge Yesu was telling me, a black American journalist, that this entire state of affairs was all the fault of "the West," personified in his view by the American ambassador, Melissa Wells.

"She is white," he told me in an interview in French in his office at the top of an empty skyscraper. "This is our country. She is a white woman. Do you know of any of her ancestors in Zaire?" He was right about one thing—Wells indeed was white, a tall, blond woman who could dominate any room. She was also a veteran diplomat, a professional tested under fire in other African hot spots. Zaireans recognized her on the streets and widely respected her for standing up to Mobutu.

Kitenge also had a few choice words for the Western media, which were apparently also part of the grand conspiracy. "CNN is not for the blacks," he said. "It's for the white people." He continued, "It's the same as in 1960s—the West is for neocolonialism and imperialism."

If I had closed my eyes, the conversation could have been in the office of some city hall political operative in Washington instead of in Kinshasa, the capital of a country that was falling apart around me. The words were in French. But the antiwhite sentiment and the belief in a white, antiblack conspiracy were strikingly, sadly similar.

I encountered much the same attitude wherever I traveled around Africa, from a State House adviser to the president in Kenya to a Nigerian drug czar complaining about American bias against innocent Nigerian travelers. I suspected that my white colleagues didn't hear it as often, that the Africans may have expressed their paranoia more openly to me, as a black reporter. After all, I was black, a brother. I was supposed to understand.

"The British are very jealous of a Sudanese asserting this much independence, especially if he's a nigger, a black African boy."

This time I was in Khartoum, the capital of Sudan, interviewing Hassan Turabi, the Sudanese Islamic theorist who has led an Islamization campaign there ever since a group of generals seized power in 1989 with the backing of the country's virulently anti-Western Moslem fundamentalists. Some in the Western intelligence community also believe that Turabi is the driving force behind worldwide Islamic terrorism. Turabi had recently survived an assassination attempt in Canada, where he was stabbed in the head, and I had heard that the near murder had left him incoherent, his speech slurred. But I found Turabi sitting in the offices of the Islamic Foundation he heads, and to my surprise he seemed remarkably lucid as he explained the origins of his thinking about the West.

Turabi traveled to the United States during the 1960s as part of a U.S. government–sponsored student exchange program. He decided to go to the American South and to the Indian reservations. "I ran into a few problems," he told me. "I went into a barber shop. I didn't know you had to go into a black barber shop. He said, 'What do you want?' And then when he noticed my accent wasn't American, he said 'It's all right to receive a foreigner, even if he is a nigger.'

"I still see African Americans even today are not integrated into society," Turabi continued. "Socially, the African Americans are still isolated. . . . Socially, the society is still separated." In the legal system, for example, he said, "The juries don't decide according to law. If you are black, you are guilty."

And all of that was even before I was able to ask my first question; in fact, it came just after I walked into the room and handed him my business card, and Turabi saw that I was black.

Turabi is the spiritual leader of the Islamic revolution in Sudan, Africa's largest country and one deeply divided between its Arabized Moslem north and its Africanized Christian and animist south. For sixteen years, Sudan was led by a dictator-president named Jaafar Nimeri, who had taken power in a 1969 coup. Nimeri initially showed himself willing to compromise with his political opponents for the sake of a broader national reconciliation, but later veered toward a more radical brand of Islam, imposing the strict Islamic justice code of *sharia* law, and in the process reigniting a dormant but long-simmering civil war against the non-Moslem and black population in the South. Nimeri was himself overthrown in 1985 by a secular coalition of trade unionists and army officers, and eventually a British-educated politician, Sadiq al-Mahdi, became prime minister after generally free elections. Sadiq promised to reverse *sharia* law, but four years later, he too was overthrown, this time by a group of more radical Islamic army officers intent on turning Sudan into a strictly fundamentalist Moslem republic. A brigadier general named Omar Hassan Ahmed al-Bashir became Sudan's president. But Hassan Turabi, the intellectual force of the revolution, is widely considered the power behind the throne.

Sudan also emerged under Bashir as one of the most brutal regimes in Africa, with one of the world's worst human rights records. In 1994, Human Rights Watch/Africa labeled Sudan's human rights record "abysmal" and reported that "all forms of political opposition remained banned, both legally and through systematic terror." There were forced removals of southern refugees to isolated desert camps, there were arrests of political prisoners, including Sadiq al-Mahdi, and there were the "ghost houses"—the unofficial prisons where dissidents were held in secret, with no communication with their families. Restrictions were placed on the movements of Christian clergy, on the number of churches that could be built, and on the importation of Bibles and books for Christian theological schools. And, of course, there was the relentless prosecution of the war against blacks and Christians in the South, including bombing of villages.

Yet I sat there as Hassan Turabi, the architect of much of the terror, a man responsible for fueling a brutal war against black Africans in the south, lectured me about the history of oppression against blacks in America. Let's talk about the oppression of blacks in south Sudan, I wanted to ask him. Tell me about all the hands and feet that have been chopped off under *sharia* law. Tell me about the arrests, the torture, the executions, the bombings of villages.

Objectivity is supposed to be one of the cardinal rules of journalism. The reporter questions, and questions critically. But we are supposed to stop at the line where our questions become challenges, where we find ourselves debating and criticizing the people we are interviewing. And that was one of the hardest parts of the job of reporting in Africa: seeing injustice, and being forced to sit and listen to hypocrisy and outright lies—all while staying silent.

When I finished my interview with Turabi, I returned to the Khartoum Hilton hotel. I could have used a drink, but since Islamic law was imposed over Sudan, the strongest thing available in the hotel lobby was either the four-flavored fruit juice or the foul-tasting nonalcoholic beer. I opted for the fruit juice.

In the lobby, I ran into a group of black Americans staying at the hotel, there on some kind of a fact-finding trip and being given VIP treatment by the Sudanese regime. Some of the men had dressed for the part, in flowing white African robes and white turbans wrapped around their heads. Several of the women in the group had cloaked their heads in Moslem veils, and I guessed they must be Moslems from the States.

The next day, I learned that the U.S. ambassador in Khartoum, Donald Petterson, had hosted the group at his house for a small reception. Across the front page of the government-controlled newspaper was splashed a story about how the black American delegation had berated the ambassador over U.S. policy toward Sudan. Some members of the group had told Petterson that it was unfair for Sudan to be labeled by the State Department as a worldwide sponsor of terrorism and as one of the world's most oppressive regimes. After all, they said, they themselves had been treated with the utmost courtesy by their Sudanese hosts, and they had found the dusty streets of this capital safer than those of most crime-ridden American cities.

As I read the paper I was nearly shaking with rage. Couldn't these people see they were being used, manipulated, by one of the world's most notorious terrorist states? Couldn't these black Americans see that they were being made willing tools of a ruling clique that was busy persecuting black Africans in the name of Islam? Couldn't they see how stupid they looked, how stupid they were being?

I wanted to confront them, to shout at them. But instead, I deliberately avoided them. I crossed to the far side of the lobby whenever I had to, just to avoid the temptation of trying to shout sense into them, and maybe even end up hitting someone in the nose.

I went back to my hotel room, saw that it was nearly the top of the hour, and turned on CNN for the headlines. And I froze instantly when I heard the anchor announcing the death of an Italian journalist and her cameraman in Mogadishu.

My mind raced. I thought immediately: It must be Ilaria.

I had met Ilaria during my frequent forays into Somalia and had taken an instant liking to her. She was a good-natured reporter for one of the Italian national television stations, the one affiliated with the Communist Party. She seemed genuinely friendly and had a quietly wicked sense of humor that I quite enjoyed around the dinner table at the Al-Sahafi Hotel. Please God, I thought, don't let it be Ilaria.

I called the *Post*'s office in Washington and got Yasmine Bahrani, the longtime foreign-desk news aide, on the line. I braced myself hard and asked her to read me the wire story on the death of the journalists in Somalia. And then I heard the name and got the confirmation I dreaded. It was Ilaria. She and her cameraman had been slain in an apparent carjacking attempt in north Mogadishu, shot and left to bleed to death in their bullet-riddled car. Oh, God, No! I thought. Ilaria was dead. And for what? A botched car theft in the dying days of a failed UN mission.

I paced the hotel room, anger and pain coiled up inside of me. I really wanted a drink, but remembered alcohol was forbidden. I needed to get out of the room, so I crossed to the front door, opened it, and then paused when I thought about the black Americans sitting in the lobby in their African robes praising the Sudanese regime. I didn't want to face them, risk getting into an argument that would likely turn into a fistfight. I had way too much swirling in my head right now. So I closed the door, stretched out on the bed, and alone there in the room I cried. I cried for Ilaria. And I cried for everyone else I knew who had died senselessly on this senseless continent.

Sometimes I wonder whether it ever would have been possible for me to be like those black Americans in Khartoum. Maybe if I had kept my interests purely academic, like in college, when I was able to remain detached while reading about African socialism and liberation theory and the development philosophies of Kenneth Kaunda and Julius Nyrere and Kwame Nkrumah. Maybe then I could have read about Africa from afar and adopted the same knowing platitudes about the evils of colonialism and the sins of the West. Maybe I would have been better off if I had never come to Africa at all, except on a weeklong tourist trip, staying in the five-star hotels, buying tourist souvenirs, wearing African kente cloth. Maybe then I, too, could have spouted the same vacuous criticisms of American meddling as the sole root of all the continent's ills. I, too, could have been a fervent supporter of the land of my roots.

But it's too late for me now because I've lived here too long. And it's not only me, but other black people, black Americans who come here to live and to work, not the ones for whom Africa is a stamp on the passport. Take the case of Linda Thomas-Greenfield, the embassy official who was almost killed in Rwanda. But that wasn't the only part of her Africa experience that made her, like me, cynical and ready to go home.

She was no novice when I met her in Nairobi; she was in her third African posting for the U.S. State Department, after having spent three years in Gambia and two and a half in Nigeria. And before that she had lived in Liberia, just after completing her studies at the University of Wisconsin. "I remember the plane coming down," she said. "I couldn't wait to touch down."

But nine months after Thomas-Greenfield's arrival in Kenya, and just after her horrifying experience in Rwanda, we chatted over coffee at the outdoor terrace of Nairobi's Inter-Continental Hotel downtown. And, like me, she was fed up, burned out, and ready to go home.

Her house in Nairobi had been burglarized five times, so she had an electric fence installed. "When they put up the electric fence, I told them to put in enough volts to barbecue anybody who came over," she said. But the fence didn't help—the break-ins continued. So she went to the local police station, and the police agreed to post two guards on her property. And then the police guards posted there began demanding she pay them extra money for their services. "I've gotten to the point where I'm more afraid not to give them money," she said. "They're sitting outside with automatic weapons."

Finally, she had a higher fence, ten feet high, built around her grounds. And when I met her, she had become so exasperated that she told me, "I'm ready to sit outside myself with an AK-47."

The crime in Nairobi wore her down. The brush with death in Kigali during the Rwandan nightmare forever changed her view of Africa. But more than ever, what seemed to break the spirit of even this hardened, longtime Africa lover was the attitude of the Africans themselves. In Kenya, she said, she had never been invited into a Kenyan home. And even going about daily chores, she was met constantly with the Kenyans' own perverse form of racism, a kind of lingering inferiority complex that makes black Kenyans bestow prefer-

ential treatment on whites at the expense of their supposed "brothers."

"There's nothing that annoys me more," she said, "than sitting in
a restaurant and seeing two white people getting waited on, and I
can't get my service." Once, at a beach resort hotel on the Kenyan
coast, Thomas-Greenfield complained to the manager about the
abysmal service from the waiters and staff. The manager explained,
apologetically, "It's because they think you're a Kenyan."

A similar incident occurred when Thomas-Greenfield, her husband, and another black American went to a popular restaurant at
the Safari Park Hotel on the outskirts of Nairobi. Thomas-Greenfield was doing some advance work for a twenty-two-member congressional delegation (congressmen, spouses, and staff) that was
scheduled to visit East Africa, and she decided to go to the restaurant to try out the menu and test the service. They sat endlessly,
waiting for a waiter to take their drink orders, until finally, again, she
found a manager and complained. And the manager replied, "We
didn't know who you were." They thought she and the other black
Americans were Kenyan. "Here the colonial mentality runs deep,"
Thomas-Greenfield said, shaking her head in disgust. "But I don't
want to wear an 'honorary white' sign over my head."

She then made the depth of her frustration clear in the strongest
terms she could find: "I'd rather be black in South Africa under
apartheid than go through what I'm going through here in Kenya."

Sadly, I knew exactly what she meant. I thought of all the petty
slights, the raised eyebrows, the inconveniences large and small, the
appeals to "brotherhood" by Africans with their hands outstretched,
and, above all, the suspicions that always greeted me when I
explained that, yes, I really am an American, a black American, in
Africa. I thought of a conversation I had in a Nairobi bar soon after
my arrival. A young woman asked me where I was from, and when I
told her, she replied, "I think you're a Kenyan."

"No," I said, "I'm American."

"You don't look like an American. You look like a Kenyan."

"No," I insisted, "I really am American. Trust me."

"I know you're a Kenyan," she said firmly, turning away. "You're just trying to pretend you don't speak Swahili."

"Okay," I said, resigned. "You found me out. I'm really a Kenyan."

"Aha!" she said, turning back to me, pleased with herself now. "I knew it!"

I also thought of the time once, late at night, when I was sitting in my dingy Nairobi office in Chester House trying to catch up on some paperwork, and I looked up and saw a rather disheveled-looking street person in torn pants and a filthy brown blazer standing in my doorway. He walked in, apologized for startling me, and explained that he was a Somali refugee living in the Eastleigh district of the city, and he was trying to get back to Somalia but had no money for bus fare.

"I was going to ask those white people, those Europeans," he said, nodding down the hallway to where some of my colleagues in the press corps were also working late. "But I felt ashamed. We are the same color, so I asked you."

I apologized and told him I had no change. And then he turned angry. "You black Americans are all like that!" he shouted. "You think you are better than we are!"

I shoved him out of the office and made sure, from then on, to keep the door locked.

I also thought of a particularly amusing exchange once at a Zairean border crossing as I was trying to enter the town of Bukavu, where I was staying in a hotel after having spent the day across the border in Rwanda.

"Where are you from?" the immigration officer asked me suspiciously, fingering my battered blue American passport, thick now with extra pages. It was evening, but the officer was still wearing his sunglasses, which by now I had determined must be a staple of the African bureaucratic uniform.

I found the question a bit silly, since he was holding my passport in his hands. "*Etats-Unis,*" I replied in French. "The United States."

"I think you are a Zairean," he said, moving his eyes from the passport photo to me and back again. "You look like a Zairean."

"I'm not a Zairean," I said again. I was tired, it was late, and I just wanted to get back to my room at the Hotel Residence, where, if the water was running, I would at least be able to take a shower, even if it would be ice cold. I tried to control my temper, since border guards seem to love it—and make your agony last longer—when they see you losing your temper. "Look," I said, "that's an American passport. I'm an American."

"What about your father—was he Zairean?" The immigration officer was not convinced.

"My parents, my grandparents, everybody was American," I said, speaking just a decibel below a shout. "Maybe four hundred years ago, there was a Zairean somewhere, but I can assure you, I'm American!"

"You have the face of a Zairean," he said, calling over his colleagues so this ad hoc joint committee could try to guess which tribe, which region of Zaire I might spring from.

Finally, I thought of one thing, the only thing, that would convince him. "Okay," I said, pushing my schoolboy French to its limit. "Suppose I was a Zairean. And suppose I did manage to get myself a fake American passport." I could see his eyes light up at the thought. "So, I'm a Zairean with a fake American passport. Tell me, why on earth would I be trying to sneak back into Zaire?"

The immigration officer pondered this for a moment, churning over in his mind the dizzying array of possibilities that a fake U.S. passport might offer; surely, using it to come back into Zaire was not among the likely options. "You are right," he concluded, picking up his rubber stamp. "You are American—black American."

And I remembered thinking then how there is no sound in the world so sweet as that final pounding of the rubber stamp in the passport, the sound that says I made it through another border control.

Of all the slights one suffers as a black American in Africa, however, none are quite so annoying as the put-downs by whites—the white Africans, or European residents of Africa. Whites in Africa constitute a tiny minority on a black continent, but many act as if colonialism never really ended, that they still really own the place.

Once I was waiting in line with an armload of groceries at a shopping center supermarket. Just as it was my turn in front of the cashier, an older white woman stepped directly in front of me and put her own basket of groceries down on the counter in front of me.

"Excuse me, lady," I said, not even trying to hide my indignation. "Can't you see I'm standing here."

She apparently heard my American twang and became flustered. "Oh, I'm so terrrr-ibly sorry," she said in her thick British accent. "I thought you were an African!"

It's strange how it works sometimes. You have a lot of black Americans hankering after Mother Africa, as if Africa is the answer to all the problems they face at home in America. And at the same time, you meet some Africans who have left, lived in America, and quickly find themselves more at home eating McDonald's hamburgers, watching football on cable TV, and driving taxicabs around Washington, D.C.

That's what happened with a group of Somali Americans I met back in 1993 during the U.S. intervention there.

About a hundred Somali-born volunteers—nearly 80 percent from the Washington, D.C., area—answered the call in December 1992 to accompany the twenty-eight thousand or so American troops being sent to Somalia as part of Operation Restore Hope. The Pentagon desperately needed Somali translators, and a McLean, Virginia, consulting firm called BDM hastily put together the translator pool, offering a $2,000-a-month stipend and the chance to breathe dust, eat military rations, sleep on army-issue cots, wear desert camouflage fatigues, dodge sniper bullets and mortar fire, and see, firsthand, the devastation that had racked their homeland. And a hundred signed up to go.

I met a few of the Somali Americans after they first arrived, and I became interested in pursuing a story about them. At first, I found them all eager and earnest, anxious to come back and contribute to a country most had left when they were children. Some wanted to track down lost relatives who were scattered through the displaced-persons camps. Some wanted to check on family property that had been left behind. Others were plain curious.

But it didn't take them long to become disappointed and discouraged. The Somalis they came back to help treated them with suspicion. They got wrapped up in Somalia's clan rivalries when in fact most of them had been away for so long that they didn't feel much affiliation with any clan. As Linda Thomas-Greenfield would discover in Kigali, the Somali Americans learned that Africa's wars are ethnic, tribal. And if you are black, there is no such thing as being neutral; you are forced to choose sides.

When I met one Somali American, Jamila Abdi, she was wearing fatigues, army boots, and fashionable sunglasses. Posted near the sandbagged front gates of the bombed-out U.S. embassy compound, she was serving as a translator for Somalis who came to the gates each day to make some kind of claim against the American troops—a claim for a relative injured by a stray bullet, or compensation for a goat or chicken run over by an errant American humvee. Jamila was twenty-six years old and had been working as a merchandising assistant for the Woodward and Lothrop department store at Tysons Corner mall in Virginia. She decided to enlist as a translator, she told me, because "the Americans were risking their lives, and they needed translators, so I came here to help out."

When I found her a few weeks later, however, she seemed tired, even a bit bitter. "I can't wait to get back to the United States," she said in our second meeting. "There has been so much blood, so much hatred. They don't see us as individuals—all they see is my clan. . . . They dislike us. They think we're betraying them. They call us names.

"It makes me very angry, very disappointed," she said. "I mean, I didn't have to come here. . . . I'm more American than Somali. The people here—well, basically I feel like I have no ties with them."

Hassan Hussein and his roommate, Mohamed Santur, were both driving taxicabs part-time in northern Virginia when they signed up for Operation Restore Hope. Hussein was thirty-four when I met him, and had been away from Somalia since 1982. Santur, too, had been gone for more than a decade, leaving Mogadishu to study at George Mason University, and he worked at the American Geological Institute when he wasn't driving a cab. At the end of their tours, they were both ready to go back home.

"Believe me, I appreciate all of the things that I have now," Hussein told me. "I'm a U.S. citizen, but I'm a real Somali. Even after ten, twenty, thirty years, I will still be a Somali. But now, they don't have the value system. . . . I noticed it the first day I arrived. You see it in their eyes. Before, to make eye contact with an elder was a real taboo. Now the children look at you like they want to kill you."

Hussein spent as much time as he could in Mogadishu talking to small groups of Somalis. He had to talk through the metal bars at the gate to the fortified U.S. compound, because if he had ventured outside on the street, he might have been hacked to pieces just for his T-shirt and sunglasses. "I started giving speeches, telling them that tribalism caused all these problems," he said. "The sad thing is, no one is hearing your voice. That's the downside of coming on this trip, seeing that you could not make the difference you had hoped, that the problems are so big."

Hussein's roommate, Santur, is a strapping six-foot five-inch Somali who used to play on the national basketball team, back when Somalia was still a nation. Sometimes, when he was out on the streets with a marine patrol, Somalis would recognize him, reach out to touch him. And, more painful, Santur would occasionally run into old teammates. "Some of them are difficult to recognize," he said. "People I used to play with, you see them and they've lost sixty pounds. There's nothing much you can do for them. It's really depressing. It's worse than I thought. . . . I see myself when I see them on the other side of the gates. I'm not smarter or better than them. I just had the opportunity."

And I listened quietly, and thought: There but for the grace of God go I.

Once, while on a trip to Senegal, I took the ferry boat over to Goree Island, just off the Atlantic coast. In the seventeenth and eighteenth centuries, Goree was the main transit point for African slaves heading off to America. They were brought there from the African interior and held in small, cavelike eight-by-six-foot cement cells, fifteen or twenty per cell. And there they stayed until the cargo ships were ready for loading, and then some twenty million able-bodied Africans, chained at the neck and at the ankles, made their final passage into slavery through a small door, down a wooden plank, and on to the New World.

Joseph Ndiaye, the director of the slave house museum at Goree, keeps an inscription book for visitors to write their impressions. I spent more than an hour there, flipping through the book, jotting down some of the comments in my notebook.

"Yes, mother, I have returned—440 years-plus later," wrote a black woman who came here from Sacramento. "I felt the presence of my ancestors and I know why we are a strong people. Black I will always be. Mother Africa I love you."

"I have come home, and I pledge to myself, this will never happen again," wrote another.

"I'm just a born-again African," said a Brooklyn native.

And from this angry black woman, who left no home address: "The only language white people understand is the gun. I will supply the weapons for revolution. It is the only way black people will be free."

It went on and on. Some of the tributes were moving, some poetic, some angry. For many black Americans who had come across the Atlantic, this trip was clearly a near religious pilgrimage.

I felt disturbed as I stood there. I shuddered slightly, reading the various comments in the inscription book. I, too, had come to Goree hoping to feel that same kind of spiritual connection, to find some emotional frame of reference. And I tried to make myself feel something that simply wouldn't come.

I felt distant, apart. I felt revulsion at the horrendous crime of slavery—sort of the same feeling I had experienced years earlier, as a student backpacker in Europe, when I visited the Auschwitz concentration camp. It was just like that, really; a reminder of a past atrocity, and one that must not be forgotten. But for some reason I felt little personal connection or pain. Goree was a powerful historical setting, one that makes visitors reflect on the evil nature of mankind. But for me it was nothing more. I thought about all the other evils I had seen around Africa, and in some way, I suppose, I was thinking about the evil and the darkness I had not yet seen, but which I knew awaited me.

And then I thought: Would I have been better off if this great tragedy, this crime of slavery, had not occurred? What would my life be like now? Would I be standing here now as a journalist with my notebook in hand and a camera slung over my shoulder?

And then I stopped, because I started hating myself for what I was thinking, what I was about to think. Those questions cut straight to the heart of what had been troubling me ever since I had set foot here in the land of my ancestors. But the answers were so unspeakable, so unthinkable, really, that I closed my eyes and literally forced the entire train of thought out of my head. I knew what I thought, but I didn't want to think, so I willed myself not to think my own thoughts.

I should have come to Goree long ago, I decided then. Yes, that was my problem. Back in my youth, when I was traveling around Europe and Asia and had avoided traveling to Africa for whatever reason—yes, that is when I should have come. Because then I would likely have come from the other direction, from across the Atlantic, from America, and my head would have been empty of the sights and sounds now swirling around there. Then I, too, would have added my inscription to the book, paid my own moving tribute to those who had passed here before me. And I would have gone back home, to America, and my soul would have been left pure.

But it was too late now. I had come to Goree from the East, from the darkness, and I had already seen way too much of Mother Africa, and what I had seen had already made me sick.

And I left there that day wondering how I could ever be whole again.

8

Wake-up Calls

"What we have done, and what we will continue to do,
is to demand the rights of the African people as human
beings."
—Jomo Kenyatta

There wasn't much left of Kibassa Maliba's son. I saw the grisly photographs, and there were only his charred remains.

Kibassa was a key leader of Zaire's united opposition movement, the "Sacred Union." When unpaid army troops went on a rampage in Kinshasa in 1994, some soldiers loyal to President Mobutu Sese Seko went straight to Kibassa's house and blasted open the steel front gate with seven rockets. Once inside, they shot Kibassa's twenty-eight-year-old son, who had been sleeping in the front room. Just for spite, they doused the body with gasoline or some other flammable liquid and set him on fire.

It's tough in Africa when you decide to oppose the Big Man. It may be even tougher in Zaire, where Mobutu has shown time and again that he's willing to take any action, no matter how brutal, to hang on to power.

Of all the things a newspaper reporter has to do, I find none so distasteful as having to talk to the relatives of someone who has just died. That's particularly true when the death was violent and the family members are still shocked and grieving. I never liked doing it as a young reporter in Washington, when I had to call the relatives of a murder victim for some kind of comment. And I didn't like it any more in Africa—even though I ended up talking quite a lot to the relatives of people who had just died, and had usually died violently.

It didn't get any easier when I already knew the family, and Kibassa was one of my best contacts in Kinshasa, and one of the few Zairean politicians whom I admired for his straight talk. That day, I found him holding court in the covered courtyard of a new house he had just moved to, and he was receiving a stream of political supporters and hangers-on who had come to offer their sympathies. When it was my turn, we sat down opposite each other, and to my surprise, Kibassa was in a defiant mood. "My son has paid the price," he told me, "but I will continue the fight."

I asked him if he was certain Mobutu was behind the attack that killed his son, and Kibassa didn't miss a beat. Of course it was Mobutu, he said with such force I was startled. This was the dictator's heavy-handed attempt at intimidation. Then Kibassa shook his head, resigned, and he stared off as if in deep contemplation. Finally, he said, "In the middle of the twentieth century, why should people act this way?"

Why indeed? It was a damn good question, and one I found myself asking repeatedly as I traversed the continent, seeing not just famines and massacres but also the everyday human suffering, the abuses of rights, the trampling on individual liberties, the police harassment, the beatings in detention, the closing down and fire-bombing of newspapers, the arrests of opposition politicians, and the outright murder of those with the courage to speak up against injustice.

It's what really hit me about Africa, not the Somalias or the Rwandas or the Liberias, because in many ways, those are the exceptions, the basket cases, the places where somebody flipped the switch. No, the real story occurs in the places you never really read much about, but where I spent a lot of time—Zaire and Kenya, Cameroon and Gabon, and the giant of them all, Nigeria. These are the places where every day, with each new interview, I found a new and disheartening tale of some brave and anonymous African, somebody like Kibassa Maliba, who was trying his best and paying the price. I saw their courage and their self-sacrifice and it ripped my heart out, I mean it really touched my soul. But in the end it was just plain depressing, because deep down I knew that in Africa it's all too rare for such struggles to end in victory. In Africa, the good guys don't win; they usually get tossed in prison, tortured, killed, beaten up, or sometimes just beaten down. They get beaten so hard they finally give up. And the rest? They just stop trying because they're too busy simply trying to survive.

When I wasn't depressed about it, I was in a rage. Angry at the monumental unfairness of it all, and angry that there's so little the outside world, anybody, really, can do to help. The world did try once to help, in Somalia, and I had been on hand to witness how that had turned into a multibillion-dollar fiasco. Now, for the most part, all the outside world would ever want to do would be to sit on the sidelines.

I tried to document the unfairness as best I could, tried to give some little voice to the voiceless. But in the end I know it won't matter much. The Big Men will still be there, arrogant, extravagant, enjoying the benefits of foreign-aid dollars. They'll still have their marble palaces carved out of the jungle and their bank accounts in Switzerland, their villas in the south of France, and their apartments on the Avenue Foch in Paris. They'll have their fleets of Mercedes limousines and their private jets. They'll build basilicas with their own likeness in the murals with the apostles, and they'll open universities that bear their name but where students can't afford books and will have no jobs if they ever get out. They'll equip their armies with shiny boots and their security forces with the latest weapons, but the hospitals will run short of needles and bandages, and college students will be using cardboard cutouts to learn the keys on a computer keypad because they don't have a real computer to use.

And I keeping asking myself Kibassa Maliba's question: Why?

Of course, it wasn't supposed to be this way, not when I first set out for Africa. The 1990s were to be Africa's "decade of democracy," or so I had been told. The Western donor nations were finally getting tough, demanding open elections, legal opposition parties, more monitoring of foreign dollars. Internally, too, an explosive new combination of forces was said to be eroding the decades-old acquiescence to authoritarianism: Urban populations had more access to information, and a younger generation of Africans carried no living memory of white colonialism, only black repression. Under such pressures, from the outside and within, the old African strongmen were starting to wobble, one by one. Or so it was said.

But sadly, as I survey the African landscape, little has really changed; like so much else—like my own heady optimism in Somalia before the disaster—the great promise of African democracy lies largely in ruins. It was stamped out by a military thug named Sani Abacha in Nigeria, who replaced Babangida and jailed the winner of the country's free election and Nigeria's real president, Moshood Abiola. It was made a mockery of in Cameroon, where sinister strongman Paul Biya was able to manipulate the voting rolls and control the ballot boxes to have himself declared the winner of a presidential election that foreign observers concluded was too fraudulent to be fair. It never really had much of a chance in Zaire, where Mobutu, the most obdurate of the African strongmen, has reduced his country to a shambles rather than surrender his power and the chance to plunder whatever can still be scraped out of the nation's resources. And the promise of democracy was set to the torch in Kenya, where Daniel arap Moi's ruling party instigated tribal clashes that left tens of thousands displaced, all to provide the proof of the prophecy I heard from one of Moi's top State House aides, that "democracy cannot work here in Africa."

That's not to say there were no bright spots. I went to Malawi and watched the demise of the oldest and longest-serving of the strongmen, "Life President" Hastings Kamuzu Banda, the self-described "Black Cock" known for his dark sunglasses, horsetail fly whisk, and the red-shirted "youth brigade" gangsters who terrorized the population. I saw him go down to an election he was forced to call at the hands of a little-known businessman named Bakili Muluzi, whom I had once interviewed riding around in the backseat of a car when it was too dangerous to be seen meeting in a public place. Yes, that one was sweet, if only because Malawi was perhaps the most sinister of Africa's strongman dictatorships, personified by Banda, who had nurtured a personality cult so powerful that it was prohibited in public to even utter his name without using his full exalted title: "His Excellency, the Life President . . ." Malawi was one place where the international donor community was as good as its word, actually using aid dollars as leverage to force the shift to a multiparty system and the election that was the life president's downfall. But the circumstances were ripe there; Banda was in his nineties and ailing, barely able to see or speak, basically a walking corpse propped up by greedy palace aides who didn't want to lose their place at the trough. Banda wasn't so much beaten; his regime just withered away.

And there was Mozambique, one of my last stops before leaving Africa, one of the last notebooks on the top of the pile. That election was the final step in a peace process that ended one of southern Africa's nastiest civil wars. It was also, after Somalia, one of the few places where the UN got one right. There was a massive demobilization of the warring armies. Foreign troops and election monitors fanned out throughout the country. And when the rebel leader threatened a last-minute poll boycott, the United States and the UN stepped in with heavy pressure and kept the elections on track. It was costly; the UN basically paid the combatants to stop fighting. Whether it could serve as any kind of a model was far less certain.

The tiny West African nation of Benin also jumps to mind. In March 1991, Benin held an election and tossed out an entrenched strongman, and suddenly this obscure little country on the Gulf of Guinea was being touted by the enlightened Africanists as the democratic wave of Africa's future. Yet this, too, was to prove short-lived. A subsequent election in 1996 brought the former ruler back to power.

And of course there was Zambia. In 1991, a little-known, diminutive union leader named Frederick Chiluba managed to oust one of Africa's towering figures, Kenneth Kaunda, from the presidency of the nation Kaunda himself had founded. To many in the West, Kaunda seemed a relatively benign dictator, but his true crime was his crackpot policies that had run Zambia's economy into the ground. After periodic suspensions of aid, the international lenders had finally forced the old man to hold a multiparty election, and to the world's surprise—not to mention his own—Kaunda lost. Resoundingly. And in Chiluba, much of Africa came to see the possibilities of a new, democratic future.

But if the success of that election was exhilarating, what followed was the source of widespread disillusionment. Chiluba's Movement for Multiparty Democracy itself became entrenched as a new ruling clique. Far from wiping out corruption, Chiluba presided over a system as corrupt and incompetent as the one he replaced. Government officials were implicated in drug smuggling. The few honest officials resigned in disgust, claiming the new leaders had lost their direction. Newspapers critical of the new government were taken to court, their editors harassed. And in a sign that the new rulers were as authoritarian and undemocratic as the old, Chiluba drafted a new law to bar Kaunda from running for office again, by imposing a term limit on the president and also declaring Kaunda was ineligible because his parents were not born in Zambia but in the neighboring territory that is now Malawi.

After the 1991 elections, it seemed everything had changed in Zambia. By 1996, it had become painfully clear that the more things change, the more they really do remain the same.

While even the success stories were heartening, they were still too few in number. In many cases, the stories remain incomplete at best.

And the few successes did little to repair the overarching despair that washed over me as I saw an election stolen in Cameroon, an election rigged in Kenya, an election annulled in Nigeria, and heavily flawed elections conducted mainly to ratify the status quo, or to ensure the continued flow of aid dollars in places like Zimbabwe, Ethiopia, Tanzania, and Uganda.

I know that many black Americans feel a sense of alienation in the United States and like to look longingly to Africa as a mecca of black empowerment. It's a seductive image, almost too good to be true, and an uplifting counterpoint to the feelings of deprivation and discrimination as a minority in America. Here, after all, are black nations, ruled by blacks, the mirror opposite of the condition back home where many blacks are made to feel like a permanent and unwanted minority in the country of their birth.

But that's the problem with the image—if it sounds too good to be true, that's because it is. It's a mirage. It's not the reality of Africa today, where in most places blacks are still waiting to be empowered three decades after the last Europeans packed up and went home. Of course, the countries became independent, the flags changed, the names were Africanized, new national anthems were sung, new holidays observed. The picture of the Big Man replaced the portrait of the Queen. But in country after country, power simply passed from a white colonial dictatorship to an indigenous black one—and the result has been more repression, more brutality. For the Africans, the ordinary, decent, long-suffering Africans, precious little has changed.

This analysis may sound too harsh, an exaggeration. But for that I can offer no excuses, because I've been there, and I'm trying to tell it to you straight, just like I've seen it. Because that's been one of Africa's biggest problems, the lack of any straight talk even from— or should I say *particularly* from—Africa's friends in the West who want to help.

And so I return to Kibassa Maliba's question: Why in the twentieth century? Why do Africa's leaders behave the way they do, plundering their national treasuries and allowing their countries to collapse around them? Why do they cling to power through all means, long after they have accumulated their billions? Why here, in black Africa?

Before my arrival in Africa, I had spent four years reporting from Southeast Asia. I also spent a year on a journalistic fellowship at the East-West Center in Honolulu, which allowed me to travel back to Asia for research. What I found in Asia was a region of amazing economic dynamism, a place largely defined by more than a decade of steady growth and development, vastly improved living standards, and expanded opportunities. Almost all of the Southeast Asian countries had risen from poverty to relative prosperity, creating huge and stable middle classes and entering the first tier of newly industrialized economies.

Why has East Asia emerged as the model for economic success, while Africa has seen mostly poverty, hunger, and economies propped up by foreign aid? Why are East Asians now expanding their telecommunications capabilities when in most of Africa it's still hard to make a phone call next door? Why are East Asians now wrestling with ways to control access to the Internet, while African students still must use cardboard drawings of computer keyboards because they don't have real computers in their classrooms? Why are East Asian airlines upgrading their long-haul fleets, while bankrupt African carriers let planes rust on weed-strewn runways because they can't afford fuel and repair costs? Why are the leaders of Southeast Asia negotiating ways to ease trade barriers and create a free-trade zone, while Africans still levy some of the most prohibitive tariffs on earth, even for interregional trade?

There was nothing inevitable abut Asia's success and Africa's despair. Both regions emerged from colonialism at about the same time and faced many of the same obstacles. In 1957, when Ghana gained its independence from Britain, it was one of the brightest hopes of black Africa, with a higher gross national product than South Korea, which was itself still recovering from a destructive war, and before that, from thirty-five years as a Japanese colony. Today South Korea is recognized as one of Asia's "dragons," an economic powerhouse expanding into new markets throughout the region and the world. Ghana, meanwhile, has slid backward. Its gross national product today is lower than it was at independence. World Bank economists like to point to Ghana as an example of an African country that is "recovering" under a strict fiscal discipline program; what they don't tell you is that the economy today is propped up by foreign aid.

It's an ugly truth, but it needs to be laid out here, because for too long now Africa's failings have been hidden behind a veil of excuses and apologies. I realize that I'm on explosive ground here, and so I'll tread carefully. It's all too easy to stumble into the pitfall of old racial stereotypes—that Africans are lazy, that Asians are simply smarter, that blacks still possess a more savage, primitive side. But I am black, though not an African, and so I am going to push ahead here, mindful of the dangers, knowing full well that some will say I am doing a disservice to my race by pointing out these painful realities. But we have come too far now to pull back; the greater disservice now, I think, would be to leave the rest unsaid.

First let's look at the statistics, the cold and hard realities, many of them depressingly familiar. According to the World Bank, Africa is home to the world's poorest nations—and that doesn't even really count places like Somalia, where no meaningful statistics are available because there is no government around to collect them. Africa's children are the most likely on earth to die before the age of five. Its adults are least likely to live beyond the age of fifty. Africans are, on average, more malnourished, less educated, and more likely to be infected by fatal diseases than the inhabitants of any other place on earth.

Africa's economy has contracted. Its share of world markets has fallen by half since the 1970s, and the dollar value of the continent's global trade actually declined during the 1980s. African trade accounts for less than 0.1 percent of American imports. With the exception of South Africa, the African continent has been largely relegated to the economic sidelines, to the irrelevant margins of the world trading system.

Talk to me about Africa's legacy of European colonialism, and I'll give you Malaysia and Singapore, ruled by the British and occupied by Japan during World War II. Or Indonesia, exploited by the Dutch for over three hundred years. And let's toss in Vietnam, a French colony later divided between North and South, with famously tragic consequences. Like Africa, most Asian countries only achieved true independence in the postwar years; unlike the Africans, the Asians knew what to do with it.

Talk to me about the problem of tribalism in Africa, about different ethnic and linguistic groups having been lumped together by Europeans inside artificial national borders. Then I'll throw back at you Indonesia, some 13,700 scattered islands comprising more than 360 distinct tribes and ethnic groups and a mix of languages and religions; Indonesia has had its own turbulent past, including a bloody 1965 army-led massacre that left as many as a million people dead. But it has also had thirty years since of relative stability and prosperity.

Now talk to me about some African countries' lack of natural resources, or their reliance on single commodities, and I'll ask you to account for tiny Singapore, an island city-state with absolutely no resources—with a population barely large enough to sustain an independent nation. Singapore today is one of the world's most successful economies.

I used to bring up the question of Asia's success wherever I traveled around Africa, to see how the Africans themselves—government officials, diplomats, academics—would explain their continent's predicament. What I got was defensiveness, followed by anger, and then accusations that I did not understand the history. And then I got a long list of excuses. I was told about the Cold War, how the United States and the Soviet Union played out their superpower rivalry through proxy wars in Africa, which prolonged the continent's suffering. And I would respond that the Cold War's longest-running and costliest conflicts took place not in Africa but in Korea and Vietnam; now tell me which continent was the biggest playing field for superpower rivalry.

When the talk turns to corruption—official, top-level plunder—then at last we are moving closer to brass tacks. Corruption is the cancer eating at the heart of the African state. It is what sustains Africa's strongmen in power, and the money they pilfer, when spread generously throughout the system, is what allows them to continue to command allegiance long after their last shreds of legitimacy are gone.

Of course there's corruption in East Asia, too. Wide-scale corruption. South Korea's former president has been jailed for corruption after having admitted to taking bribes from the country's powerful business conglomerates. In Indonesia, the business dealings of President Suharto's children have become so nefarious and so ubiquitous that it is said that anytime you take a taxi, check into a hotel, smoke a clove cigarette, make a phone call on a cellular phone, or buy a Mercedes in Jakarta you are putting money into the pockets of one of the president's relatives. One watchdog group ranked Indonesia as the world's most corrupt country, and Hong Kong risk consultants have placed it third in Asia, behind only Communist China and Vietnam. And in Thailand, army generals have long enjoyed a cozy relationship with business, including holding seats on the boards of major corporations.

Yet Korea is an economic superpower, Indonesia has reduced poverty more per year for the last quarter century than any other developing country on earth, and Thailand, Vietnam, and China have all been posting annual growth rates of about 8 to 10 percent.

Contrast that now with Africa, where corruption is similarly rife, but the results quite different. Consider again Zaire, where Mobutu in his thirty years of power has taken corruption to unimaginable new heights (or depths, depending on your point of view), establishing a kleptocracy rivaled only by what Ferdinand E. Marcos was able to erect in the Philippines. It has been estimated that Mobutu stashed as much as $10 billion in overseas bank accounts, mostly money pilfered from Zaire's diamond and copper revenues and from raking off the proceeds of state-run corporations.

Living under such an overt kleptocracy inspires corruption and thievery at the bottom, and that's exactly what Zaire had been reduced to in the 1990s. It's everyone out for himself, as I learned from the time I landed at the confused Ndili International Airport. First, I was met by a dizzying array of soldiers and police, customs inspectors, immigration officers, hustlers, pickpockets, pimps, lowlifes, baggage handlers, swindlers, con artists, and hangers-on. They each claim some "function"—checking your yellow vaccination card, clearing your bag through customs, stamping your passport—and then they hold out their hand for the "fee," usually about twenty dollars. It made Mogadishu's international airport look calm and orderly by comparison.

To avoid this loud and confusing gamut of thieves, I decided to opt for "the VIP service"—meaning that I paid a hundred bucks to one uniformed soldier who got me through the row of extended hands quite quickly and rode in the taxi with me all the way from the airport, his machine gun between his legs. Imagine an ad that said: "Unpaid soldiers for hire, for personal escort service." Zaire, I thought, is really not so far removed from Somalia.

So endemic is African corruption—and so much more destructive than its Asian counterpart—that the comparison has even spawned a common joke that goes like this:

An Asian and an African become friends while they are both attending graduate school in the West. Years later, they each rise to become the finance minister of their respective countries. One day, the African ventures to Asia to visit his old friend, and is startled by the Asian's palatial home, the three Mercedes-Benzes in the circular drive, the swimming pool, the servants.

"My God!" the African exclaims. "We were just poor students before! How on earth can you now afford all this?"

And the Asian takes his African friend to the window and points to a sparkling new elevated highway in the distance. "You see that toll road?" says the Asian, and then he proudly taps himself on the chest. "Ten percent." And the African nods approvingly.

A few years later, the Asian ventures to Africa, to return the visit to his old friend. He finds the African living in a massive estate sprawling over several acres. There's a fleet of dozens of Mercedes-Benzes in the driveway, an indoor pool and tennis courts, an army of uniformed chauffeurs and servants. "My God!" says the Asian. "How on earth do you afford all this?"

This time the African takes his Asian friend to the window and points. "You see that highway?" he asks. But the Asian looks and sees nothing, just an open field with a few cows grazing.

"I don't see any highway," the Asian says, straining his eyes.

At this, the African smiles, taps himself on the chest, and boasts, "One hundred percent!"

The joke was first told to me by an American diplomat in Nigeria who had also spent time in Indonesia. It carried a poignant message about the debilitating effects of corruption in Africa versus its more benign counterpart in Asia. "In Indonesia, the president's daughter might get the contract to build the toll roads," the diplomat told me, "but the roads do get built and they do facilitate traffic flow." In Africa, the roads never get built. It was the difference, he said, between "productive corruption and malignant corruption."

It's this problem of corruption, from the president all the way down to the customs officials at the border posts, that seems to me about as good an explanation as any for Africa's plight. But it still begs the question: Why? Is there something in the nature of Africans that makes them more prone to corruption? Why does Asia produce a Lee Kuan Yew and a Suharto, while Africa offers instead so many Mobutus and Mois and Aideeds and Hastings Bandas?

Is there some flaw in the African culture?

I did manage to find one pretty good answer, from a fairly unlikely source—Yoweri Museveni, the president of Uganda.

Museveni came to power the old-fashioned way; he formed a ragtag guerrilla army and shot his way into the capital, Kampala, in 1986. He also is, in many ways, an old-fashioned African Big Man. He brooks little dissent. He does not put much store in Western-style democracy, believing that pluralism brings only chaos. His solution is a kind of "no-party democracy," which is a fancy way of saying he is a one-man authoritarian ruler. Yet Museveni rarely comes under criticism from his many and generous Western aid donors mainly because they remember the nightmare he replaced—the chaos of two successive, brutal dictators, the clownish Idi Amin Dada and his sinister successor, Milton Obote.

All that being said, Museveni is still a thinker who sounds more like a scholar than a soldier. He's also a straight talker when it comes to Africa and its problems. I saw him in person for the first time at an international forum of government officials, diplomats, and academics he was hosting in Kampala. Museveni used the opening ceremonies of the conference and his prerogative as president of the host country to expound on his theory of why Africa had failed to develop.

I sat and listened as he rattled off the same tired old explanations—excuses, really—that I'd heard time and again. First, he said, was that for five hundred years, Africa had no independence in decision making, most exemplified during the Cold War period by the question: "Are you pro-East or are you pro-West?" He called this "primarily a mistake of the Africans" to allow the superpower rivalry to divide the continent. Then he spoke of Africa's "fragmented markets" and the need for more regional integration. He acknowledged the continent's "high degree of illiteracy—not enough artisans, technicians, engineers." He talked about "economic policies that have killed the incentive of producers," and he mentioned exchange rate controls, that kind of thing.

He seemed to me to be making some sound points. But when the session was opened up for members of the media to ask questions, I found my way to one of the open microphones on the floor and posed to him the question that had been nagging me. Why, I asked him, had East Asia developed so rapidly and not Africa? I ticked off each of his own earlier reasons and threw them back in his face. East Asia, I said, had also suffered colonialism, so that was not in itself an excuse, I said. Asian countries, too, are composed of multiple ethnic and linguistic groups, so diversity is not in itself the reason. Asian countries, too, have artificial borders and continuing border disputes, and some East Asian countries, like Korea, like Vietnam, were also racked by destructive civil wars in the 1950s and 1960s. But still Asia has managed to prosper while Africans seem forever mired in poverty. What happened?

Museveni considered my question for a long time. He rambled on for a few minutes about how the East Asian countries had received greater assistance from the United States, in aid and "rental" payments for U.S. military bases on their soil. And finally he came around to the thought that I could tell was really on his mind.

"Discipline," he said at last. "The discipline of the Asians compared to the Africans." He paused. "I tend to find more discipline among the Ugandan Asians than among the Africans. I am not yet ready to explain this. People who come from an area with a big population, where people are very many and therefore competing for natural resources, may tend to be more disciplined than people who take life for granted.

"Scarcity of resources instills discipline in a people," he concluded. "Too much competition for resources also instills discipline in a people."

That was one of the few times on the continent I actually found myself impressed by an African leader willing to engage in discussion, in a blunt way, about Africa and its problems. That kind of candid assessment is rarer still among Africa's friends and boosters in the West. Instead of straight talk about Africa, you're more likely to get doublespeak, apologies, excuses—and above all, hypocrisy.

It's one of the things I found most frustrating about Africa, the unwillingness of even some of the most seasoned academics and "Africa experts" to give me their honest, coldhearted, unsentimental assessment of the continent and its problems. When it came to discussing the ruthlessness of the dictators, the difficulty of democracy finding a foothold, the ever-present problem of tribalism, Africa has consistently been held to a double standard, an "African standard." There's a reluctance to push too hard, too fast for reform. There is a tendency not to want to criticize too openly, too harshly.

The reason, of course, is that Africans are black. Too much criticism from white countries in the West comes dangerously close to sounding racist. And African leaders seem willing enough to play that card, constantly raising the specter of "neocolonialism." I remember the Kenyan foreign minister, on my first day in Africa, lambasting the American ambassador for having "the mentality of a slave owner." It was a well-targeted jibe, aimed at playing on that greatest of white fears: the appearance of sounding racist.

As I see it, the reluctance to talk straight about Africa is itself the greater disservice. The old Cold War days of coddling dictators may be over, but African strongmen still aren't pushed very hard. They aren't pushed hard to get off the aid-dollar dole, and they certainly aren't forced to follow accepted international behavior when it comes to the treatment of their own citizens.

If I sound tired of all the old excuses, it may be because I've heard so many of them before. Or variations on a theme, in a different context. And I'm not just talking about Africa here—I'm talking about America, too.

Ever try to have a meaningful conversation in America about the problems of the black underclass? About drug abuse and teenage pregnancy in black neighborhoods? About the breakdown of the black family, the school dropout rates, the spiraling black-on-black crime? Daniel Patrick Moynihan tried, a long time ago, before he was a senator, when he warned about the disintegration of black families. And did he get trounced—branded a racist and worse. But go back and look now at what he said; sounds to me like Pat had that one just about right, and way before such talk was fashionable.

If white people are uncomfortable talking about problems plaguing the black community, you sure as hell don't find much straight talk among blacks themselves. I try to talk about these things all the time, every time I'm back in Detroit for one of those family holiday gatherings. I hear a lot of talk about white racism. I hear all about Jim Crow and legal segregation and unfair housing practices and all the rest. I hear a lot of excuses, but not much more—and what I hear is mostly backward-looking, not inward-looking.

It seems to me that if the race is ever going to progress, we might start by admitting that the enemy is within.

My father is a straight talker; not much formal education, a few years of college, some union training courses. But he's extremely well read, he has a keen knowledge of history, and he can sure cut through the crap to reach straight to the heart of a problem. Once when I was home from Asia and we were sitting around the dining table for a cousin's Thanksgiving turkey, I decided to deliberately broach a pretty delicate subject, just to see what responses I'd get.

I had noticed a real boom in Korean-run grocery stores and small department stores in the old neighborhood. The Koreans had bought up a lot of those old burned-out and abandoned shop fronts and turned them into profitable businesses. They worked long hours, employing mostly family members, especially behind the cash register. Why is it, I asked between helpings of turkey and stuffing, that the new immigrants to America can come into black neighborhoods and prosper, while blacks who have been here for four hundred years are still stuck on the bottom rung of the ladder? Then I told the story of a Vietnamese American friend of mine now living in Houston. She came here in 1975 when she was about nine years old, not speaking a word of English. Her family lost pretty much everything when the communists marched into Saigon, and had to start from scratch. But my friend graduated from a good university, went on to earn a master's degree, and had just been hired by a big Houston-based energy company.

Why can an immigrant kid who didn't even speak English twenty years ago do so well in the system, I asked, when so many blacks are still struggling on the streets, hustling just trying to make ends meet?

Boy, did I cause a moment of silence with that one, and they weren't pausing to bless the turkey. But it was my old man who spoke up, came to the rescue, and his blunt manner hadn't been made any smoother by his seventy-plus years. "Because," he said, "those black folks you see out there on the streets think the white man owes them something. They're still waiting for that twenty acres and a mule!"

My dad has never met Yoweri Museveni, probably never will. But I know that would be a great dinnertime conversation—no bullshit, just a lot of straight talk.

In Africa, there's a lot of that same backward-looking attitude. Most Africans were born in independent black countries, but their leaders still harp about colonialism they way black America's self-described "leaders" like to talk about slavery and Jim Crow. There's another similarity, too: Black African leaders talk about foreign aid as if they're entitled to it—it's something that is *due* to Africa, with no strings attached—the same way many American blacks see government assistance programs as a kind of entitlement of birth. In both cases, you're left with black people wallowing in a safety net of dependency.

In that sense, I guess some of the old African tyrants are right—there really is a white conspiracy out there that keeps black people down. Only it's not the conspiracy they're probably thinking of, but it's so broad and so insidious that it makes The Plan look like kid stuff. What I'm talking about is the grand conspiracy of silence, a collective willingness of white people in the West to bury their heads when the talk turns to Africa. It's so pervasive that even the word "tribe" gives some white people the jitters because they think it's racially laden, condescending. The more polite term now is "indigenous ethnic group."

Of course blacks, too, are unindicted coconspirators in this grand silence. Here I'm talking about those self-anointed spokesmen who purport to represent all of black America, as if we were a unified group with a single worldview. They make their ritual demands for debt relief. They call for ever-increasing amounts of foreign aid to these corrupt little black potentates. They have even now begun trumpeting the call for the United States to pay "reparations" to African countries for the past crime of slavery—even though some of the traditional African rulers of the time were themselves guilty of complicity in the slave trade, rounding up slaves from the interior for the white traders who created a booming market for humans. All of this talk about Africa skirts the real issue—the need for a critical reexamination of independent Africa's internal failings. What's missing is the straight talk.

But then, how can Americans talk straight about Africa when we still can't talk straight about race among ourselves?

Africans might start the process, the reexamination, by taking a cold, hard look at themselves. They might begin by looking at their own maddening propensity to accept all kinds of suffering while waiting for some outside deliverance.

As I traveled this continent, one of the questions always nagging me was this: Why don't Africans stand up more for themselves in the face of this glaring injustice? As a reporter, I saw people take to the streets against authoritarianism and oppression in Haiti, and later in Burma. I got a glimpse of the tail end of the popular protests that changed the system in South Korea. Thanks to CNN, I've been an armchair eyewitness to revolutions that toppled dictatorships across Eastern Europe and in the former Soviet Union. But in Africa, it's a rarity to see people take to the streets for their rights. In Africa, there is no People Power.

In Zaire, I once asked an opposition leader named Poppa Ileo, an elderly patriarch of the anti-Mobutu forces, to explain to me this odd absence of popular protest. What I got was a tirade about how it was America's job, not that of the Zaireans, to get rid of the dictator created by U.S. policy.

"Mobutu's military is killing the Zairean people," he said. "When the Iraqis began killing the Kurds, what did the Americans do? According to the Americans, we must not be people, because we are being killed by the army. If five white people, Europeans, are killed, there would be foreign troops here. But hundreds of Zaireans are being killed. The Americans are the champions of democracy and human rights. Because of the United States, there are many changes in Eastern Europe. Communism has broken down. Democracy is blooming everywhere.

"They aid Russia, they aid Poland because of the democracy movement. Now the movement is happening in Africa. But here in Zaire, the government is blocking democracy. Mobutu is a product of the Americans. The Zairean people want democracy, but America is not helping them. I want the United States to do what it has done in other countries where human rights are not respected. With Marcos, Duvalier, Noriega—it's always been the Americans. America is a leader in the world. People are saying, 'If you are a friend, help me!'"

I was feeling annoyed. Of course I knew the history of the CIA's complicity in the overthrow and assassination of Zaire's independence hero, Patrice Lumumba. But that was thirty years ago! I sought the advice of my friend Ipakala Abeiye Mobiko, who edits a little weekly newspaper called *La Reference Plus,* a consistent advocate for political reform in Zaire. Mobutu sees it as a mouthpiece for his political opponents. I went looking for Mobiko in his usual place, the second floor of a rundown building at a congested traffic circle. This time, though, his office wasn't there; in its place was a burned-out shell, with only the newspaper's charred name on what was left of the door. When I finally found him, Mobiko was working out of the front room of his small house—gamely putting together a newspaper with reporters and editors seated around an oblong table in the living room, banging on old manual typewriters.

Mobiko described how the soldiers came to the office on a Thursday, at seven or eight at night. First they shot their way inside. Then they looted it bare, carting away the tables and chairs and file cabinets and typewriters. What they couldn't carry, they simply destroyed, using their rifle butts as sledgehammers. And as they left, they poured gasoline and set the office on fire, a clear message from President Mobutu.

"The problem of Mobutu is difficult to solve just here," he told me. "The Zairean people believe that if Mobutu is still in power, it is with the help of the United States. Bill Clinton said one of the major problems he had to face was getting rid of these dictators all over the world. Well, people are still waiting for Bill Clinton to live up to his promise."

I was growing angry now, and desperately in need of a more intelligent assessment. Eventually, I spoke with Father Gode Iwele, a small, serious, and scholarly Catholic priest whom I sought out on several trips to Zaire. On one visit, I had asked him about this question of Zaireans constantly revisiting the past, and still waiting for others, particularly the Americans, to deliver them from Mobutu, when the opposition leaders themselves were never able to deliver more than a few hundred protesters onto the streets. Father Gode listened to me vent my frustration, then said, "People are convinced that the Americans are supporting Mobutu, and if the Americans decide to put him away, he cannot stay there any longer. But change cannot happen in this country by putting our hope on foreign countries. This is a Zairean problem."

I next saw Father Gode several months later, after yet another wave of violent rioting and looting by unpaid soldiers—and this time one of the victims was the French ambassador, shot dead while watching the chaos from his office window. A political stalemate had dragged on for more than a year, and the elephant grass overgrowing the capital had by now almost obscured the abandoned government buildings. Malnutrition had grown more serious, too, and health experts were warning about the return of sleeping sickness. Out in the eastern part of the country, in a place called Likasi, Mobutu's allies were engaged in a vicious new round of ethnic cleansing, rooting out the Kasai population, herding them on trains, shipping them out with no place to go. Some thirty thousand Kasaians were living in a tent city hastily erected by the International Red Cross. And still Zaireans had not taken to the streets against Mobutu. They were still waiting for the United States to bring them deliverance.

This time Father Gode knew what was on my mind. "Each people has its identity and its culture," he told me. "The people of Zaire are peaceful. They don't like war. Second, they are somehow realistic. In South Africa, there was suffering, but the government there still had some respect for human beings. Here, if you go out into the streets, you will just be killed. My own position is that it would not be prudent to make people go into the streets. We have a lot of people dying already. There's no medicine in the hospitals. They would just build higher walls out of the dead bodies."

On that same trip, I put the same question to a reporter friend named Jean-Louis Katambwa, whose nickname was "Mike." He was working for *Umoja,* a solidly anti-Mobutu newspaper in Kinshasa. He was laying on me his wearingly familiar line about CIA involvement in the overthrow of Lumumba, and why it was America's responsibility today to remove Mobutu. "You Americans, you have to help us," he said. "What did you do in countries with other dictators? You took the dictators away! Why don't you help the Zaireans take this dictator away? He is there now, deep in the jungle. Please help us, America. You did it with Marcos. What the Zairean population is asking is for you to help us."

At that point I interrupted him. Where, I asked him, was the People Power? If Mobutu is so unpopular, why aren't there a million people out there right now marching in the streets against him. Why should my country help you when you are not out there trying to help yourselves?

I was really angry now, shaking, slapping his desktop with my palm. Mike could see clearly that this was bugging me, and he paused for a moment, mulling over my question. Then he shifted gears a bit.

"People in Zaire, especially in Kinshasa, are not accustomed to taking to the streets," he said at last. "People are hungry. It's a problem of habit here. They want to take to the streets. But if they take to the streets today, then tomorrow they will be tired." Tired, beaten down from just trying to survive, unwilling to be mowed down by soldiers with machine guns.

"It's a problem of education," Mike continued. "Don't take the example of the Philippines. We have our own customs here. It's a problem of mentality. The process of protesting for democracy takes a long time. Step by step. It's like a person in a dream, just waking up."

* * *

But some are starting to wake up. It was one of the rare heartening things about Africa, meeting those few brave, struggling, ordinary Africans—politicians, yes, but also the doctors and priests, the newspaper editors and teachers and just plain folks—who were out there every day, teaching kids in a classroom under a tree with no books or paper, organizing a union, starting up a new newspaper, or opening a walk-in clinic where prostitutes could go for condoms before they hit the streets. As I met some of them, I caught a glimpse of that missing ray of hope. I also saw in their stories the insurmountable odds.

Eugene Nzila is the director of Project SIDA (AIDS in French), once one of the most respected, widely recognized AIDS research programs in Africa. He was the doctor who sold condoms to the Zairean prostitutes for two cents each, trying to instill a sense of responsibility and to stem the tide of the pandemic. At its peak, Project SIDA employed some thirty physicians and received $4 million in international support. But Nzila's office is largely deserted now. The computers are still there, but its links to the global database have been shut down since the office has no working telephone line. The staff hasn't been paid for months and most have stopped showing up; Nzila himself still comes to the office, trying to keep the electricity on to protect the precious blood samples that need constant refrigeration. He is hoping, praying, that perhaps someday the project can be restarted.

But the project has become another classic example of the rot that has infected what could potentially be Africa's wealthiest country. Nothing works here now—not the schools, where the teachers are unpaid; not the public hospitals, where patients must pay cash up front to get doctors to treat them. Government bureaucrats don't bother showing up at empty, cavernous offices; if you need an official permit or stamp, you find the officer in charge at his home and pay him cash for the required signature or rubber stamp. Not even the police and soldiers are paid, and most of them now moonlight as security guards, or more often just extort passersby or stage bloody street riots. It's privatization run amok.

The inmates in the jail are starving because the prison system has no money to feed them. The animals in the zoo are starving. The food situation in the capital is now so desperate that residents are digging into the ground for roots to eat and others are planting crops along little strips and patches of public grass. "Precolonial" is how one British resident of Kinshasa described the country.

And yet Eugene Nzila still dutifully comes in to his office every morning. Of course, he has no salary, so he has adopted the Zairean habit of skipping meals every other day. I ask him how he survives, and he laughs at the stupidity of my question. "I don't survive!" he says. "I'm starving!"

Edward Oyugi is not a criminal, not even a political dissident, certainly not a rabble-rouser. He's simply an academic, a professor of psychology in Nairobi, another African trying to wake people up. For his efforts, he's spent enough time in prisons to be considered something of an expert on the Kenyan penal system. He can tell you about the prison on the coast, where he was kept in isolation in a swelteringly hot cell, locked indoors day and night for four long years, with nothing to read but his Bible.

And his crime? He ran afoul of President Daniel arap Moi, who saw the universities as a major source of subversion. Oyugi was teaching at Kenyatta University when he was elected to the staff union at the university in the late 1970s, at a time when student demonstrations were taking on an antigovernment tone. Moi began an effort to weed out the so-called radical elements on the campus, and Oyugi and three others were arrested and charged with having a "seditious" document in their possession.

Oyugi was released after he went on a hunger strike, but then he was blacklisted from the system and unable to work. So like others among Kenya's best and brightest, Oyugi left, for Germany. He returned a year later, when he was allowed to resume his old post at Kenyatta, but in 1990, with multiparty fever sweeping the country, he was arrested again, no evidence, no case, just plain harrassment. This time charged with trying to overthrow the government. He was sentenced to seven years in prison, but the charges were obviously fabricated and later dropped on appeal. But he had already spent more time in jail awaiting the reversal, and when he was released he was again barred from taking up his old teaching position.

Edward Oyugi today may be a beaten man, unemployed, battered down by an unjust system and a ruthless tyrant. But he's not bitter. He's soft-spoken, self-deprecating even. Most days he just "scavenges around," he says, trying to find a few consulting jobs, trying to make a little money here, a little there, enough to buy food to eat. If he feels any remorse, it's not for himself but for Kenya's educational system and how Moi has managed to completely destroy it, bankrupting the country's future. "Most of the good teachers are gone," he says. "The ones who remain here are mostly sycophants who go to him for money. They don't publish anything. They don't produce any research. And there's no quality. So the universities are really destroyed.

"It will take a long time. There must be a new government favorable to academic freedom and respectful of the sovereignty of academic institutions. Moi is incapable of changing in the direction that would be favorable for academic institutions to flourish.

"We have lost about three generations," he says. "I see a complexity of problems that will take a long time to solve. It's really pathetic for the future of this country that the leaders should completely close their eyes."

Koigi wa Wamwere is a political activist, a member of Kenya's large Kikuyu tribe, a nemesis to President Moi and his KANU machine. Koigi is another brave and lonely soul standing against African injustice.

He has been in and out of prison for years, always for speaking out against dictatorship. He once fled to exile abroad, to Norway, when he got wind of a plot to kill him. He came back to Africa four years later, was abducted by Kenyan security agents, and charged with treason, but those charges, of course, were later dropped. In the meantime, Koigi has become founder of a new human rights group, called NDEHURIO, and he's conducting his own investigation into the government-orchestrated tribal clashes in the Rift Valley.

Koigi, along with two relatives and a friend, was arrested on a charge of masterminding a wildly concocted plot to raid a police station and steal weapons, supposedly to launch a new armed rebellion. But Moi was sure to leave nothing to chance. The presiding magistrate, William Tuiyot, a member of Moi's ethnic clan, prevented Koigi's defense lawyers from presenting their case, allowing a patently false government case built on lies to stand unrefuted. The discrepancies in the case against Koigi would have been laughable had he not been on trial for a capital offense. Medical examiners testified that one of the Koigi "raiders" shot dead at the police station the night of the raid had actually died the day before the incident took place; a second victim, pulled from a maize field, had been dead for a full month. The homemade pistol that the Koigi raiders supposedly used failed to work when it was presented as evidence in court. Witnesses could not identify suspects. Koigi even had an alibi: On the night of the supposed raid he was in Nairobi, at the home of respected human rights lawyer Gibson Kamau Kurai. But Tuiyot, that impartial arbiter of justice and seeker of truth, dismissed all the defense witnesses as "liars."

When Koigi was finally allowed to speak in his own defense, he presented an eloquent indictment of the kangaroo court that he knew would ultimately convict him. "I regret most strongly being tried by a court of law that is more of a court-martial," he said. The trial, the evidence against him, the fake raid, were all concocted by Moi, who saw Koigi as a threat and his thick dreadlocks as an intolerable act of radical defiance in a country that insists on conservative uniformity. Moi had earlier pledged to have Koigi's dreadlocks cut off, one way or another.

"If you want to kill a dog," Koigi went on, "give him a bad name." And here he proceeded to invoke the names of two other African heroes unjustly tried and convicted—Nelson Mandela and Kenya's independence leader, Jomo Kenyatta. "Why," he asked, "should a court in an independent Kenya be trying so hard to outperform colonial courts and courts of apartheid in perpetuating injustice? Such a court must surely be driven by that tribal hatred which has completely routed the rule of law in Rwanda, Somalia, and Liberia."

The truth is, Koigi concluded, "that though Kenya is independent and Africans in power today, you—a black African—will give us less justice because we are not your tribesmen than white colonialists gave Kenyatta, though Kenyatta was black and a colonial subject. . . .

"That President Moi will use a verdict of guilt against us to tell Kikuyus and other non-Kalenjin communities in Rift Valley who are in the opposition that they must either join KANU, quit Rift Valley if they don't, or risk being killed in tribal clashes or in prison through courts of law. . . .

"That President Moi will use a verdict of guilty against us to tell political opposition in this country that if one fails to agree with him, no amount of innocence, no written law or unwritten, no constitution, no amount of pleading for justice from any quarter and not even God will protect such a person from his wrath. This trial is therefore part of Moi's campaign to crush multiparty democracy in this country."

I wish I could say that Koigi's eloquence was heeded, that Tuiyot recognized the error of turning Kenya's courts into a tool of KANU. But this is Africa, and the good guys rarely win in Africa. Koigi was convicted—but of a lesser charge, which spared him the death penalty. He was given eight years in prison and six lashes of the cane. And Moi certainly got his wish—Koigi's dreadlocks were cut, I'm sure. And a prominent critic, a figure who might rally the opposition, has been locked away, well through the next scheduled elections.

I could go on and on. My notebooks overflow with tales of oppression, persecution, and injustice. So much that I sometimes wanted to punch a fist through the wall, but of course I knew that that wouldn't do any good. So instead my feelings just stay coiled up inside until another plane ride, another country, and the same injustice, the same unfairness, all over again.

* * *

Africans need to continue to wake up and listen to people like Koigi if they are ever to get on with improving their lives. Of that much, at least, I am sure. But for me, little else is so certain right now. That's because Africa has taken all my certainties, twisted them around and turned them inside out, and now I'm no longer sure what I really think.

I want to hate the dictators and believe in the brave Africans struggling for freedom. But with those rare exceptions, most Africans are not struggling; they have been too violently suppressed for too long, so many now see no other way except waiting for a big white marine in combat gear to come and rescue them from repression. I want to find heroes here among the ordinary decent Africans, but they infuriate me with their endless acquiescence to repression, their limitless tolerance, their excuses. Koigi wa Wamwere is locked away in Kenya, but there is not a peep of protest on the streets of Nairobi or Nakuru. An election is stolen in Cameroon, and a week later it's as if nothing at all happened, the Big Man's still there, always will be. The good guys aren't winning because a lot of them are no longer even willing to go on with the fight. Africa's injustices have turned me into a revolutionary, but there's no revolution to be fought, just more misery and despair. And excuses.

Except in South Africa. Yes, South Africa, the continent's great exception, the black hope. There, people did take to the streets, in Soweto and Sharpeville and all the other townships. South Africa's black masses showed they were willing to stand up against injustice, on their own with only rocks against automatic wapons, and the odds there seemed far more insurmountable. In South Africa, there were good guys and bad guys, a clear-cut case of black and white. And for once, the good guys finally did win.

If I was to find hope, I realized—if I was to stop this downward spiral of my own disillusionment—then I would have to head south.

9

Looking South, Looking North

"Keep your whites."

—MOZAMBICAN PRESIDENT
SAMORA MACHEL,
giving advice to Zimbabwean
prime minister Robert Mugabe

I GOT MOMENTARILY LOST driving around Johannesburg one night
and ended up in a high-speed car chase with two crazy white guys,
one of whom had just tried to put his fist through my window.

I was in South Africa for a brief two-week stint, filling in for
our regular Johannesburg correspondent, Paul Taylor, who was
taking a vacation break. I'd just had dinner with a friend and was

trying to navigate Johannesburg's unfamiliar streets, looking for the road that would take me back toward the freeway. I spotted the street I was looking for a few seconds too late, so I had to cut quickly across a lane of traffic. I also apparently cut across the path of the two white guys in a dark-colored sedan, and they weren't too pleased about being "dissed" by a black dude driving a sporty-looking new car.

They followed me for about a block, the driver honking his horn furiously and flashing his bright lights into my rearview mirror. When I was forced to stop at the next red light, the dark car whipped around fast in front of me, blocking me practically sideways so I couldn't go forward. Oh, shit, I thought to myself. Just what I don't need. It was a few months before South Africa's first all-race elections, and the country seemed at times teetering on the brink of civil war. There's a good chance these guys are armed, I thought.

As I was dreading what might come next, one of the white guys jumped out of the car, ran over to my side window, and started beating it with his fists like he was crazy. He punched my side-view mirror and slashed at the radio antenna. He was screaming like a crazy man, but I couldn't hear anything he was saying. The window was rolled up, and I was too busy thinking, how the hell do I get out of this one?

I jammed the car into reverse and made what I thought was a pretty impressive backwards maneuver, avoiding the guy who was banging at my window, jamming the gear into first, and swinging around the other car as fast as I could. I looked back and saw that they were soon following me again, and probably even angrier now that I'd given them the slip.

Head for Alex, I thought.

"Alex" is the popular nickname for the compact, squalid black township of Alexandria, one square mile of human misery housing four hundred thousand black men, women, and children in the shadows of the gleaming office towers, shopping centers, and well-manicured lawns of the white suburb called Sandton just across a four-lane highway. "Alex" had been declared a black area as far back as 1912, but around 1958, the architects of South Africa's apartheid policy realized that this large concentration of blacks was far too close to the city for comfort, so they embarked on a plan to remove the residents of Alex to the safer confines of faraway Soweto. When Alex's residents resisted, the authorities began forcibly removing them in 1966, and that policy lasted until Alexandria won a reprieve a dozen years later. And after the hated pass laws that restricted black movement were scrapped and blacks were allowed to live any-where in the city, Alex's population started to swell once again, mainly because of its choice location—a particular bonus for the black women housekeepers who had only to trudge across the high-way to catch a minivan taxi or maybe even walk to the houses they cleaned for well-to-do white people.

I had gone to Alex just that morning for a few interviews and to get a tour of the place from a local community organizer and peace activist, a man named Linda Twala. I knew basically how to get there, and I was pretty confident that a couple of white guys fol-lowing a black man in a car were unlikely to follow him all the way into a teeming black township. That was just the way it was in South Africa; blacks and whites lived separate lives, and whites particularly were terrified of treading where swarms of poor black people lived.

Not too different from Detroit, I thought to myself, amused.

It turns out I was right. The car on my tail followed me all the way along the highway until it became pretty clear that I was head-ing for Alex. I saw the headlights growing dimmer and dimmer in my rearview mirror, the car falling farther and farther behind, until it finally disappeared.

I breathed an audible sigh of relief and was surprised at how fast my heart was racing. I looked for the first convenient place to make a U-turn to head back to the "safety" of the white suburbs. The two white guys pursuing me probably didn't know it, but I had no particular interest in driving into Alex at night either. Truth is, I, too, was terrified.

Ironic, isn't it? Here I am, a black man in South Africa, and at the first hint of trouble from whites, I look for safety in numbers from my own kind, in Alex. My assumption was that if the township residents saw a black guy obviously in a jam, being pursued by a couple of white toughs, they would no doubt jump to my aid simply out of black solidarity; those two white guys would have been lucky to make it out of there alive.

But me, driving alone into Alex at night? Sorry, but no way. No solidarity then, I was sure; those same township blacks who might have jumped to my aid against the common white enemy would likely just as soon put a brick aside my head and leave me lying in a ditch for the keys to the car and the wallet in my pocket.

Funny place, South Africa. Its weird pathologies force people into this kind of racial groupthink. Since I was only there for brief trips, I ended up spending most of my time in Johannesburg in the comfortable and familiar air-conditioned shopping malls, the trendy restaurants of the north suburbs, and at the dinner parties of white friends and colleagues debating whether or not the country was set to slide to hell under Nelson Mandela, its first black president. It was similar to the situation I found myself in after first landing in Kenya. But I hadn't been in South Africa long before I, too, had fallen into that same kind of racial groupthink, heading for Alex, looking for shelter from my black kinfolk, as soon as I felt under threat.

I thought about that little incident for quite a long time afterward—not because the scene itself was so important or dramatic, because I'm sure it happened all the time in South Africa, but for what it represented. All my life, growing up as a black kid in a white country, I've always resisted and resented the notion that I was supposed to take sides. I had always tried to avoid being defined by the color of my skin, remembering, I suppose, Martin Luther King's vision that it was supposed to be the content of your character that mattered. That was why I chafed at the suggestion that I was supposed to be a "black reporter," not simply a good reporter. And in

Africa, it was why I refused to be lured by the various African despots and their spokesmen who suggested somehow that as a black reporter, I was supposed to report more favorably on them, that I was somehow supposed to understand. I wasn't going to be pigeonholed or forced onto any side.

Yet South Africa managed to turn all my presuppositions on their head. Here, there's no getting around the fact that everyone—myself included—is defined and categorized according to the color of his skin.

In those months before the election, South Africa was on the precipice. Even though the plan for ending white rule and electing the first black government was already in place, the country was very much in danger of sliding into a full-scale race war. Fortunately, that never happened. But during those precarious months, more than once I found myself asking: If I were in Johannesburg and a race war erupted, which side would I be on? As a reporter, of course, we're supposed to be neutral, to be able to cover all sides of a conflict. But a race war? Would a black American reporter be able to stay neutral in that kind of conflict? Could I possibly expect to be recognized as an outsider, a mere observer? Or would I find myself again retreating to the "security" of Alex? Was there any doubt, really, which side I would be on?

I traveled to South Africa four times—twice before the 1994 elections that brought Mandela and the ANC to power, and twice afterward. My time was way too short to gain more than a superficial impression, and to unravel the many layers of complexity of a huge and complicated place. But with each trip, I became more fascinated and perplexed by the place. On one level, South Africa was the one place on the continent that looked and smelled most like home, like America. From the moment you arrive at the modern Jan Smuts International Airport and breeze through the refreshingly efficient customs and immigration procedures, to the time when you are barreling along one of the supermodern freeways with the skyline of Johannesburg visible in the distance, you have the impression that this could easily be some midsized midwestern American city. The shopping malls—and Johannesburg is indeed a city of shopping malls—all have that identical look of shopping malls everywhere from D.C. to Detroit to Dallas. In fact, in one of white Johannesburg's upscale shopping malls, there is very little to remind a visitor that this indeed is Africa, except for the odd shop here or there selling African artifacts and souvenirs at inflated prices.

But if this is a Western, Americanized city, it's one that's been transplanted to the middle of a black country on a black continent, and you can be reminded of that crucial fact pretty quickly. As much as white South Africa has tried to insulate itself, it doesn't take long for Africa to intrude. This is one place on the globe where the developed world and the developing one exist, literally, on top of each other, cheek to cheek, and that volatile mixture is as comical as it often is bizarre.

On my first day working in the *Post*'s South Africa bureau, an urgent bulletin came over the South African Press Association wire: An unidentified gunman or gunmen with at least one AK-47 assault rifle had just opened fire on a group of black workers on their day off who were holding a Sunday meeting of their burial society, kind of an employee-run insurance fund that pays for the funerals of members of their families. It had happened in the eastern suburbs, in Germiston, at the Scaw Metals steel mill in the gritty industrial belt about nine miles outside the city. Some of the victims had been outside the plant, eating their lunch and drinking. At the initial count, at least twelve people were killed instantly and twenty more wounded, and an hour after the shootings the bodies could still be seen lying around the cement area in front of the factory.

The carnage itself did not strike me as odd—or even particularly newsworthy at the time, since this kind of violence had become commonplace in South Africa in the months before the elections. Most of the bloodshed was caused by the ongoing political war between supporters of Mandela's African National Congress and the rival Inkatha Freedom Party, or IFP, the largely Zulu party of Chief Mangosuthu Buthelezi; it would be revealed only much later—even though the ANC insisted as much at the time—that much of the violence was being orchestrated behind the scenes by a hard-line "third force" within South Africa's white security and intelligence branch. Inkatha was still opposed to the planned elections—Buthelezi dropped his boycott and joined in only at the last minute—and gun battles and massacres like the one outside the Scaw Metals steel mill had become an almost daily occurrence. In fact, that Sunday's shooting took place just a mile from the spot where, only a month or so earlier, seven Zulu-speaking IFP supporters had been dragged out of a minibus and shot to death by unidentified black gunmen.

Maybe I had already been on the continent too long, but to me this kind of violence was part and parcel of an African election. And twelve people killed didn't seem like a particularly large death toll by local standards. It was certainly fewer people than had been killed in any of Kenya's government-orchestrated outbursts of tribal slaughter in the Rift Valley. A dozen dead was more like the toll from a Saturday night barroom brawl in Bujumbura.

No. What surprised me was not the crime itself but the response of the police. The policemen, mostly officious-looking white officers with ruddy complexions—came and did what you might expect police to do in any midwestern American city where a crime has occurred. They cordoned off the area with police tape. They marked the spots on the ground where the victims had fallen. They combed the area apparently looking for fingerprints or whatever it is police technicians in South Africa look for. And an officious-looking senior policeman stood before the television cameras, looking somber but stern, and promising a "full investigation" to apprehend the perpetrators of this brutal, heinous attack.

I almost burst out laughing at the ridiculousness of the scene, which was absurd on several levels. First, there was the strong possibility—no, likelihood—that some of those same cops in white shirts had provided the weapons and the getaway vehicles to the killers. And of course there was the other basic fact that the South Africa Police, or SAP, had to be one of the world's most incompetent when it came to detective work or rudimentary crime-solving. For years, the SAP was mainly a tool of antiblack repression, and as a result, the officers and recruits had little training in even the basics of police work. In the old days of pass laws and influx controls under apartheid, "crime-solving" meant that if you saw a black on the streets at sundown, you hauled him in to jail. Once pass laws were abolished with the breakdown of "petty apartheid," the SAP was at a loss.

But what really struck me watching that scene was the lunacy of the pretense. This crime was never going to be solved! This was, after all, Africa, and crimes similar to this one happened every day— more nameless, faceless victims for the tally sheets.

I was reminded of a line out of the movie *Apocalypse Now*—a film loosely based on the Joseph Conrad novel *Heart of Darkness*—about the evil lurking in the mysterious Belgian Congo. In the movie, Martin Sheen, playing a U.S. Army intelligence officer, is going up the river, into Cambodia, to assassinate the renegade Colonel Kurtz, who went overboard after being charged with torturing and killing suspected Vietcong spies. Sheen, as the narrator, deadpans that charging a man with murder in this place is like handing out speeding tickets at the Indy 500. And that's exactly how I felt watching those white police officers diligently going about their "investigation" of what was basically just another African slaughter—and one that the police themselves may have orchestrated. You don't go out and catch guys with AK-47s and ski masks in Africa—you just bury the dead and move on.

But that was what was so different about this place, about South Africa. The whites here were living in a totally different world, a world where you really did go out and put down police marker tape and chalk outlines around the bodies, where you did find out the victims' names before you dumped them into mass graves, and where you actually did launch investigations and make righteous promises—no matter how disingenuous—to bring the perpetrators to justice. I was watching a collision between two different sets of values, the "Western" one and the "African" one. The "real" Africa, the Africa I had seen further north, was closing in fast on their insulated little world here, and they weren't quite willing to admit it. In South Africa, they still tried to retain some pretense of Western sensibilities and values; in South Africa, they were still counting the bodies.

There were of course other, more compelling reasons besides the development of the physical infrastructure why South Africa in those days looked a lot like America. Perhaps most important, the two countries shared a similar history of white racial oppression and legal discrimination against blacks, but with one key distinction—in the United States, blacks are a small minority while in South Africa, blacks are by far the majority. That difference is central for one major reason—in America, the white majority could, and did, eventually accede to black demands for voting rights and equal protections under the law, without any real fear of losing its own power. In South Africa, the reverse seemed largely true: Ceding voting rights to blacks meant the end of white domination, and that was something many whites, no matter how much they professed concern with the black condition, were loath to accept.

Trying to understand white attitudes, to really discern the roots of the racism—maybe to find some parallels to the United States—became a matter of intense interest to me. Maybe I found it so curious because on the surface it really did seem like a bit of an oxymoron: How could a white person living in Africa hate black people? And if he did hate black people, why the hell would he live on a black continent, surrounded by four hundred million of them? Racial attitudes in a place like South Africa seemed to me too complicated to sum up with simplistic, dismissive phrases like "white racism." That seemed like the symptom of the problem, but not necessarily the cause itself.

Still, the simple "all whites in South Africa are racist" explanation was the one I wanted to believe, at least when I first set foot in the place. The situation would be a lot easier to comprehend, after all, if blind racism itself was what had driven the white minority to impose a system as brutal as apartheid. And when I arrived, I found myself walking around with a kind of emotional chip on my shoulder. I was nervous, but maybe after my little car-chase escapade I felt a little bit emboldened. I also relished the opportunity for a firsthand encounter with a white racist, in one of those trendy shopping mall restaurants in the north suburbs, or standing waiting to be served in one of the bars in the yuppie market theater district downtown. My ears were attuned to any possible whispered slight, and I watched closely for any raised eyebrows or looks of alarm whenever I entered a bank to change money, or a curio shop to browse at postcards.

If I was anxious and on guard—and I was still a bit jittery after the car chase—it was because I came armed with a litany of tales of abuse that seemed to me to define the way South African whites regarded the black majority. Like the story of the white couple who got angry when their purebred dog mated with the dog of a black man, so they killed the black man, and actually got lenient treatment from a sympathetic white judge and a white-dominated judicial system. The white killers were Rhodesian transplants who had moved to this frontier holdout of white racism as their own country joined the ranks of black-run states.

South Africa had become the final bastion for all the white racists of the world, the supremacist scum who had descended here from points farther north on the map as country after country underwent the change from white colonial domination to black rule. Some whites, like those in Kenya, had opted to stay, had taken Kenyan citizenship, and were content to remain quietly grumbling about how much better life was in the "old days." But others had packed up and fled in the dead of night across the border to Tanzania, to Zambia, and finally to Rhodesia. Then Rhodesia had become the last stand for white supremacy in Africa, but that, too, changed in 1980 with the signing of the Lancaster House accords, which paved the way for the first democratic, all-race elections and transformed Rhodesia into the independent black nation of Zimbabwe. Again, many whites chose to flee, some to Australia and

New Zealand, but many others farther south, to South Africa, where their backs were now to the ocean and where they decided to stake out what must truly be the final stand of the white man in Africa. And there they were joined by an unsavory collection of Eastern European fascists, racists, Nazis, and skinheads all huddled there together on the southernmost tip of the world's black continent, with Africa encroaching on their protected white universe more and more each day.

That was what was running through my mind as I wandered around South Africa—a black American in the last bastion of white supremacy. These are the world's craziest white people, I thought, and they are really going to hate this black dude from America because I represent the future they despise.

For the most part, though, I was the one who was disillusioned. My car chase notwithstanding, I couldn't find the fight I came looking for. In fact, more disappointing and confusing in a way, the white South Africans I encountered were quite courteous and polite. Almost instantly they knew from my accent that I wasn't from the place, and they would begin with the basics. Where are you from? How long have you been here? And then invariably they would want to know what Americans thought of the situation in South Africa and how I thought things would turn out. It was almost as if they were looking for reassurance.

On my first day in Johannesburg, I started feeling a niggling pain in my jaw, sort of behind my bottom row of teeth and extending all the way up into my ear. After a few days, the pain became intense, and when I couldn't stand it anymore, I went to a doctor. A white doctor in the suburb of Richmond gave me only a cursory examination, and then told me that the problem was an infection in the spot where a long-removed wisdom tooth had been. He immediately sent me off to a dentist for emergency root-canal work.

The dentist's office was above a movie theater in a quaint-looking low-rise suburban community called Norwood, not far from where I was staying. And quite frankly, I was terrified. What if this guy is a white supremacist? What if he's never before treated a black patient and he doesn't want to stick his white fingers into my black mouth? What if he's one of those whites who can't stand the thought of the white man in Africa ceding power to the black majority, and he will see in me—a well-dressed black man from America—all of his internal angst about black political aspirations? I remembered the movie *Marathon Man*, where the evil dentist took the drill to Dustin Hoffman in what must have been the most excruciating form of on-screen torture I could imagine. I decided I really didn't want to go through with my trip to the dentist. I parked my car and walked around the block a couple of times, until finally the pain in my jaw overcame the fear in the pit of my stomach. I went inside.

The dentist was not, in fact, an evil white supremacist, but a kindly fellow with a silver-gray beard who looked a lot like Santa Claus. He was also wearing a small strip of yellow ribbon on the breast pocket of his white coat—a sign that he was one of the silent majority of South Africans in favor of peace. And as he worked away in my mouth, he gave me a view of the local political scene that I found surprisingly insightful. The danger, he said, was from the extremists on both sides who were trying to sabotage the upcoming elections. The majority of whites had long ago accepted the need for change, and indeed had supported President F. W. de Klerk's reforms in an earlier whites-only referendum. But now the gun-toting white rejectionists in battle fatigues and ski masks, and the gun-toting black militiamen engaged in the running ANC-Inkatha feud, were through violence threatening to derail the country's well-orchestrated plans for peaceful evolution. And after a while, the dentist looked up at me and said, "But of course as a foreigner here, I suppose you think we're all crazy here."

Yes, I really did think South Africans were all crazy. Here they had built the most modern, best developed country on the continent, and now the white extremists seemed pretty hell-bent on destroying the whole thing, simply because in their blind racism they couldn't stomach the inevitability of black majority rule. They had relied on the time-honored practice of divide and rule, first dividing the black majority along ethnic and tribal lines with the ten so-called homelands, and then covertly orchestrating a decade-long dirty war between Inkatha and the ANC. And now those same simpleminded racists were smugly pointing to the black-on-black violence as proof-positive of their self-fullfilling prophecy that black rule would mean a slide to violence and anarchy. The South African press had already revealed the tip of the orchestration with the 1991 scandal called "Inkathagate"—hundreds of millions of dollars in covert payments from police slush funds to Inkatha and an affiliated labor union. And while the extent of the collusion would only come out later, there was already ample evidence that the police involvement was more direct than simple funding, like actually planning attacks, providing the weapons, even using official vehicles to shuttle IFP attackers to the site of their attacks. Thousands were being killed in the campaign of violence, and the country appeared for a while to be sliding into a civil war—and all because of the crazy white extremists who'd just as soon see the place collapse as turn over power to Nelson Mandela.

I also thought the blacks were equally crazy for allowing themselves to fall into the trap. If the white extremists' resort to the divide-and-rule strategy made me angry, what made me more furious still was seeing how easy it was for whites to stir up black emotions, to flip the switch and unleash the orgy of bloodshed. The violence soon turned into a series of tit-for-tat raids and assassinations that sullied both sides, the Inkatha as well as the ANC, which was staging its own retaliatory attacks in the townships. The warfare here was less about tribe than about power, and Buthelezi's fear that his own ethnic power base in KwaZulu/Natal would be eroded under an ANC-dominated government. But to me the troubling question was: Why did the black majority allow this to happen? Couldn't they see how their violent feuding was playing directly into the hands of the white right wing? Could they not unite behind a common enemy, at least bury their differences for the short term, until the ultimate goal—the end of white minority rule—was fully realized?

* * *

Perhaps much of my anger grew from my own perspective, and my view of the anti-apartheid struggle as not just for South Africa's black population but a struggle for the dignity of black people everywhere. I remember writing editorials for the student newspaper at the University of Michigan denouncing the racist regime in Pretoria and demanding the university divest itself of stocks in companies that failed to adopt the Sullivan Principles. From the time I had first developed a political consciousness, South Africa had loomed as the world's last great morality play, a noble struggle between good and evil, black and white—no ambiguities, only the certainties in my own mind. But now I was here, and I was watching with dismay as the struggle—my struggle—was being stained by the bloodshed of escalating violence. The realities were not as simple as I wanted, the complexities mind-rending. The bad guys were bad, that much was clear—but the good guys weren't all good—and sometimes it was difficult to remember who were the good guys in the first place.

Sometime later, I went to a business seminar where a mostly white crowd of a hundred or more executives and managers had gathered to hear a lecture from a black American psychiatrist and academic named Price Cobbs, who had coauthored a book called *Black Rage*. Cobbs's theme was affirmative action in America, and he was in South Africa to try to help these white professionals grapple with similar issues of workplace diversity and multiculturalism.

The crucial question, as Cobbs put it, was how South Africans together were going to be able to manage "that volatile interface between black rage and white fear." Black rage was understandable enough—it was the rage of being subjected to humiliating repression in their own country, a rage built up after decades of enduring a codified, legalized system of racial segregation. And white fear? "People have the fear that somehow their gardener is going to be the banker next Monday," as Cobbs put it.

I thought long and hard about that concept: black rage and white fear. Certainly black rage was evident—it was evident from the township uprisings that ultimately forced the former president, P. W. Botha, to warn his white countrymen to "adapt or die." And I also came to see the rising tide of black crime as a kind of expression of rage, a righting of the past wrong of apartheid. In fact, what I found difficult to understand was how such justifiable rage had been contained as well as it had, why hordes of blacks were not swarming over the north suburbs meting out bloody vengeance against every white family with a swimming pool and an electric fence.

When I had been in Alex, getting a township tour from Linda Twala, we had walked through a filthy squatter camp on the banks of a little river that was clogged with garbage and debris. And I asked him why it was that the black residents of Alex didn't just move en masse across that four-lane highway, away from the misery, and claim those shopping malls and spacious homes as their own. And all he could tell me was that it could indeed happen that way, one day, if the white people across the road did not start paying attention to the problems of these townships. "Across the road, you've got thousands of whites who don't know the living conditions here," Twala told me. "One day, if a fire breaks out, many blacks are going to start killing whites. One day, if people say, 'Enough is enough, here is our enemy,' then many innocent people will die.

"To cross over to the white area, you don't need a car," Twala observed, pointing out the high-rise hotel and shopping malls across the road. "You can walk—and carry your AK-47. And what could they do? Nothing. Many innocent people will die, even the ones who tried to give us food, because their color will be the same."

Black rage and white fear. Now it was starting to make some sense to me.

Black rage had gotten most of the world's attention, but I found white fear the more intriguing concept. Perhaps that was the core emotion I had been looking for to explain white racism in South Africa. It was fear. Fear of blacks. Fear of living as a tiny and privileged minority on a continent of four hundred million black people whom they had oppressed for three-and-a-half centuries. Fear now of living in a country run by blacks. Fear of black retribution for past injustices. Fear that South Africa would follow the path of other African countries. Fear of the future.

In his searing autobiographical book *My Traitor's Heart*, the white South African journalist Rian Malan describes in haunting prose his own dawning realization that despite a gnawing sense of revulsion at the injustices of his society, his fear—the fear of blacks—lay at the dark center of his own racial attitudes. "I sometimes think the fear was always with me, even when I was a child and loved all natives, indiscriminately," Malan writes. "It is the lot of children to be stalked by amorphous fears and nocturnal terrors, by the feeling that there is something out there in the dark, something threatening. It seems to me that must be true everywhere, but in South Africa's white suburbs, the terror always had a black face. You'd lie with your head under the covers, frozen with fear, listening to the window rattling in the wind, and you knew it was a black out there."

At another point in the book, Malan describes his fear of walking back to his car after a drinking binge with black friends in Soweto, and how the terror wells up inside of him—wildly, irrationally—when he passes a group of young blacks loitering on the roadside. "I had seen the fear for what it was," he writes, "and it became my constant companion. It came upon me whenever the black comrades punched the sky at the sight of me, when their stones thundered down on the roof of my car, when I couldn't understand what blacks were saying about me, when I searched the eyes of black hitchhikers, and even when I opened the newspapers. It doesn't help to say that the fear was irrational, or even psychotic. You are what you think, and white men who think blacks pose a mortal danger are in mortal danger. After that night, I knew there was no way to purge the black fear from my white heart. Unless I did that—unless we all did it—there was no hope for any of us. Whites and blacks would tear one another apart like dogs in a war that left the victor standing in a landscape of graves and ruins."

Strong words. But it helped me start understanding just a little of the fear that South Africa's white population was starting to feel.

Crime—violent, random crime—had long been a feature of daily life for South Africa's black majority. Blacks lived with crime every day in the lawless townships—and not just the political assassinations, but the armed robberies, the murders, the attacks on commuter trains, the gun battles between rival taxicab operators over the lucrative routes to shuttle black workers into Johannesburg. Under the white minority regime, crime, as long as it was confined to black townships, was rarely, if ever, investigated—out of sight and, so, out of mind. And since it was often difficult to untangle the political crimes from the ongoing township violence, many times the statistics were lumped together, painting a chilling picture of South Africa as one of the world's most dangerous countries, with some twenty thousand homicides each year, or about fifty-five people killed each and every day. Several surveys, based on police blotters, placed Johannesburg well ahead of New York, Los Angeles, and Rio de Janeiro for the number of murders per one hundred thousand inhabitants. Between 1990 and the fall of 1993, some 52,800 South Africans had died violently—more than twice the number of South Africans killed during the two world wars and just a few hundred short of the total casualties for the Boer War at the turn of the century.

But what was new was that South Africa's violence was spilling over the walls into South Africa's white community, particularly in Johannesburg's prosperous northern suburbs. The fear that blacks lived with every day was now entering the once-insulated world of white privilege. The pyschological sandbags that whites had erected to protect themselves from the country's endemic violence were quite quickly being washed away in an angry black surge, and that one-time seemingly powerful police force that was more used to oppressing black people than dealing with the mundane matters of crime prevention seemed incapable of coping. Crime was now an obsession among whites, the topic of almost every dinnertime conversation, every social gathering—much as it had been in Nairobi when I first arrived there and found a similarly besieged white expatriate community talking in hushed and fearful tones about the latest atrocities committed by the teeming masses beyond the walls. That it was black crime was left unsaid. But it was always understood.

There were, of course, lots of reasons for this sudden surge of crime into white neighborhoods, most of them rooted in the legacy of apartheid and the aftermath of the evil system's collapse. With freedom of movement, blacks could now go anywhere in their country, and areas once designated off-limits were suddenly teeming with black faces. With more movement, the yawning inequities between the white "haves" and the black "have-nots" became even more glaring. The liberation struggle, the white government's "total onslaught" campaign against anti-apartheid groups, and now the white-orchestrated dirty war between the ANC and Inkatha had all left the country awash in firearms. And years of strife, struggle, and school boycotts had produced in the townships a generation of unemployed, angry, bitter young men for whom crime against whites was just retribution. The hordes weren't yet crossing the highways with their AK-47s, like Linda Twala in Alex had warned me they could. But some were crossing over, one at a time, to take what they thought was theirs.

And yet the raw statistics on crime fail to paint the full picture of white fear. It was the stories, shown every day on television and recounted in everyday conversation, that fueled the white terror of the black onslaught. Like the story of the elderly white couple found tied and suffocated in their burglarized suburban home. Or the story of the American Fulbright scholar, Amy Biehl, a Californian who went to South Africa as an outspoken critic of apartheid and ended up being chased, stabbed, and beaten to death in a township outside of Cape Town by a black mob shouting the slogan of the militant Pan-Africanist Congress—"One settler, one bullet."

Of course Amy Biehl's death doesn't fall into the category of random criminal violence; she was killed specifically because she was white. And maybe that's why her death, more than the other daily incidents of crime and mayhem, terrified white South Africa even more. A black mob had set upon a white exchange student—

an American, no less—and killed her because she was in the wrong place at the wrong time, an incident that reached to the dreaded core of white terror—the fear of black retribution for decades of oppression, and whites being targeted randomly for their color.

It's a fear fueled by guilt, if nothing else. Even among those whites who did not support apartheid, there is still that nagging sense of guilt that they didn't do more to actively oppose it, that they let this evil system persist for as long as they did. I thought it would be revealing to write a story on white guilt and the heightened stress of the transition in South Africa, so I called a woman named Merle Friedman, who was director of the psychology department at the University of the Witwatersrand. She invited me over to her home, a rather grand and spacious affair behind a huge fence and up a long, narrow driveway. We sat on the verandah having drinks while she gave me her theory of white anxiety in black South Africa. "We're all frightened for our personal safety," she told me. "I don't walk anywhere anymore."

She continued, "I think whites are really frightened of their economic future and what they're going to be deprived of." And then she paused and added, "For most of us, it's unremitting guilt. After the Holocaust, people said they didn't understand. In a way, we, too, say we didn't know. But we knew a lot. You had to deny or pretend not to see what was going on. And the government did a very good job to help that, because the press was censored."

We sat there for a long time, sipping cold drinks from long glasses, and she told me more horrendous stories of crime, black-on-white, black-on-black, white-on-black, Asians being attacked, violence by or against mixed-race "coloreds"—South Africa was truly a racial hodgepodge. She talked of whites being killed in their homes by blacks, of carjackings in broad daylight, of "taxicab wars" in the black townships between rival minivan operators, of daring bank robberies—so many bank robberies that banks had begun having regular counseling sessions for employees. Friedman herself ran weekly "trauma clinics" in the black townships to try to help the black victims of violence who couldn't afford the fancy psychiatrists and counseling that whites in the suburbs might routinely seek out. She remembered one woman in particular, the lone survivor of a township massacre, who had been left for dead, dumped into a pit with the dead bodies of her friends and neighbors, and had to claw her way up from the pile. And when the woman related the story in Friedman's trauma clinic, she found herself again writhing on the floor from the pain of the memory.

The stress of the rising crime and the uncertainty was taking its toll. Suicides were up. Alcoholism was up. Divorce was up. There were a spate of home killings, white farmers going home at the end of the day, killing their entire families, then turning their guns on themselves. A doctor in the north suburbs, the one I first went to see when I had the problem with my teeth, told me he was prescribing more antidepressants than ever before.

And as Friedman and I sat there under the cool shade on the verandah, talking about a society splitting apart, what struck me most was the dissonance. Here we were talking about some pretty horrific goings-on from the peaceful, idyllic surroundings of the psychologist's front porch, surrounded by shrubbery and high trees, far removed from the "Africa" that was encroaching from somewhere just beyond the top of the high fence.

And then I felt an odd sensation stirring inside of me and I knew instantly that it was empathy.

That wasn't what I was supposed to feel. It wasn't the emotion I wanted to have, not here, not in South Africa, the last bastion of white supremacy. No, I was supposed to despise this place and dismiss all the white people as racist. But here I was, sitting on this verandah on a peaceful afternoon, actually feeling sorry for this white woman and her family because I know that everything they have—the house, the greenery, the high fence—is really just an illusion. It's an illusion because no matter how "Westernized" their lives seem, they live in Africa, and I know what darkness lurks out there, beyond the fence, beyond the borders, further north, in the "real Africa." My mind flashed back to all the scenes of misery and despair, to the faces of the starving people along the roadside in Somalia, and the wide-opened and pleading eyes of the young woman lying dead atop the pile of corpses in the Rwandan refugee camp at Goma. I see the photo of Kibassa Maliba's son, charred black from the flames that engulfed his body and killed him. The prison cells of Kigali filled with lifeless figures. And then I think of the ANC-Inkatha feud, and how South Africans seem to be taking their own country down that same, bloody path.

But then I start hating myself again. Certainly a black man cannot admit to harboring even the slightest iota of empathy for the perpetrators of apartheid, one of history's greatest evils. I wanted to feel no sympathy for these people, I didn't want to try to understand their position. It would be so much easier if South Africa were not such a confusing racial and tribal conundrum, but just a simple case of black and white, good and evil, the just and righteous cause triumphant in the face of the historic injustice. To think otherwise, to even raise questions, would be to diminish the nobility of the struggle against racial oppression.

After so much disillusionment, so much disappointment, in the black-ruled nations of Africa, I had so relished this chance to take a break, to come here to South Africa, to find for a change a story with a certain moral clarity. I had always envied those journalists who were based here, because they never had to deal with the more vexing emotional and moral dilemmas of black Africa, where the perpetrators were often indistinguishable from the victims. Such horrors existed here, too, of course—that ubiquitous "black-on-black violence," as we so often dubbed it in the press. But in South Africa, blacks killing blacks became the sideshow to the main event: the epic struggle of good against evil. Further north, in Somalia, in Rwanda, in Liberia, in Zaire, there was no main event—just the killings, the brutality, the sideshow as reality.

That was what I thought when I came here. South Africa would finally give me a chance to find some clarity, verify my own certainties. Yet here I was again, feeling confused and angry at myself for feeling that way. Hating those blacks involved in the ongoing violence for tarnishing my long-cherished notion of their epic struggle. Hating the Inkatha party and its leader, Buthelezi, for allowing himself to become a willing stooge of the evil regime. Hating the ANC for not being purer than pure, for having in its ranks young militants who put flaming tires around the necks of their rivals and engage in the same kind of bloody attacks as the other side. And I'm hating the whites—the psychiatrist, the dentist, all those shopkeepers who treated me gingerly—for not hating me, for not giving me an excuse to hate them.

South Africa may have been "Western," but it was, I decided, at its core more complex, more confusing—more African. No less than Somalia or Rwanda, South Africa defied all my preconceived notions and assumptions, mixing up my head by creating all these confusing paradoxes, and before I knew it, before I could stop it, I found myself thinking things that one shouldn't really be thinking, feeling what I know must not be felt.

"The decadence, the corruption, the falling of standards—things are not going well."

I am in Zimbabwe now, sitting on the living-room couch in the home of Ian Smith, the prime minister of what was called Rhodesia when this land was a breakaway British colony run by its defiant white settler minority. Smith is a very bitter man, that much is clear. And he has little good to say about the man who replaced him, Robert Mugabe, whom Smith still considers a communist, a dictator, and worse.

What a strange world this is. When I was a college newspaper editor at the University of Michigan in the 1970s, I used to write strident editorials railing against Ian Smith as the embodiment of stern-faced white racist intransigence. I remember the euphoria in our campus newsroom when the Lancaster House accords were announced, paving the way for the transition from Smith's evil regime to the independent black-run nation of Zimbabwe. And now, here I am, a black man, sitting in the living room of that hated icon of repression, sipping his coffee and taking notes while he rails on to me about all the problems black rule has wrought.

This seemed to me like an important stop to make in my understanding of Africa, especially South Africa. In my short time in Johannesburg, I heard a lot about all the problems happening "up north," as the rest of Africa was called, with hushed tones of trepidation bordering on outright dread. And of all those supposed hellholes "up north," Zimbabwe was most frequently mentioned as a place where whites had once been promised that lifestyles and living standards would not suffer under a black government. And Zimbabwe now was held out as everything South Africa had to fear—a place where everything familiar had collapsed. Dictatorship was encroaching; white land was slowly being confiscated by the communist ex-guerrillas in power; crime in the largest city, Harare, was rampant. Zimbabwe, in short, had become South Africa's worst nightmare.

Of course the real Zimbabwe that I discovered was nothing like these dark depictions. In its first decade of independence, from 1980 until 1991, Zimbabwe had averaged 3.6 percent economic growth per year—miraculous on a continent where the trend for many national economies was to contract. Adult illiteracy was down to under a third. Per capita GNP was about $570, more than twice the level of many other African countries. Zimbabwe still suffered from natural calamities, including a devastating drought in 1991, but it still had a lot it could boast about. Most impressively, it was one of the few African countries at peace with itself, displaying a remarkable measure of racial reconciliation. I was particularly impressed after combing through Harare's late-night discos and bars and seeing how black and white kids of all ages mingled easily. It seemed to me a model of how to overcome the past and really build a multiracial society.

Not, of course, according to Ian Smith. He was droning on about "standards." He was telling me that this had been the great fear of the white minority regime, and the main reason they had fought so hard in the fifteen-year guerrilla war to stop the encroachment of "Africa" onto their protected white universe. "We always had very high standards here," he was saying. "We wanted to maintain those standards."

I interrupted, "I've been to Zaire, Liberia, Somalia, Rwanda.

Surely you're not saying that Zimbabwe is now as bad as some of the other places in Africa."

To my surprise, Smith agreed. "Compared to all those other dreadful places, this is a good place," he said. "If you come from one of those places to the north, this place is more efficient and organized." The danger, he said, was slippage. Rwanda, Somalia, Liberia, Zaire, were never very far from the surface if you let things slide. Africa was always just around the corner.

After our interview, Smith offered to give me a ride back into town. As I stood in the driveway waiting for him to get ready, a friend of his, a white guy in a truck, pulled up to say hello to the former prime minister. The friend and I shook hands, and I told him I was a reporter just visiting from Kenya.

"Kenya, huh?" the white guy said. "Well, then, you know what we're worried about down here. Kenya! That place is really falling apart, isn't it? And that fellow up there, Moi, is a real bad one—worse than the fellow we've got here. He's just letting the place collapse up there. Shame, too. Well, we're trying to keep it from happening here."

I wanted to hate this guy, call him a racist, give him the line about how a black country falling apart under a black government is still better than blacks in Africa living under white repression. But at the same time, I also wanted to agree with him, to tell him, yes, you're right, Moi is ruining Kenya and it is a shame, and yes, you'd better watch it, because it can happen here too, because no one ever thought it would happen in all the other places where it did happen. But that's exactly what makes Africa so confusing. I wanted to say both of those things. But I didn't know which to say. So I said nothing—and hoped he didn't see me nodding my head in agreement. I know this probably sounds confusing—that's because it's confusing to me, too. Africa was like that, forever tearing apart my brain.

One of the dirty little secrets of Zimbabwe's success as an independent black nation is something that most blacks—Americans or

Africans—probably would rather not hear. It has something to do with a piece of advice that Mozambican president Samora Machel gave to Robert Mugabe well before independence. Machel told him simply, "Keep your whites."

Machel had learned this lesson the hard way, because when his country gained independence from Portugal in 1975, the whites packed up and left. Out of a population of some two hundred thousand Portuguese settlers, just twenty thousand stayed behind. And the whites that left took with them pretty much everything of value, leaving behind a ravaged country with virtually no infrastructure and only a handful of skilled or educated blacks. And it's not that Machel didn't try to convince the Portuguese settlers to stay. *Los Angeles Times* correspondent David Lamb, in his book *The Africans,* quotes Machel telling the Europeans after independence: "We want harmony among the races. For the sake of national construction, we must have the support of all people on every continent and of every race." But his plea fell on deaf ears. The Portuguese didn't believe there was any future for the white man in independent black Africa. So they left, and Mozambique was decimated.

And Mugabe, a protégé of Machel's who had kept sanctuary in Mozambique during his guerrilla war, learned the lesson well. When Zimbabwe became independent, Mugabe made sure to keep his whites—many of them, anyway—and the country managed to avoid that most common of the continent's ritualistic dances, the African Downhill Slide.

In the mid-1990s, there were still about a hundred thousand whites living in Zimbabwe, out of a population of some 11.2 million—less than half the pre-independence population, but still substantial. At the same time, some 60 percent of the country's most productive farmland was still in the hands of about 4,500 white farmers. The Lancaster House agreements had imposed a ten-year constitutional constraint on redistributing land, so that emotive issue was conveniently avoided for a decade. But in the early 1990s, with the expiration of that constitutional prohibition, black Zimbabweans became impatient. Land, after all, was one of the key issues that had fueled the fifteen-year guerrilla war, and the victors some fourteen years after independence were still waiting for their spoils. The government did make some early, tentative steps toward confiscating white land for redistribution, but most of those attempts were successfully bottled up in court challenges. A land tenure commission was set up to hash out the problem. But all the while, Mugabe remained ambivalent, recognizing, apparently, that despite the popular appeal of land confiscation, the white commercial farmers still constituted the backbone of Zimbabwe's economy.

The offices of the Zimbabwe Farmers Union are on the top floor of a building in the congested, bustling commercial heart of Harare. The ZFU represents the country's small-scale, black farmers, and is the African equivalent of the more powerful, predominantly white Commercial Farmers Union, representing the white commercial farmers. Funny how it is, a decade and a half after black rule, and you still have two separate farmers unions, one black, one white.

Emerson Zhou is an economist for the black union. When I climbed the stairs to the ZFU offices, I got mostly a few curious looks, and was told that the top officials I needed to see were either out of the office or too busy. Zhou was chosen to brief the American journalist, and we walked to a tiny, cluttered, and barely lit backroom office.

He treaded a careful line when describing for me the condition of black farmers in his country in the fourteen years since independence—much improved, with much left to be done. The most important thing, he said, was that Zimbabwe had achieved racial reconciliation. "It's a different racial environment," he said. But the biggest problem lingering was that blacks under a black government still didn't have their share of the economic pie. "There are a lot more blacks occupying high positions in business sectors," he said, "but from an ownership point of view, blacks are still in a peripheral kind of role."

Zhou recounted for me the familiar litany of Zimbabwe's problems—mostly the disaffection over the failure to redistribute more land to blacks, the lingering inequality between the privileged white minority and the impatient black majority. But would he have had it any other way, given the chaos that befell so many of Africa's other newly independent black states? "When one reads about what is happening in other places," he told me, "we seem to have a near perfect situation here."

One need not venture too far to find a pretty stark example of residual power of Zimbabwe's white establishment. In fact, just walk a few blocks to the rival headquarters of the white Commercial Farmers Union, which occupies a couple of floors of a sleek highrise. No walk-ins, there. When I called, a crisply curt and efficient secretary gave me a specific appointment time. My interview was with Jerry Grant, the deputy director, an affable enough fellow who instantly noted my accent and said, "You're obviously not from around here." Then he proceeded to speak quite candidly—far more frankly, I thought, than if his interviewer had been a black African instead of a black American.

Grant described to me the long exodus of white farmers during the guerrilla war and in the years immediately after independence, when Mugabe's chief political rival, Joshua Nkomo, refused to accept the 1980 election results and his supporters, from the Ndebele tribe, retreated to their stronghold of Matabeleland and launched a low-level campaign of terror. The "dissidents," as Mugabe dubbed the Ndebele guerrillas, sought to undercut the government by deliberately striking at the heart of the fragile new country's economy—its remaining white population. White farmers were attacked in their homes. White families were attacked while driving in their cars or riding buses. Grant estimates that more whites were killed in the Matabeleland tribal conflict than in the entire fifteen years of the liberation war that preceded it. The farmers union kept a pretty precise list of attacks—dates, places, names of whites who lost their lives. It may have been black Africa now, but the white people still counted their dead.

Mugabe eventually crushed the insurrection, and he did it the old-fashioned way—through brute force. In 1983 he unleashed his crack army unit, the North Korean–trained Fifth Brigade, which proceeded to lay waste to Matabeleland and the insurgents. Somewhere between five thousand and thirty thousand people were killed in what has come to be known as one of Africa's most brutal, and effective, counterinsurgency campaigns. Nobody knows the real number, because Zimbabwe had graduated into the ranks of an independent black African country, and one of the criteria for membership in the club is that you stop counting the bodies.

In those early days of independence, Zimbabwe looked likely to tumble down the same slope of bloodshed, chaos, and instability that has engulfed much of the rest of sub-Saharan Africa. If that war is not well remembered, it may be because not much got reported in Western newspapers; a lot of people were rooting for Zimbabwe as an African "success story." Its liberation war was particularly popular, especially on college campuses like mine, because it was one of the few clear-cut cases of black and white, good and evil. And Robert Mugabe was widely respected in Africanist circles abroad as one of the continent's most brilliant independence leaders. So why let the truth of a nasty guerrilla war and a brutal counterinsurgency campaign spoil the picture?

"We all thought it was heading for Zaire," Grant said, recalling those turbulent early days. "It could have easily gone that way." And why not, I asked him. He replied, "Our black people were very pragmatic. The black people were just as concerned as the white people about the future of the country. It could have gone wrong, but it went right, and I don't think it can go wrong now."

It seems I had found one of the few points on which blacks and whites and even Ian Smith could agree: They had seen what horrors lay "up north," in Africa, and it had frightened them into their senses. Now they were grateful that Zimbabwe, with all its faults, hadn't fallen down that abyss. Africa was there, briefly, pounding at the gates, but in Zimbabwe they had managed to keep the continent at bay.

Nelson Mandela spent twenty-seven years in prison, but he is one African leader who seems to understand well the lessons of Africa's sad history. Not only is he a hero to South Africa's black majority, but he also manages to cut a reassuring presence to jittery whites, convincing them that they, too, have a stake in the new South Africa.

A lesser politician may not be able to pull off that balancing act, between the angry young township blacks who want rapid change—the kind of kids Linda Twala in Alex told me might be ready to go over the highway and attack the white suburbs—and the white population looking for any excuse to say the country is heading downhill. With the blacks, Mandela's credibility grows out of his own moral authority, drawn from his twenty-seven years in an apartheid prison. Only Mandela can stand before an angry black crowd and calm them by asking if anyone there has suffered more than he. But for whites, he is also a kindly, soft-spoken, healing figure. As one white South African woman told me after the elections, "I'm so proud to be from a country with a president everyone else would like to have!"

I was able to get a glimpse of the Mandela magic only once, before he became president, when he held a press conference at the ANC headquarters at Shell House. The topic was an embarrassing one for the ANC, the release of a report detailing torture and even execution in some of the ANC guerrilla camps when the group was still in exile. The ANC "spin" on the revelations was to say that any disciplinary action against ANC members should be coupled with similar actions against whites in the apartheid system who abused human rights. It was an issue that threatened to undercut the ANC's moral standing—and add to my own despair about whether these were really the good guys—but Mandela handled it deftly.

"What you must appreciate is that the alleged abuses were committed in a state of siege," Mandela told the reporters packed into the Shell House conference room. "We don't think it is in the interests of justice for us to punish only a few individuals," he said, when far larger human rights abuses "have been committed as part of a systematic policy by the government of this country.

"We are looking at this matter globally," Mandela went on, in the kind of tone a teacher might use in lecturing a class. He said that the ANC was calling for the establishment of a commission to investigate all past human rights abuses, and to offer reparations to victims where necessary. Then, alluding to his own twenty-seven years as a prisoner, he added quietly, "Maybe I should apply for reparations!"

It was a brilliant performance, I thought. He was not a great speaker, but he sure knew how to mesmerize a room, even a room of cynical hacks. His very presence went a long way toward convincing me that if the good guys weren't perfectly clean, well, at least they were the best of the lot. Warts and all, the ANC with Mandela at the helm was head and shoulders above the rest—and at least willing to admit their mistakes. And I found myself thinking then, if only more countries in Africa could have leaders like Mandela instead of the lot of buffoons and misfits they're stuck with, the continent would be a lot better off.

I asked myself many times while traveling around the continent: Can South Africa manage to avoid the slippery African slope of economic decline, creeping totalitarianism, societal breakdown, and violent anarchy? As long as Mandela stays in charge, there's little doubt it can. But he's repeatedly said he intends to step down when his term ends in 1999, and without him, South Africa's future seems far less certain. The government-spawned political violence largely abated after the elections, but KwaZulu/Natal remained a killing ground, largely away from the front pages. Crime raged on unabated, prompting even Mandela later to admit that the situation was "out of control."

Optimists were quickly willing to see South Africa as the rare African exception—a modern, industrialized country with a diversified economy and a strong private sector, something most other African countries lack. There's a vibrant and free press and a strong sense of the importance of a constitution and the rule of law. Perhaps more important, the ANC government, so far, has shied away from the the the more radical demands of some of its followers, including the kind of confiscatory economic policies that would generate capital flight and make racial reconciliation more difficult. Moreover, South Africa has the benefit of hindsight, having viewed the sorry history of the rest of the continent and, therefore, not being doomed to repeat it.

But if one thing leaves me less optimistic than most, it's the unfortunate accident of South Africa's geography. Coming here only briefly from the rest of the continent—from Kenya, from Rwanda, from Somalia, from Zaire—has left me largely unable to see the place outside the prism of my own disillusionment. I had also gone to Goree Island at the wrong time and from the wrong direction, and all I could see was the brutality and violence behind me. South Africa was like that, too. If I had come here first, maybe I would have felt differently; but I had come here from "up there," and I had seen too much. I knew already that Africa has a way of brutally burying almost all optimistic predictions and scenarios.

I wanted to look south and see hope. But instead, I could only look north.

Back in Rwanda some weeks after South Africa's elections, I was in a small truck traveling along the highway from the town of Gikongoro in the southwest. My traveling companion was Sam Msibi, a black South African cameraman for Worldwide Television News. I was stuck there, in Gikongoro, and needed a ride back to Bukavu, on the Zaire side of the border. Sam was going that way in a vehicle loaded down with WTN television equipment. Grateful for the lift, I squeezed into the front seat, Sam's camera on my lap.

Sam could tell you something about being a black reporter in Africa. But unlike me, he's an African, a South African, and he earned his reporter's stripes covering his country's bloody township wars between rival supporters of Inkatha and the ANC. One of Sam's stories exposed Inkatha's clandestine support from South Africa's police and security forces, a sensitive issue since at the time the white minority government was denying any involvement in the black-on-black violence. For his exposé, Sam ended up shot five times, in Tokoza, one of the bloodiest of the township killing fields. This was no random shooting. The gunmen had followed him, targeted him. And he lived to show the scars on his body.

"Before, it was great to work in the townships," Sam recalled. "But as the election got closer, they all said the press was working for the ANC. So it got dangerous.

"It's a problem in Africa," he went on, navigating the winding mountain road. "When you're black, you have to worry about black-on-black violence."

As he spoke, we were passing a pretty depressing scene of Rwandan refugees on the move toward Zaire, fleeing for what they think is safety and carrying with them their rolled sleeping mats and their plastic water cans, and with all of their belongings on their back or balanced on their heads. Some walked with herds of cattle and goats in front, and always with small children, barefoot, trailing behind.

They break your heart, the children. Most of them were limping along on blistered, bleeding little feet. They propped themselves up on sticks like old men; their tiny legs are buckled from the pain. With each little step they grimaced. But they dared not stop and rest because they would likely get left behind.

"Sometimes I want to stop to take pictures," Sam said, staring out sadly at the scene. "But I don't know how these people will react." I mentioned, naively, that I had just traveled the same road about a week or so earlier with a Belgian TV crew, and they had encountered no problems filming along the highway. "Yeah, but they're white," Sam explained patiently. "They might think I'm a Hutu or something."

We drove in silence for a long time, looking out at the landscape of misery passing by our windows. "Goodness," Sam said softly at one point, more to himself than to me. "How would you like to see your mother or father or child walking ninety-eight kilometers to get away from a war? Listen to that—a child crying. That's life, man. A lot of pain in it."

The drive was long, nearly four hours, but I didn't mind because I was enjoying Sam's company. I was even enjoying our long silences because I knew that he, as a black South African, and I, a black American, were thinking many of the same thoughts. This African tragedy was as different from downtown Johannesburg as it was from Washington, D.C., or Detroit.

"Africa is the worst place—Somalia, Zaire," Sam said at last, breaking the silence, expressing our common thoughts. "When you see something like this, you pray your own country will never go this way. Who wants to see children walking like that?

"I feel I'm related to these people. I feel they're my own people. I pity them—and not just here. In Kenya, in Zambia, in Angola. I always feel pain in my heart to see this.

"I love my country," he said. "I love it now more than ever." And he displayed his patriotism openly in the form of a small South African flag on his shirt. "It's the twentieth century—and more black folks are suffering than ever before. In South Africa, you hear on the radio that a million people got killed somewhere in Africa, and there you are brushing your teeth, and it doesn't mean anything to you. It's like in America."

Exactly like in America. And that's when I knew that this was not my place. I knew then, on that long drive sitting next to a South African, that while in America I may sometimes feel alien, it is here in this place, the land of my distant ancestors, that I truly am the alien. This was another world for me, just like it was for Sam. I knew I didn't belong here.

10

Retreat

"I knew that I had travelled far, and wondered how I had had the courage to live for so long in a place so far away."

—V. S. NAIPAUL,
A Bend in the River

IT'S BEEN A LONG JOURNEY now, and I'll be leaving Africa soon. I'm beaten down, weary, ready to leave all of these lurid images behind me, ready to go home. I've seen too much death, too much misery, too much hatred, and I find I no longer care.

Africa. Birthplace of civilization. My ancestral homeland. I came here thinking I might find a little bit of that missing piece of myself. But Africa chewed me up and spit me back out again. It took out a machete and slashed into my brain the images that have become my nightmares. I close my eyes now and I am staring at a young woman atop a pile of corpses. I see an old man on the side of the road imploring me for a last drop of water before he dies in the dirt. I see my friends surrounded by an angry mob as they try to fend off the stones that rain down to crush their skulls. I see the grotesquely charred body of a young man set on fire. I see a church altar desecrated by the blood of the dead, and bullet holes forming a halo around Christ's likeness on the cross. Then I see Ilaria, beautiful Ilaria, bleeding to death in her car on the side of the road. There is an old man, broken and bent, who still limps from the pain of the torture that destroyed his limbs. There are the limbless beggars pressing their bloodied stumps against a car window. There is a child, smiling at me, while he aims his loaded grenade launcher at my passing car.

My eyes snap open, but I remain frightened of these ghosts that I know are out there, in the darkness, in Africa. I tried my best to get to know this place, to know the people. But instead I am sitting here alone in my house in Nairobi, frightened, staring into the blackness of the African night. It's quiet outside and I'm feeling scared and lonely. I am surrounded by a high fence and protected by two large dogs. I have a paid security guard patrolling the perimeter, a silent alarm system, and a large metal door with a sliding bolt that I keep firmly closed, all to prevent Africa from sneaking across my front yard and bashing in my brains with a panga knife for the two hundred dollars and change I keep in my top desk drawer.

It wasn't supposed to turn out this way. I really did come here with an open mind, wanting to love the place, love the people. I would love to end this journey now on a high note, to see hope amid the chaos. I'd love to talk about the smiles of the African people, their generosity and perseverance, their love of life, their music and dance, their respect for elders, their sense of family and community. I could point out the seeds of democracy, the formation of a "civil society," the emergence of an urban middle class, the establishment of independent institutions, and the rule of law. I wish I could end my story this way, but it would all be a lie.

How can anyone talk about democracy and constitutions and the rule of law in places where paramilitary security forces firebomb the offices of opposition newspapers? Where entire villages get burned down and thousands of people made homeless because of competing political loyalties? Where whole chunks of countries are under the sway of armed guerrillas? And where traditional belief runs so deep that a politician can be arrested and charged with casting magic spells over poor villagers to force them to vote for him?

My language may seem dark and disturbing, but that's what the reality was for me—almost all dark and disturbing. More than three years here have left me bitter and largely devoid of hope, and largely drained of compassion.

Now when I hear the latest reports of the latest African tragedy—a tribal slaughter in Burundi, perhaps, a riot in a refugee camp in a remote corner of Zaire, maybe a new flood of refugees streaming across a border in Uganda or Sierra Leone—I can watch with more than casual interest because I have been there. I feel sorrow for the victims. I shake my head in frustration at the continent's continuing anguish. I might even rush off a contribution to the Red Cross or one of the other aid agencies struggling to help. But I feel nothing more.

Maybe I would care more if I had not been here myself, if I had not seen the suffering up close, if I hadn't watched the bodies tumbling over the waterfall, smelled the rotting flesh. Yes, perhaps from a different vantage point, I would still have the luxury of falling back on the old platitudes. Maybe if I had never set foot here, I could celebrate my own blackness, my "African-ness." Then I might feel a part of this place, and Africa's pain might be my own. But while I know that "Afrocentrism" has become fashionable for many black Americans searching for identity, I know it cannot work for me. I have been here, I have lived here and seen Africa in all its horror. I know now that I am a stranger here. I am an American, a black American, and I feel no connection to this strange and violent place.

You see? I just wrote "black American." I couldn't even bring myself to write "African American." It's a phrase that, for me, doesn't roll naturally off the tongue: "African American." Is that what we really are? Is there anything really "African" left in the descendants of those original slaves who made that torturous journey across the Atlantic? Are white Americans whose ancestors sailed west across the same ocean as long ago as the slaves still considered "English Americans" or "Dutch Americans"? And haven't the centuries on America's shores erased all those ancient connections, so that we descendants of Africa and England and Holland and Ireland and China are now simply "Americans"?

If you want to establish some kind of ethnic pecking order, based on the number of years in the New World, then blacks would be at the top of the list; the first slaves from Africa arrived in Virginia before the Mayflower even set sail. Black influence today is visible in so many aspects of American culture, from jazz to basketball to slang and hip-hop, from black literature to the picture screen, from prime time to poetry. Spaghetti and dim sum and sushi have all become part of the American culinary scene, but what can be more American than down-home southern cooking—fried chicken and biscuits, barbecued spare ribs, grits and greens—and in the big houses of the old South, there was invariably a black face in the back, preparing the meals.

Yet despite our "American-ness," despite the black contributions to the culture America claims as its own, black Americans have consistently been made to feel like strangers in our own land, the land where we have lived for some four hundred years. I know, because I have felt that way too. It's subtle sometimes, that sense of not belonging. But in ways large and small, most black people in America would probably say they feel it every day.

I myself feel it whenever I'm "dressed down," not wearing a suit and tie, in a well-worn pair of old jeans and a T-shirt perhaps, and I walk into a department store or a corner shop. I can feel the store detectives' eyes following me through the aisles, making sure I'm not there to shoplift the merchandise. And if I have a newspaper under my arm when I enter the store, I make a point of waving it openly to the sales clerk, just so she doesn't think later that I'm trying to pilfer it off the rack.

I feel it when I'm standing on a street corner in Washington or

New York, trying to hail a taxi. If I'm on the way home from work, I remember to open my overcoat so the cab driver can see my dress shirt and necktie, so he will think: This is not some street thug who might rob me; this is a respectable black man on the way home from the office. And if I am in Washington and it's night, and I'm going west of Rock Creek Park, to Georgetown or one of the city's more affluent "white" neighborhoods, I make sure to stand on the correct side of the street so I am not mistaken for a black man heading east, to the black neighborhoods, to the areas where I know taxi drivers, even black ones, fear to tread.

I feel it, too, when I'm driving a car in America, anywhere in America. If I am pulled over by the police, I keep my hands clearly visible on the steering wheel; if I am wearing sunglasses, I remove them. Because I know I am a black man in America and I might be seen as a threat, a danger.

Once, when I was a kid shopping at some big department store with my mother, I broke off and went to browse through the paperbacks on the bookrack. When my mother had finished whatever she was doing and found me, and we headed together for the door, I was immediately stopped by the security guard, a gruff and burly white guy who demanded I empty my pockets. It was winter in Michigan, and I had gloves, a knit cap, maybe a scarf, shoved into the deep pockets of my coat, and I pulled them all out methodically, one by one. My mother, I recall, was incensed; she cursed that burly white security guard up and down and threatened to sue the store. She said I had been stopped only because they thought a black kid wouldn't be interested in browsing at books unless he was trying to steal one. I remember at the time thinking it was no big deal, but then again, I didn't really understand.

I never thought much about that incident, about what it all meant, until I was about sixteen or seventeen, when a high school classmate named Curt and I went to the neighborhood bank near our school to deposit the money for our class treasury or something. It was in that leafy Detroit suburb called Grosse Pointe, the kind of place where they are not used to seeing many blacks. My friend went to the teller's window to make the deposit, and I lingered around just behind him. I think I was wearing my sunglasses, trying to look cool, looking very high school. It was chilly outside, and my coat collar was turned up.

Within a few minutes, pandemonium broke out in the bank. Cops were racing in the front door, jumping behind furniture, kicking over chairs, taking up position. The startled customers spun around and put their hands in the air. And the teller, a young white woman, told Curt and me to take our hands out of our pockets and put them slowly in the air and everything would be fine. No sudden moves. And Curt blurted out, "What's up? Is the bank being robbed? Who is it?" And about then one of the cops walked up and informed us that we—Curt and I—were the ones suspected of holding up the bank. One of the tellers had seen a black kid walking into the bank with sunglasses and his hands in his pockets, following a white kid. That alert teller, whoever it was, thought that I was forcing the white guy inside, holding a concealed weapon on him while he withdrew all his cash. The teller had hit the silent alarm button that had alerted Grosse Pointe's finest.

It was all a big joke at the time, or so we thought. We had a good laugh and a story to tell back at school. The bank sent a letter of apology to the headmaster. But I learned a more important lesson that day, something about white fear of black people in America. I remember that little scene and smile to myself every time I walk into a bank today. And I always remember to take off my sunglasses—exactly as if I were walking up to a Pakistani checkpoint on a Mogadishu street.

This is not paranoia; it's everyday survival, and black people in America, particularly young black teenagers in that most threatening looking of age groups, learn the lessons well until it all just comes naturally—how to dress, how to talk, how to walk so as to appear as nonthreatening as possible. And a key part of the lesson is knowing how to feign indifference, too, at the unintended insults, the little jibes even from well-intentioned white people who still can't see past a black person's skin color enough to just treat a black American like another human being. You'll tell them you've just been at the beach, and they'll say "nice tan," and think you're supposed to chuckle along with them. Or they'll make some comment about the wind blowing their hair out of place, and add, "Of course, you don't have to worry about that." So black people just kind of smile, and say, "Oh, sure," try to change the subject before it gets any more awkward. And the worst ones, of course, are the ones who try to show you how liberal they are, how they really are not prejudiced, and you can spot them right away because the conversation always turns around to "So, what do you think of Jesse Jackson?" or "That Colin Powell is really something."

Yes, that is what America is if you are black. I've learned to shrug it off, to laugh along with the little wisecracks, the jokes. But deep down it hurts because it is a constant reminder that being black means being different, alien, never quite belonging.

So I became a foreign correspondent. For me, traveling abroad and writing about the people and places I encountered provided the ultimate escape from being constantly defined and evaluated by the color of my skin. In the mid-1980s, after a monthlong trip in Hong Kong and Taiwan visiting friends in the foreign service and a two-week reporting trip to Japan as the *Post*'s national education reporter, I became fascinated by Asia, one place, it seemed, where a black man—a black American—was judged not so much by the blackness of his skin but by the greenness of his wallet. We were all aliens in Asia, whites and blacks alike. The Hong Kong Cantonese called me "black devil" and they called white Americans "white devils," but that was fine with me—we were all devils in their eyes.

Then my foreign assignments brought me here, to Africa, finally forcing me to confront my identity, my race, my color, my nationality. After a lifetime spent in countries where I was different, apart, I have come to the only continent where I blend in with the crowds around me. If I belong anywhere—if there is one place on earth where I am not alien—it ought to be here, in Africa.

And I am hating it.

I'm conscious that some people will say that by hating Africa, I am really hating myself. Malcolm X said so in a speech back in 1965, when I was just six years old. He talked of how European colonialists had projected a negative view of Africa to make us hate it, and how the strategy largely worked. "We didn't want anybody telling us anything about Africa, much less calling us Africans," Malcolm said. "In hating Africa, and in hating the Africans, we ended up hating ourselves, without even realizing it. Because you can't hate the roots of a tree and not hate the tree. You can't hate your origin and not end up hating yourself. You can't hate Africa and not hate yourself.

"You know yourself that we have been a people who hated our African characteristics," Malcolm continued. "We hated our heads, we hated the shape of our nose, we wanted one of those long dog-like noses, you know; we hated the color of our skin, hated the blood of Africa that was in our veins. And in hating our features and our skin and our blood, why, we had to end up hating ourselves. And we hated ourselves."

If Malcolm were alive today, he might call me one of those "brainwashed" Negroes he referred to in that speech. He might call me one of those self-hating black people, and that's why it so pains me to write down these thoughts that have been locked up in my head. That's why it's necessary to be painfully clear about what I am saying—and what I am not saying.

I do not hate Africa or the Africans. What I hate is the senseless brutality, the waste of human life. I hate the unfairness, the injustice, the way repressive systems strip decent people of their dignity. I hate the way my driver in Somalia passes a starving woman on the road-side and will not stop to let me give her a bottle of water. I hate the kids swaggering outside the gates of the feeding center with machine guns on their shoulders, thrashing the old people waiting in line for a handful of gruel. I hate the Big Man who forces the entire government, the entire diplomatic community, to line up on a red carpet at the airport tarmac under a scorching sun to see him off on a foreign trip. And I hate the dictator's information officer, sitting in his hot, airless office with no electricity, lecturing me about how "the whites" have brought his country to ruin. I hate the immigration clerk at the dusty border outpost who is officiously studying my passport he's holding in one hand while the other hand is stretched out, waiting for a bribe.

Perhaps more than all that, I hate this maddening propensity of Africans to wallow in their own suffering, to simply roll over when kicked, and to express unswerving faith that some outside force, some divine intervention, will bring deliverance from their misery.

I know now that while I can walk anonymously down the streets of Nairobi or Lagos or Kinshasa or Khartoum, while I can pass through the sea of black faces and remain unnoticed, I am not one of them. I am a stranger here, adrift. I see the people, but I cannot see what lies beyond their blank stares. I look like them, I can even alter my clothes a bit to appear less "Western," but I cannot understand what it is like to be of them. True, my ancestors came from this place, and these are my distant cousins. But a chasm has opened up, a chasm of four hundred years and ten thousand miles. Nothing in my own past, nothing in my upbringing, has instilled in me any sense of what it must be like to be an African. Malcolm X said we black people in America are more African than American—"You're nothing but Africans"—but I don't feel it. I feel more lonely here in Africa than I have ever felt in America. In America, I may feel like an alien, but in Africa, I *am* an alien.

But the loneliness is only part of this feeling that is gnawing away at me. There is more, something far deeper, something that I am ashamed to admit: I am terrified of Africa. I don't want to be from this place. In my darkest heart here on this pitch black African night, I am quietly celebrating the passage of my ancestor who made it out.

There are some photographs I have kept here in my desk drawer, clipped out of one of the local English-language newspapers. I think I saved them for a possible story that I never got around to writing. The first, taken on the streets of downtown Nairobi, shows a Kenyan man in a sports coat, trussed up like a chicken, tied down to what looks like a wheelbarrow, and he is surrounded by a jubilant mob, smiling white teeth at the camera, flashing the victory sign. The man tied down to the wheelbarrow has a strange look on his face—fear, yes, but also what seems to me like complete resignation to his fate.

The lengthy caption states that this man works in an office somewhere downtown and was boasting about his prowess with the opposite sex, how he was a "total man." One of the women in the office, a woman who had been the object of his earlier advances, then pointed out that she knew for a fact that the man was uncircumcised. Upon hearing this, the man's co-workers had surrounded him, stripped off his pants, verified the presence of foreskin, and arranged for a ritualistic circumcision right there, on the spot. He was tied down to the wheelbarrow and rolled ceremoniously through Nairobi's streets, the procession attracting more and more onlookers en route. He was being wheeled to a tribal chieftain who would perform this rite of passage to manhood with no anesthesia, probably using a dull, rusted, unclean blade. The unfortunate victim, the caption read, was on his way to "face the knife."

There was another photograph I saved, this one from a rural village, that showed three men seated and staring forlornly at the camera. The caption here explains that the three have all undergone forced circumcisions, held down while an elder with a knife performed the rite, not bothering to properly sterilize the blade between the three. And an editorial in the same paper a few days later calls on Kenyans to stop this spate of forced circumcisions, which it says has now reached alarming numbers, with new incidents reported regularly. In dire language, the editorial warns that the practice can indeed prove harmful if the instruments are unclean and there are no trained medical personnel on hand to supervise.

There is one last photograph, a more recent one, and I still shiver when I look at it. This one, taken in a Nairobi slum not far from my home, shows a boy, maybe a teenager, lying flat on his back, being held down by a mob, screaming with terror. One of his hands has been chopped off. An older man is standing over him, gleefully holding what looks like a giant meat cleaver. The older man with the weapon is smiling, preparing to drop down hard and chop off the other hand. The caption explains that this boy has been caught stealing, and the crowd is now imposing street justice. I became fixated first on the boy's screaming face, but then on the faces of the crowd in the background; they are all laughing and smiling. And I ask myself, what on earth could these people possibly be thinking?

How could anyone stand by and laugh at such torture? How can a human being find glee in another person's agony? And this was not Rwanda or Somalia or Liberia, where I might have expected such callous inhumanity. This was Nairobi, supposedly one of the most modern capitals of black Africa. And these scenes were happening within walking distance of my own home.

How could I possibly relate to these Africans, when we are separated by such a wide gulf of culture and background and emotion and sensitivity? How could I ever understand what is going through the minds of the people, average people, who would stand in the background and smile in the face of such suffering?

And what frightens me most of all is that these smiling people in the photographs look just like me.

Had my ancestor not made it out of here, I might have ended up there in that crowd, smiling gleefully, while a man with a cleaver cuts off the hands of a thief. Or maybe I would have been one of those bodies, arms and legs bound together, washing over the waterfall in Tanzania. Or maybe my son would have been set ablaze by soldiers. Or I would be limping now from the torture I received in some rancid police cell.

And then maybe I would be thinking: How lucky those black Americans are!

It's been said time and again that nothing makes you appreciate your own country like traveling away from it, and America has been like that for me. I see the flaws, I curse the intolerance, I recoil from the racial and ethnic tensions. And I become infuriated at the often mindless political debate that to me never seems to cut deeper than the crispest sound bite. But even with all that—maybe because of it—I recognize that it's the only place I truly belong. It's home.

When Thomas Jefferson was ambassador to France, he wrote a letter back to James Monroe, urging him to pay a visit sometime. "I

235

sincerely wish you may find it convenient to come here," Jefferson wrote. "The pleasure of the trip will be less than you expect, but the utility greater. It will make you adore your own country, its soil, its climate, its equality, liberty, laws, people and manners. My God! how little do my countrymen know what precious blessings they are in possession of, and which no other people on earth can enjoy. I confess I had no idea of it myself."

Nor I, until I set foot in a place of such violent passions and brutality, this land of my ancestors.

My conclusion may cut against the more popular trend these days among black Americans, many of whom seem to favor a new kind of voluntary resegregation from the mainstream. And there's a compelling argument, to be sure, that more than forty years after the Supreme Court ordered desegregation with "all deliberate speed," America still hasn't come anywhere close to the dream of a color-blind, multiracial society that was one of the guiding tenets of the old civil rights crusaders. Turned off and tuned out by the white mainstream, a lot more blacks are preaching solace through retreat into our own separate communities, separate schools, separate neighborhoods, separate businesses, separate identities. Wrapped up in that is a desire to reaffirm an African identity, an African ancestry, and you see it in the growing trend of kente cloth caps and Kwanza celebrations—even though in three years on the continent I never met an African who celebrated Kwanza or could even tell me what it was.

My view is that separation is the wrong approach, that we need instead to go back to the original idea of America as a melting pot and create a society that's truly color-blind, not carved up into racial and ethnic duchies. Sorry, but I've seen what happens when societies become sundered by their divisions, when the short people start to kill the tall, when the shape of your head or the hue of your complexion determines whether you get a panga knife to the back of the head. We in America have so far managed to escape that kind of violent reckoning that tears at so much of the world—and not only in Africa—and this despite our being a nation created from multiple colors, religions, ethnic groupings. Surely the answer for avoiding that kind of violence in the future lies in expanding American inclusiveness, not voluntarily segregating or separating ourselves. I've seen what happens when separateness and division is taken to extremes—you have Rwanda, you have Liberia, you have Somalia. Why on earth would we want to start heading down that dangerous path?

And for black Americans, I think, the reaffirmation of some kind of lost African identity is rooted more in fantasy than reality. Why would we, as Americans, want to embrace a continent so riven by tribal, ethnic, and religions hatreds? And besides, how can we, sons and daughters of America's soil, reaffirm an identity that for us never existed in the first place?

No, America is home. There's no point in talking about going "back" to anywhere, in finding some missing "roots," in finding a homeland. I've lived here in Africa, and I can tell you that no part of me feels any attachment to this strange place. Far better that we all put our energies into making America work better, into realizing the dream of a multiracial society, than in clinging to the myth that we belong anyplace else.

So what future do I see for Africa, this strange and forbidding place? What future can I see for a place where kids don Donald Duck masks and ball gowns before inflicting untold horrors on each other, and on innocent civilians caught in between? What future has a place where the best and brightest minds languish in dank prison cells? Where a ruthless warlord aims mortar shells into a crowded marketplace, and where teenagers strip down cars and fit them with antiaircraft guns to roam through the streets terrorizing and looting? Where a dictator begs the international community for food aid to avert mass hunger even as he erects a new international airport in his dirt-poor hometown? What future is there in a place where the poets are hanged by the soldiers, and where the soldiers riot and kill when they are unpaid? Where entire villages are left so ravaged by disease that only the very old and very young still linger?

I've looked in my crystal ball and tried to see some slivers of light. I've really tried. But all I can see is more darkness.

Is there no solution, then, for Africa's predicament? It's the question I'm most often asked. It's in our nature, I suppose, to want to be optimists, to want to think that all problems have solutions, that even Africa might somehow, in its own time, be "fixed." But this strange place defies even the staunchest of optimists; it drains you of hope, and believe me, I know. I'd like to say I have some magic solution, the untested remedy for the continent's myriad ills. But the problem in Africa is that just about everything has already been tried.

Democracy and multiparty politics were supposed to be the answer—the much-hyped, much-hoped-for solution being bandied about by all those well-meaning academics and Africa specialists who briefed me on my way here. But in covering election after election I have seen that a lot more work needs to be done first. Elections are too easily manipulated and stolen, and in many cases end up doing more harm than good, allowing dictators to wrap themselves in a new aura of legitimacy. Before elections are held, constitutions need to be rewritten to reduce the role of imperial presidencies and level the playing field for opposition parties. Government control over the media needs to be broken, and that especially applies to radio, which most Africans rely on for their news. Security and police forces, now mostly tools of repression, need to be brought under neutral command and control. Election laws that are impartial and fair must be drafted. Voters must be properly registered. Mechanisms must be put in place to monitor funding, to prevent entrenched Big Men from simply printing more money to buy votes. Laws that now make it a crime to "insult" the president or the government must be repealed. Parliaments and judiciaries must be strengthened. Voter education must be conducted, especially in rural areas, to teach those who cannot read or write why their vote is important for their own future. And election losers need to be given a constitutional role, a stake in the system, so that elections no longer become the kind of "winner-take-all" contests that now produce factional warfare.

Until all those things are done, and not before, it is useless to talk about elections in African countries. Without those basic steps, any election becomes a sham, a charade of democracy. The rest of the continent might take a lesson here from South Africa, which did go through that lengthy exercise first of laying the groundwork for the transition to democracy; the election itself was just the final step. The lesson was already well received in Kenya, where opposition parties pushed ahead for quick elections—and Moi and his ruling party were able to use intimidation and fraud to claim a new mandate. One opposition member of parliament who did win, Paul Muite, conceded later, "We never should have gone forward with elections under the existing constitutional order."

Africa also needs to try a little bit more decentralization, more "devolution," to borrow a phrase from the American political lexicon. Most of the civil wars and conflicts around the continent are, in one way or another, caused by separatist sentiment—the Hutu don't want to live under the Tutsi, the Habre Gedir think it's their turn to rule Somalia, the Kikuyu won't vote for a Luo for president, the Zulus demand an autonomous homeland, the Eritreans have already broken from Ethiopia and gotten their homeland, and on and on.

For the last three and a half decades of independence, those secessionist claims were either swept under the carpet or ruthlessly crushed. The Organization of African Unity even established as one of its inviolable tenets the idea that the old colonial boundaries could never be altered for fear that recognizing the claim of any one group could lead to disintegration and chaos.

This attitude must change if Africa is to have any chance of surviving. The Africans might want to take a lesson from the former Soviet Union, which did break up into its component parts, or from Czechoslovakia, which split into separate Czech and Slovak republics. Countries can indeed split up and nationalist claims to self-determination can be recognized without the sky falling in.

If Africa should take a new look at breaking up, it needs at the same time to find more ways to come together. The worldwide trend today is for states to form stronger regional economic groupings—

the European Community, the North American Free Trade Area, the Association of Southeast Asian Nations, and the Asia-Pacific Economic Cooperation forum. Africa has regional groups, too, most promising being the southern African economic and trade group called SADEC and the Economic Community of West African States (ECOWAS). The West African grouping has been held as a possible model for how African states themselves can solve problems in their own backyards, with a West African peace-keeping force in charge of policing Liberia. But the performance of that peace-keeping force has been dismal—and in some cases, soldiers supposedly there to protect the population have joined the drug-crazed militia kids in looting the city bare.

One West African regional model that seems to work is Air Afrique, jointly owned by several West African countries and offering one of the continent's most efficient airlines. And there have been tentative steps in East Africa toward reviving the old East African Community, and a rail line between Nairobi and Kampala has reopened after a long hiatus.

For the most part, though, African regional groupings remain largely elaborate talking shops; African Big Men are loath to cede any of their precious autonomy to a wider regional authority. So we are left with the lunacy of all the countries of East Africa running small, money-losing, and outright dangerous national airlines using ill-maintained planes, instead of pooling their resources for one common, efficient, and potentially profitable regional carrier.

Tribalism remains the single most corrosive, debilitating influence plaguing modern Africa in its quest for democracy and development. To blame Africa's ills on tribalism is a cliché, to be sure. But like many clichés, this one has a basis in truth.

I remember first arriving in Kenya and going to see one of those old colonial Brits, a man named Douglas—I never knew his first name—who worked in a cramped, dingy, smoke-stained office above a souvenir shop, surrounded by stacks and stacks of paper files in blue and pink and yellow cardboard folders. He was a large man with white hair and a thick white mustache, and his suspenders pulled his pants so high up his waist they looked like they were touching his armpits. He was the real estate agent for the house I was renting, and I had to go to his office to drop off my check. And I remember him sitting back imperiously with his hands over his wide stomach and appraising me, the newcomer to Africa, and then announcing, "You Americans don't know anything about the African. It's all tribes—tribes! And you don't understand that." And I recall thinking at the time, how pompous this old man was, how utterly full of himself, bandying about that old worn cliché, tribalism, to explain Africa's ills.

I set out to prove old Douglas wrong. One of my earliest trips was to Tanzania, and there I found a country that had actually managed to purge itself of the evil of tribalism. Under Julius Nyerere and his ruling socialists, the government was able to imbue a true sense of nationalism that transcended the country's natural ethnic divisions, among other things by vigorous campaigns to upgrade education and to make Swahili a truly national language. Swahili today is widely spoken everywhere and has become the medium of instruction at Tanzanian universities, where I met a professor of Swahili studies who was busy translating the latest American computer program into Swahili. Tanzania is one place that has succeeded in removing the linguistic barrier that separates so many of Africa's warring factions.

But after three years traveling the continent, I've found that Tanzania is the exception, not the rule. In Africa, as old man Douglas said, it *is* all about tribes. Tribalism is what prompted tens of thousands of Rwandan Hutus to pick up machetes and hoes and panga knives and farming tools to bash in the skulls and sever the limbs of their Tutsi neighbors. Tribalism is why entire swaths of Kenya's scenic Rift Valley lie in scorched ruins, why Zulu gunmen in ski masks mow down Xhosa workers outside a factory gate in South Africa, and why thousands of hungry displaced Kasai huddle under plastic sheeting at a remote train station in eastern Zaire. And it's tribalism under another name—clans, subclans, factions—that caused young men in Mogadishu to shell the city to oblivion and loot what was left of the rubble.

The key seems to be whether a particular African leader, for his own purpose, is willing to play the tribal card, to unleash tribal passions and rivalries for his own sinister aims, usually to create the kind of violent chaos he needs to justify his own grip on power. Sadly, all too many—Doe and Habyarimana, Siad Barre and Ethiopia's Mengistu before, Moi and Mobutu today—have proven more than willing to do just that.

But tribalism need not necessarily be a corrosive influence—and that's where again the questions of separation, secession, and self-determination arise. Africa could do with a healthy dose of federalism to defuse tribalism; a tribe that can vote for its own kind, to control a regional or local government, is less likely to feel oppressed by a central government controlled by another tribe. Regions and provinces and towns given true autonomy will empower the peoples who live there. Right now, countries that call themselves "federal," like Nigeria, really only make a mockery of the term. If there's a precedent for a federal system that works, it's America.

America also has its "tribes," as anyone familiar with big-city politics can attest. We have our Italian tribe and our Irish tribe, our Polish tribe and our Jewish tribe, and, of course, our black tribe. Show me the ethnic makeup of a congressional voting district in Chicago or Boston or Baltimore, and I can usually predict with some accuracy whether the congressman elected will be black, Italian, Irish, or Jewish. It's tribal politics—but the American version is not typically associated with violence.

It's also changing. A black American can be elected mayor of Denver, a city with a minimal black population. Or mayor of Minneapolis. Or to a congressional seat in an East Coast district. People are voting across tribal lines. The old urban duchies are breaking down. Maybe there's a chance that the old dream of a multiracial, color-blind society is slowly being realized. It had better be, because I've been here and seen the alternative.

I'd like to think the same might be true of Africa one day, that the pull of tribe will also begin to break down. But I've been here too long now to see light at the end of that long, dark tunnel; Africa has a way of defying most optimistic predictions. My most optimistic illusions were smashed in the rubble of a house in Somalia, buried under a mountain of election fraud in Kenya, bulldozed up and dropped into a mass grave in Goma. Now I know better than to hope.

Three years now I've been here, and Liberia is still gripped by anarchy as the warlords battle for control and the young kids with the AK-47s still roam the streets, killing wantonly. Somalia remains a shambles, still on the edge of famine, and with its own rival warlords still lobbing artillery shells across the devastated capital long after the world has turned out the lights and gone home. (My old friend General Aideed finally met his end in August 1996, when he died several days after being hit by at least two stray bullets during an outburst of clan fighting in Mogadishu. His son, Hussein Aideed, was immediately chosen to succeed him as the head of his faction.) The civil war in Sudan now grinds into its second decade of continuous slaughter, the refugees continue to move back and forth, the aid agencies continue their lifeline of support. Mobutu, now stricken with cancer, still clings to power in Zaire, while the jungle continues to claim more of the decrepit capital, Kinshasa, and the country continues to splinter into de facto mini-states. Mugabe is still enthroned in Zimbabwe; his well-earned reputation for statesmanship for keeping the economy largely on track and averting a white exodus is now growing sullied as he becomes increasingly authoritarian—even while he cloaks himself in the mantle of electoral legitimacy. Chiluba is also still in power in Zambia, the democratic dream there now roundly trampled. The thuggish generals still run Nigeria, and still hold out empty promises of democracy. Museveni still runs Uganda, Paul Biya still runs Cameroon, Omar Bongo with his platform shoes still runs Gabon. AIDS continues to ravage the cities, and if it's abating, it's only because those most susceptible are already dead. The border between Rwanda and Zaire remains a perpetual crisis zone, and the Tutsi government in Kigali still complains about the slow pace of justice. Meanwhile, Burundi next door remains an ethnic caldron ready to boil over but one that never quite does. There are more coups, more elections, more riots, and more refugees. That's how it was when I arrived, and it's how it's likely to be years from now.

In Africa, things stay the same until they fall apart.

Nairobi remains much the same, too, even while some of the familiar faces change. Moi, of course, is still there, still clinging to power, still deftly playing the aid donors with promises of reform, even while cracking down on his erstwhile critics. And his political opponents still gather, forlorn, shaking their heads at the continued repression, analyzing, conspiring, planning, plotting, and vowing that if not in the next election, then maybe the one after that, perhaps, with luck, the old man might be toppled.

But many of the old faces at Chester House are gone now. Todd Shields has finally left Africa—and not a minute too soon, as he would likely say. Julian Ozanne has moved on as well, to another assignment in the Middle East. Ruth Burnett, the redhead from my Rwanda trip, is back in London; Gary Strieker from CNN, my neighbor across the hall, seems finally to have gotten his wish, and will also be leaving soon. The *Times*'s Sam Kiley is still around, even more jaded, more cynical than ever, and he, too, is talking about the need to get out, to try new horizons in Russia, perhaps, or somewhere in the ex-Soviet republics. A new generation of reporters is moving in, some so full of hope and optimism and ideas, so anxious to hop on the next plane to Sudan, or to discover the forgotten conflict still being waged in Mogadishu.

I'm driving the battered old Peugeot down one of Nairobi's treacherously dark streets, swerving to avoid crater-sized potholes and the barely visible pedestrians trudging silently down the side lane. Up ahead I can discern in the shadows a very large shape barreling toward me, and I know immediately that it is an oncoming car, with no headlights on even in the pitch black of the African night.

I jerk the car hard to one side to avoid a head-on collision, flashing my own bright lights, laying on the horn, and muttering some obscenity all at the same time.

"Oh, my God!" my successor, Stephen Buckley, says to me. "Why do they drive like that, with no lights on?"

Stephen has been named to replace me as the *Washington Post*'s Africa bureau chief. He is here now on a two-week "look around," to get the lay of the land and familiarize himself with his new surroundings. We're on the way back from dinner at the Carnivore restaurant.

"They think it saves the lights longer not to use them," I explain. "Or that guy may not have even had headlights. Who knows?"

"But didn't they learn in driver's ed school how dangerous that can be?" he asks, innocently enough. Then he immediately catches himself. "I know, I know. I guess I'm going to have to stop thinking like an American here, huh?" Indeed.

Stephen is a young black kid from New York, a Jamaican by birth, who only recently switched to a U.S. passport. He's about a decade younger than I am, newly married, starting his first foreign assignment for the *Post*, and full of energy and ideas. I'm trying hard not to infect him with my cynicism; I'm not sure how well I'm succeeding.

We go together to Chester House for Stephen to see our cramped little office and to meet some of the other correspondents on the floor. I turn over to him the heavy green bulletproof vest I used to carry with me on trips into Somalia, with instructions to always keep it handy for flying into combat zones. There's mosquito netting and a tent in one of the closets back at the house. And I introduce Stephen to George, and explain how George takes care of the office accounts; I wait until later to tell him that George is also a thief who more than once has dipped into the bureau accounts, and whom he should feel free to fire if there are ever any additional transgressions.

I suggest that we take a quick trip together to Kigali, the war-torn Rwandan capital, as a good chance for me to show him how correspondents operate on the road. We hop a UN plane there and check into the newly reopened Mille Collines ("Thousand Hills") hotel, the place where just a few months earlier thousands of Tutsi refugees had gathered to escape the marauding Hutu militiamen rampaging through the city. They've cleaned most of the blood off the walls and out of the stairwells now, the electricity is back on for most of the day, and there's even running water again in the bathroom.

It's been a hard, hot day, running around Kigali trying to find one of the Tutsi military spokesmen. At one point, our rental car breaks down on one of the city's infamous thousand hills, forcing us to hitchhike our way back up to the hotel. At the end of the day, we're both exhausted and stretch out next to each other on the two small beds in the room.

"You know," Stephen says to me then, "this has got to be one of the worst places I've ever stayed."

I think about this for a long time. "I've got some bad news for you," I reply. "After you've traveled around Africa a bit, you're going to pray to get back here. This is one of the *best* places you're going to stay for the next three years!"

I spend my last couple of nights in Africa in a hotel, the Norfolk, that most colonial of spots at the edge of downtown Nairobi where tourists in safari gear still gather on the verandah to drink gin and tonics while the sun sets. My belongings have been packed up and shipped out, and I've paid my last visit to the old house to say good-bye to Hezekiah and Reuben. It was a teary farewell. "I hope things improve in Kenya," I told them. "Maybe by the time I come back, you will have gotten rid of Moi."

I wasn't really confident it would happen anytime soon.

I stop by the office one last time to say good-bye to George. "Watch yourself," I warn him. "There's a new *bwana* in town. He may not be as tolerant as I was." And George promises me he'll clean up his act and become more responsible—but, of course, I know he's lying.

And then I take a taxi to Jomo Kenyatta International Airport, and sometime before midnight I step onto a British Airways plane heading north, out of Africa, home.

There's not much to see from the plane window at midnight; the airport runway lights, a few lights from downtown far away. And as the plane gains altitude, Africa recedes further and further away into the distance, further into my mind. And I'm asking myself: Was that all just a bad dream? Think of all the horror I've seen, back on that vast stretch of earth now beneath me, that dark spot on the globe called Africa.

I open the little plastic bag with my headset and plug the earphones into the armrest in time for the start of the BBC news just coming across the television screen at the front of the cabin. The story is about Rwanda; something about a new outbreak of violence at the border and worries about fresh incursions from Hutu rebels based over the border in Zaire who are plotting their return.

I close my eyes and switch channels to a music station. I'm leaving Africa now, so I don't care anymore about the turmoil in Rwanda and have no interest in this latest tragic development. I've seen it all before, and I'm sure I'll see it again. But from now on, I will be seeing it from afar, maybe watching it on television like millions of other Americans. I'll watch the latest footage of refugees crossing a border someplace, soldiers looting, kids with grenade launchers blasting apart yet another quaint but rundown African capital. I will watch with more than passing interest, since I have been here. I will understand now the complexities behind the conflicts. I will also know that the problems are too intractable, that the outside world can do nothing, until Africa is ready to save itself. I'll also know that none of it affects me, because I feel no attachment to the place or the people.

And why should I feel anything more? Because my skin is black? Because some ancestor of mine, four centuries ago, was wrenched from this place and sent to America, and because I now look like those others whose ancestors were left behind? Does that make me still a part of this place? Should their suffering now somehow still be mine?

Maybe I would care more if I had never come here and never seen what Africa is today. But I have been here, and I have seen—and frankly, I want no part of it.

So am I a coldhearted cynic? An Africa hater? A racist, maybe, or perhaps a lost and lonely self-hating black man who has forgotten his African roots? Maybe I am, all that and more. But by an accident of birth, I am a black man born in America, and everything I am today—my culture and attitudes, my sensibilities, loves, and desires—derives from that one simple and irrefutable truth.

Afterword

WHEN THIS BOOK was first published, in early 1997, it generated an immediate flood of comments and commentary, critique, and some harsh criticism. Hundreds of people—black and white, as well as Americans of Hispanic and of Asian descent—sent me letters, post-cards, and E-mail, thanking me for sharing my journey and telling my story so vividly, and agreeing with my concluding observation that for those of us born on American soil, our commonality transcends the differences of our origin.

Such an assertion of an American identity is not new, not even from an American of African ancestry. The idea of returning to Africa is an old one within black America, but for decades blacks have found the African experience wanting. Langston Hughes reported his amazement at being called "white" by black Africans who saw him not as a native, but as an American. Harold R. Isaacs traveled to Africa in the summer of 1960 and wrote a lengthy article for the "Reporter At Large" column of the *New Yorker,* in which he describes meeting "American Negroes" in West Africa who "had come looking for freedom from racism and prejudice, or at least for a racial situation that counted them in instead of out—that provided solace and a sense of identity in a world in which everyone was black." But instead, he wrote, "the Negro pilgrim in Africa soon finds himself not free at all, more than ever without solace and a sense of identity, fighting new patterns of prejudice, and suffering the pangs of a new kind of outsiderness. He had thought that he was alien in America, but he discovers that he is much more alien in Africa." And more recently, in 1992, the black American writer Eddy L. Harris, in his book, *Native Stranger,* writes of his travails traveling around Africa—contracting dysentery, being thrown in jail—and finally ending up on a riverboat in Zaire along with a small group of English, Dutch, and Australian tourists. "Suddenly I didn't know where I belonged," Harris writes. "It was so strange to be among so many black people and yet to have so much more in common with the handful of whites."

Yet oddly, the underlying premise of my book—that Africa showed me how our very Americanness makes us one—seemed to have generated a considerable amount of debate and controversy. For a small but vocal number of critics, that sentiment amounted to a kind of declaration of racial betrayal.

Some said I was too emotional in my descriptions of Africa and its problems, too harsh and too sweeping in my judgments. Others said the book was too narrow in scope, accusing me of ignoring the "good news stories" and focusing on only a few war zones or bad news stories—this despite the fact that I traveled the length and breadth of the vast continent, by car, by train, in small propeller planes, and overcrowded ferry boats, visiting and reporting from twenty-one sub-Saharan African countries in a little more than three years as an Africa correspondent (my byline in the *Washington Post* appears from nineteen of those countries; with two others, Congo and the Ivory Coast serving as springboards into other nearby conflicts). Some reviewers criticized not the book that I wrote, but the one that I did not write. A few, particularly in academic circles, accused me of ignoring or neglecting key factors of Africa's history, the legacy of colonialism, the depopulation caused by slavery, the superpowers' Cold War rivalry and the meddling of the Central Intelligence Agency in places like the former Zaire. One self-styled Africa expert from the Council on Foreign Relations went on national television to accuse me of "missing the real story" on the continent, which he dubbed a new "African renaissance" of good government and economic prosperity. And there were others who said that while they accepted the premise of my book and agreed with much of my description of Africa and its failings, they feared my ideas, laid out so starkly in a book, might fall into the wrong hands and become fodder for those with an agenda for cutting economic assistance to Africa or promulgating theories of black racial inferiority.

Many of those critics missed the point; *Out of America* is first and foremost a journalist's book. It was never intended as an academic tome or a work of political science. It is a personal memoir, a first-person diary, if you will, of my experiences as a reporter—a black American reporter—covering Africa during one of its most fascinating three-year stretches, starting at the end of the Cold War in 1991.

There is of course room for other books to take a broader scope on those same tumultuous years, but that was never my intention. And to have written anything other than the book that I wrote would not have been true to my own experiences. To those who say I was too emotional, too harsh in my critiques, too unforgiving, I say, guilty.

Take the journey with me, see Africa as I did, as a reporter with a front-line seat for some of the continent's worst horrors, disasters, and crises, and try to come to any different conclusion. If much of the book focuses on a few African trouble spots, such as Somalia, Rwanda, Kenya, and Zaire, then again, I say, guilty; this book was never meant to be an encyclopedic catalogue of all African countries or even of all the countries I visited. These were the biggest news stories during the years I was on the continent, the places that left the most searing images in my mind and most shaped my view of the continent. And more important, they were each in their own way emblematic of larger, continent-wide problems.

As I traveled around the United States in the spring of 1997, following the publication of the hardcover edition of *Out of America*, one of the most intriguing questions I was asked, from the proprietor of a black-run bookstore in Dallas specializing in Afro-centric literature, was whether the tone of my book was so angry because I was still too close to the topic. Or, as the woman questioner more precisely phrased it, would I have written the same book with the advantage of more time and distance between myself and my African experience?

It was a question that I turned over in my mind as I sat down to write these brief remarks for the paperback edition of *Out of America*, now that much time has passed since my last visit to the African continent, in December, 1994. Since then there has been some good news generated out of Africa. But so much more of the news is still depressingly familiar. On the "good news" side, there have been a few bright spots, including an overall average economic growth of 4 percent on the continent in 1996, led by Uganda—a perennial favorite of the international lending community—which has surged along at a tigerish 8 percent a year since 1992. And there has been much made of a "new breed" of African leader on the continent, younger, more technocratic than ideological, not democratically minded, but also less interested in blaming European colonialism for Africa's modern-day ills. Politically, too, there have been some encouraging signs on an often too-bleak African landscape. Mali, which held its first free election in 1992, is stumbling along and trying to entrench its democracy, even though opposition leaders accuse President Alpha Oumar Konare of trying to reimpose one-party rule. Liberia under international supervision and against long odds managed to stage an election in which the winner was longtime guerrilla leader Charles Tayler, whose commitment to democratic principles remains to be proven. And Zaire's Mobutu Sese Seko, perhaps the world's worst kleptocrat, was finally chased from power in 1997, and soon succumbed to cancer.

Yet for all the small signs of hope and progress, there is much to despair. Laurent Kabila kicked out Mobutu, but he lately has been showing worrysome undemocratic tendencies. His security forces in the capital, Kinshasa, have violently suppressed protests, killing several protesters, and Kabila has balked at cooperating with United Nations teams wanting to investigate alleged massacres committed in areas of Eastern Zaire from which he launched his rebellion. Kabila has surrounded himself with soldiers and advisors from Angola and from Rwanda's minority Tutsi tribe, further alienating himself from the majority of the people who once welcomed him as a conquering hero. And in the East, various rebellions continuously threaten to tear the country apart along ethnic lines.

Congo-Brazzaville, across the river, was also torn apart in mid-1997 by a violent rebellion that destroyed much of the capital, over-threw the democratically elected president, and returned the country's former Marxist dictator, Denis Sassou-Nguesso, to power. Congo's implosion was particularly painful for me to watch, even from afar via CNN; Congo had always been a lazy rest-spot, the quiet back-water I traversed regularly on my frequent trips into and out of neighboring Kinshasa. Watching the scenes of the victorious Cobra militia sweeping through Brazzaville, brandishing their AK-47s and looting anything left in the city, brought back to me those scenes of anarchy from Mogadishu and Monrovia—yet another once-tranquil African capital gone down the familiar path of insanity. I wrote about a coup in Sierra Leone in 1992; since then, there's been another one, in early 1997, led by another junior officer, Major Johnny Paul Koroma. And in a stretch of even African-sized hypocrisy, it has been Nigeria's brutal military dictator, General Sani Abacha, leading the regional effort to try to oust Koroma and restore democracy to Sierra Leone—all while the winner of Nigeria's own presidential election, Moshood Abiola, still languishes in prison.

The Great Lakes region of central Africa remains explosive, with the Hutu-Tutsi massacres continuing in Burundi, Eastern Zaire, and in Rwanda, where the Tutsti-led security forces have become increasingly violent against Hutu extremists. Meanwhile, more than

100,000 Hutu remain in prison without trials in Rwanda for their suspected roles in the 1994 genocide. Peace—let alone democracy—remains a long way off.

Violence has flared again in Kenya, in advance of scheduled elections, with bandits burning down homes and shops along Kenya's Indian Ocean coast, and police using tear gas and bullets against peaceful protesters in Nairobi. Angola's fragile peace looks shakier still due to UNITA's continued intransigence. Zambia survived a botched coup attempt, making the president, Chiluba, even more authoritarian. Somalia has receded from the headlines, but remains a country without a government, a forbidding place carved up by rival warlords.

South Africa continues to offer one of the continent's best black hopes. The most persistent question in Africanist circles is: How is South Africa going? The assessment so far is that with qualifications and one big exception, it is still heading in the right direction. Foreign investment has continued to flow in steadily, and South Africa seems to be emerging as the engine of growth and investment that the continent so long lacked. The qualifications are that growth remains slow at about 2 percent a year and unemployment stubbornly high, leaving as much as 30 percent of the labor force idle. Politics in the post-Mandela era remain a question mark. But the "big exception" to the generally positive outlook is crime. South Africa has what is perhaps the highest murder rate in the world, sixty-one per 100,000 residents, and robberies, carjackings, and house-breakings are rife. More troubling is that the government seems at a loss as to what to do to stem the carnage.

So again, the question arises: Would the advantage of time and distance have changed my perceptions? And the continuing litany of Africa's tragedies—the few shimmers of hope so overwhelmed by the continued despair—makes the answer sadly apparent. The tide of democracy has subsided in Africa, and democratic government has not taken root. Human rights and dignity for the majority of Africans are appallingly lacking, and the continent continues to be plagued by coups, violent rebellions, tribalism, and repressive, unrepresentative governments.

Out of America stands as a testament to a particular time in Africa's modern, post-Cold War history, three tumultuous years beginning in 1991, that I was able to witness firsthand as a journalist traveling to the worst of the trouble spots. Much has changed since then—but much, much more has remained stubbornly the same.

Keith Richburg
Hong Kong
November, 1997

Acknowledgments

THIS BOOK IS THE PRODUCT of my three-years-plus journey through Africa as a correspondent for the *Washington Post*, and I owe a debt of gratitude to my editors at the paper who sent me there in the first place. They provided support and encouragement along the way, gave me the freedom to roam the continent in search of stories and themes, and—perhaps most important—paid all the bills. I particularly want to thank Mike Getler, formerly the *Post*'s assistant managing editor for foreign news, who called me while I was on a sabbatical in Hawaii and first asked if I was interested in the Africa job. Over lunch, Mike and then foreign editor David Ignatius listened while I outlined some of the ideas I wanted to explore in Africa, and heard me give voice to some of my initial misgivings about venturing into the land of my ancestors. David later helped me conceptualize many of the earlier stories from Africa, and I credit his deft editing with getting many of the stories, particularly about Somalia's civil war and famine, onto the *Post*'s front pages. Jackson Diehl and Eugene Robinson, my current editors, also provided endless support, allowing me a long tether to travel widely and to explore new and creative ways to get complicated ideas into print. When I was leaving Africa and decided to write a magazine article summing up my experiences, Bob Thompson and Peter Perl were enormously receptive and helped refine the final version that became the genesis for this book.

I also want to extend my deep appreciation to the *Post*'s executive editor, Len Downie, managing editor Bob Kaiser, and to *Post* publisher Donald Graham, all of whom have supported me throughout my career.

I'd also like to thank my colleagues at the foreign desk, the life-support system for the foreign correspondent. I'd like to single out Ed Cody, who took direct responsibility for editing the Africa stories, as well as Denny McAuliffe and Andy Mosher. Peter Harris kept the checks coming and the credit-card collectors at bay. And the indefatigable Yasmine Bahrani always managed to sound cheerful at the other end of the phone line.

As I was preparing for my Africa assignment, I was fortunate to meet several academics and Africa specialists in the United States on whose wise counsel I would rely over the years, and many of their thoughts and ideas have crept into the text, particularly the sections on Africa's politics and prescriptions for the future. Among those I want to thank are Makau wa Mutua at Harvard, Carol Lancaster at Georgetown, Pauline Baker of the Aspen Institute, and Michael Chege, also now at Harvard.

Many African friends and colleagues also helped me over the years to understand the continent and provided insights that often made it into my stories. In Kenya, Paul Muite and Gitobu Imanyara were particularly helpful. In Somalia, Hussein Mursal and Rakiya Omaar helped me sort through the country's byzantine clan makeup.

Over three years in Africa, I met many dedicated and tireless aid workers who continued toiling away even under the most arduous circumstances imaginable. They not only shared with me their insights, but occasionally even found space to put me up and provided me with more than a few hot meals and cold beers. Journalists in many places couldn't function without their generosity. I specifically want to thank Mike McDonagh of Irish Concern, Brenda Barton of WFP, and Paul Mitchell, formerly of the same, Samantha Bolton of MSF, and Stephen Tomlin and the gang at IMC, who put up with my repeat visits and always found spare seats on airplanes. And a special thanks to Lindsey Fielder Cook, who was there at a particularly rough time.

My colleagues at Chester House—who endured my occasional rants—encouraged me to put my thoughts down into the "swan song" magazine piece that became the thesis for this book. Jennifer Parmelee in Addis Ababa was always there to back me up, Karl Maier introduced me to "The Shrine" in Lagos, and David Chazan always let me sneak in a few minutes on his satellite phone in Mogadishu so I could file my stories in time to hit the roof. I also shared many adventures—some wonderful, some tragic, some bizarre, and all memorable—with Eric Ransdell of *U.S. News & World Report*, Liz Sly of the *Chicago Tribune*, and Nina Winquist of the International Red Cross. One of the things that I will always miss about Africa is the camaraderie you build up on the road.

While I've relied on so many others for their friendship and support, the ideas and arguments in this book—like the mistakes—are of course entirely my own.

This book would not have been written without the encouragement of Paul Golob, my editor at BasicBooks, who plucked the thread of an idea out of a breakfast conversation we had in early 1994. He spun out the idea, helped me weave it together, and provided valuable ideas and editing until it became this final product, so I am particularly grateful to him for encouraging me to go through with it.

In my final year in Kenya I was fortunate enough to meet Louise Tunbridge, who became my constant companion and best friend. We talked endlessly over dinners and red wine about Africa in general and Kenyan politics specifically, and I found no other journalist in Nairobi who knows more or cares more about Kenya than Louise. She understood my frustrations, listened to my occasional ravings, gave me wise advice, and was always there when I returned from long and sometimes emotionally exhausting trips away from home. For her love and quiet companionship I will always be grateful.

Index

INDEX